THE
HAMMER

THE
HAMMER

Tom DeLay

God, Money, and the Rise of
the Republican Congress

Lou Dubose and Jan Reid

PUBLICAFFAIRS
New York

Published in the United States by PublicAffairs™,
a member of the Perseus Books Group.

Book design by Jane Raese

Library of Congress Cataloging-in-Publication Data
Dubose, Lou.
The hammer: Tom DeLay, God, money, and the rise of the Republican
Congress/Lou Dubose and Jan Reid.—1st ed.
p. cm.
Includes index.
ISBN 1-58648-238-6
1. DeLay, Tom D., 1947– . 2. Legislators—United States—Biography.
3. United States. Congress. House—Biography.
I. Reid, Jan. II. Title.
E840.8.D455D83 2004
328.73'092—dc22
[B]
2004053469

FIRST EDITION
10 9 8 7 6 5 4 3 2 1

To Dorothy and Jeanne

Contents

Acknowledgments

This book would not have been possible without the generous support of Audre and Bernard Rapoport, who not only supported us but proposed that such a book be written. We are also indebted to Charlotte McCann, a tireless and thorough researcher and fact-checker who always seems to know the difference between the Alaska National Wildlife Refuge and Alaska National Wildlife Reserve, the latter of which exists only on an early version of our manuscript. The staff at the Newspaper Center in the Madison Building at the Library of Congress was resourceful and generous. The staffs at Democracy 21 and Public Citizen provided a wealth of information on our subject. Susan Morris, a misplaced Washingtonian trying to improve the political landscape of Texas, connected us to the well-connected in Washington. Rebecca Webber, a misplaced Texan doing campaign finance advocacy in Washington, reminded us that a book that offers little hope in its conclusion is not a book worth writing. Dennis Greenia and Michael Berryhill shared their prodigious research and documentation of aspects of the story. Fred Lewis of Campaigns for People was a knowing guide to the Byzantine world of fundraising and redistricting in Texas. In Washington our good friends Beverly Lowry and Tom Johnson provided moral support, meals, and good cheer. We found Murky Coffee at 7th and Pennsylvania a fine place to get connected—to Wireless Internet, extraordinary sources, and some of the more interesting people in the District.

Writing about a powerful political operator is not unlike writing about a Mafia don; few people will talk for fear of retribution. We are grateful to those sources both on and off the record

who met with us and provided us information. PublicAffairs
Publisher Peter Osnos recognized the public's interest in a book
about a man who is arguably the most powerful member of
Congress, and helped shape the book. Our patient and dedicated editors at PublicAffairs, Lisa Kaufman and David Patter-
son, helped turn a manuscript into a book. And of course we
thank our spouses, Jeanne Goka and Dorothy Browne, for putting up with the discontents that result from writing any book—
this one in particular.

Lou Dubose and Jan Reid

THE
HAMMER

Kicking Ass and Taking Names

WASHINGTON, D.C., NOVEMBER 2003: By mid-morning on this Wednesday in mid-November it was evident that something big was about to play itself out in the House of Representatives. Most members were in their seats and quieter and more focused than usual. Aides hovered under the faux candelabras by the four doors on the east and west sides of the chamber. The leadership had brought in former Speaker Newt Gingrich to buck up conservatives who feared a deficit deeper than the big dig that will house a visitors' center at the east Capitol steps. Now standing before a video screen bearing the Capitol logo behind the slogan "Fulfilling America's Progress" was Majority Whip Roy Blunt—starting a process known as "whipping the bill." As Blunt, his deputies, and the morning ground on, the message was clear and consistent. President Bush wanted this Medicare prescription-drug bill. The integrity and viability of the Republican House majority were on the line. It was up to the Republican majority to send a strong bill to the Senate. Conservative members who failed to vote the party line were betraying their leadership, failing their president, and creating the same intramural dissent that reduced the Democrats to a minority party after they had dominated the House for forty-five years.

Sam Johnson, a craggy Dallas Republican hardened by the time he spent as a POW in Vietnam, rose from his seat below the huge chandelier and walked toward the southeast exit. As the speaker at the front of the chamber cranked up the volume and intensity, DeLay fixed his gaze on Johnson, who turned to face the front of the chamber and listen. "You saw what happened to them," said a deputy whip who had stepped up to the lectern. "You saw how they became the minority party. Do we want to follow them into the minority? We need every member, including those on our right flank."

To Blunt's left, almost directly beneath an alabaster sculpture of a screaming American eagle, was the House majority leader. Dressed in a dark blue suit and sitting with his arms folded across his chest, Tom DeLay appeared to be presiding as much as he was observing. During the eight years he had served as whip, the short and now somewhat paunchy Texas congressman had elevated the political art of whipping to a science. Blunt had gained his chops as DeLay's deputy whip, and now the Missouri congressman was raising the stakes for conservatives in the Republican Conference, composed of all the Republican House members, just as his boss used to do when the numbers were close. Now and then an aide would lean over to confer with "The Leader." But even as DeLay listened, he remained focused on the members out on the floor, his gaze sweeping the room.

The buzz among House Republicans was that DeLay wasn't happy with Blunt, his handpicked choice to succeed him as whip. Blunt didn't work as hard, was too amiable and at times too eager to please. He didn't have the organizational skills DeLay had developed when he held the position. Nor did he inspire the fear and respect DeLay did.

"It's never easy to watch someone who has taken your old job," said a committee staffer who went to work in the House five years before DeLay arrived. "You always think you could be doing it better. DeLay thinks Blunt is a little lazy."

Even if DeLay were fair and open-minded, Roy Blunt would lose out. Anyone would. Few members of the House, perhaps no member of the current House, could work the whip operation as did DeLay, who practices a confrontational, competitive politics from the time he leaves his modest, high-rise Arlington condo until he walks out of the downtown restaurant hosting the final fundraiser of the night.

Since his arrival in the House eight years earlier, DeLay had overcome Newt Gingrich's opposition to win a place in the leadership in the big Republican year of 1995. Then he built a whip's organization that pushed as much of Gingrich's program as possible through the House. He alone managed the succession crisis when Gingrich resigned in 1998, designating Denny Hastert Speaker, and all but declared himself majority leader (without a whisper of opposition) when Dick Armey left that position in 2003. If he was sitting at the front of the caucus and breathing down Blunt's neck, it was because he knew how to count votes when it counted and move votes when it mattered. The Medicare vote was the biggest single issue for the Republican Congress and the president in 2003 and DeLay was there to make sure Blunt didn't blow it.

It was going to be close. House Republicans practice what *Washington Post* congressional reporter Juliet Eilperin has described as "the art of the one-vote victory." In an October 2003 story, Eilperin describes a 216–215 win on a Medicare vote, a 217–216 vote on federal Head Start, and a 209–208 win on vouchers for Washington, D.C., schools. "Hastert and team virtually always ignore the 205 House Democrats and one independent," she wrote. They concentrate instead "on the pool of 229 Republicans, from which [they] can lose no more than 11 moderates in order to have a bare majority."

Tony Blankley, who is editor of the *Washington Times'* editorial page and a Sunday morning talking head on television, marveled at the close votes DeLay had orchestrated. Blankley worked for Gingrich in the House and was particularly impressed with the work DeLay had done as whip. "They didn't have anything close to what you would call a working majority," Blankley said of those days when Bill Clinton, though wounded, was still president and had power and popularity that confounded Republicans. "Go back and look at those votes; what they did again and again was extraordinary."

As the Medicare vote moved to the floor, the leadership was playing the same high-stakes Texas Hold'em that Eilperin and Blankley described. On this occasion, it was the conservatives who were bolting—objecting to a Medicare bill that would add $400 billion to an already huge deficit and expand an existing entitlement. DeLay was in a difficult position. George W. Bush badly wanted two major pieces of legislation passed: an energy bill and Medicare reform. DeLay had single-handedly killed the energy bill by refusing to remove a provision that shielded from lawsuits producers of the gasoline additive MTBE. (DeLay had even insisted on retroactive protection, reaching back and eliminating lawsuits already filed, which many considered the real deal-killer.) So he had damn well better deliver this Medicare bill, and the only way to do it was by imposing discipline on the conservatives threatening to vote with the Democrats. When the vote was cast, Republicans would have to vote as if the three Latin words chiseled into the marble eagle's perch above DeLay's left shoulder were their operational imperative: *E Pluribus Unum*.

This one-party rule was unprecedented in American government. As discussion of the Medicare bill began, the Democrats whom DeLay's staff openly derided as irrelevant were again ignored. In fact, they were not even in the chamber. When the bill finally would come to the floor under a closed rule, they would not be allowed to alter it in any way. They would not be allowed to offer amendments. The chamber where Blunt and DeLay were counting the votes for the biggest entitlement bill Congress had undertaken in decades was closed to Democrats. And to the press.* The Republican House Conference had convened in the ornate Ways and Means Committee chamber in the

---

*One of the authors read the House Ways and Means Committee sign on the door in the Longworth Building and walked in on a day that Tom DeLay was (later in the afternoon) scheduled to testify before a Ways and Means subcom-

Longworth Building. They might as well have been in the House chamber. Because here, across Independence Avenue from the Capitol, the future of Medicare was being decided. The 208 Democratic and one independent members of the United States House of Representatives would have no role in it. Democrats could complain, as did an angry and incredulous Barney Frank, who was left sputtering on the floor at 6:30 in the morning after the bill had been on the floor for three hours: "Mr. Speaker. Mr. Speaker, a parliamentary inquiry!" But that was all they could do.

It wasn't always this way. This is the New Republican House, which began with the bang of the oversized gavel a supporter made for Newt Gingrich to convene the 1995 session. Gingrich, who would flame out in three years, ushered in changes that drastically affect how laws are made. Since DeLay was elected to the leadership in 1995, he had fully exploited the new system that Gingrich, fellow Texan Dick Armey, and he had put in place. DeLay worked with a remarkable sense of focus and ruthless political skill, making law as he remade the House. Now, as the Medicare prescription drug bill moved toward the floor, he was the only surviving Republican elevated to a leadership position by the celebrated Class of '94. The New Republican House was Tom DeLay's House.

The changes have been drastic, and the House over which DeLay presides today is far different from the one he encountered

---

mittee. After he realized he was the only reporter in the room and quickly departed, Republican Conference Chair Deborah Pryce wondered who the interloper was. Along with a member of DeLay's staff, Pryce gave chase. The gentlewoman from Ohio was generous and forgiving. "This is not your fault," she said. "This is a security breach. I intend to find out how you walked by the people we have posted at the door." We trust that she did, and that we didn't cause the Republican Conference security detail any great inconvenience.

as a minority party freshman in 1985. Gone are the powerful committee chairmen, who presided with baronial independence over the belabored business of creating legislation. Their independence, rooted in a rigid system of seniority, once provided a check on the power of the leadership. Gone is the bipartisan nature of committee work, where bills were drafted as the public and the press looked on. When Democrats offer amendments at committee meetings, Republicans call the question and use a straight party-line vote to cut off debate. Committees now draft bills in closed minority sessions or working groups. Only when the majority on the committee completes a draft is a bill brought to the full committee for a formal vote that usually divides along party lines. Gone are the floor debate and the long days of making law in the House chamber. Most Americans don't know that the House now meets only two days a week, doesn't debate, and disposes of legislation in rolling votes, in which long lines of unrelated bills are rolled out for up or down votes with an efficiency rarely achieved by O'Hare Airport air traffic controllers. Bills are also brought to the floor under closed rules, or amended closed rules, which allow no amendments and only an up or down vote. The committee system, floor debate, bipartisan collaboration, social relations across party lines—all are as dated as the brass spittoons that once graced the members' lounges.

"The House of Representatives is no longer a deliberative body," said Massachusetts Democrat Barney Frank. "It's a plebiscitary system." Frank, a skilled debater and parliamentary tactician, says it is futile for Democrats to try to shape legislation in committee or on the House floor. Frank has been frustrated by the constraints imposed upon committees and the closed rules that preclude amending bills on the floor. When the $400 million Medicare bill would finally come to the floor, members would have one alternative, to vote yes or no.

"It's up or down, essentially a plebiscite on the floor of the House. Republican voters are allowed to vote outside the party line as long as it is not outcome determinative," Frank said. "So whenever Republicans need votes to win something, the votes are there."

Frank is a Northeastern liberal, as far from Texan Tom DeLay in ideology as he is in geography. Norman Ornstein works in Washington. As resident congressional scholar at the American Enterprise Institute, he would have been considered conservative before Newt Gingrich and the Southern takeover of American politics left him in the center. He describes himself as "a raging moderate." Lately, in speeches and columns he has been raging about DeLay. And the way Congress is run.

Ornstein has observed that the Republicans didn't invent the abuse of House procedure. They have, however, perfected it, taking everything the Democrats did while they were in the majority and expanding on it. "As a minority party in the House," he wrote, "Democrats have been treated shabbily, ignored, shunned, left powerless repeatedly as Republicans have used closed rules and the power of the gavel to make them impotent (using and expanding on many of the tricks of the trade they learned from the Democrats when they were in the majority, while adding a few of their own)." Arizona Senator John McCain seems shocked by the conduct of the House and wonders what the payback from Democrats will look like: "We better hope they are never a majority again," he said.

This will not change any time soon. "They seem to be determined to create a permanent majority," Ornstein said in an interview.

Following the meeting of the Republican Conference convened to pass the Medicare bill, DeLay made the opening comments at the press stakeout in the hallway, telling reporters the floor schedule, explaining the merits of the legislation, and praising the Republican members of Ways and Means who had put it together. When Ways and Means Committee Chair Bill Thomas looked into the television cameras and made the case for a 1,200-page bill most members of the House would not have time to read before the vote, DeLay stood behind him and to his right, framed in the CBS News camera that Thomas addressed.

"The rumors about the [hair]piece are put to rest," a reporter said as he nodded to the bald spot on the back of the majority leader's head. DeLay didn't hear the comment. Nor did he take his eyes off Thomas. The three men—DeLay, Thomas, and Blunt—were spelling out for the country the huge changes about to be made in a Medicare program that hadn't been overhauled since it was signed into law by President Lyndon Johnson in the mid-1960s. As is often the case when committee chairmen are talking to the press, the majority leader positioned himself so he could be seen looking over the chairman's shoulder. Tom DeLay was running the show. House Speaker Denny Hastert was nowhere to be seen. Nor was there a single Democratic representative in sight. No Democrat on the Ways and Means Committee played a part in shaping the bill. No House Democrat would be appointed to the House-Senate conference committee.

In Tom DeLay's Congress, Democrats don't matter.

AUSTIN, TEXAS, JUNE 2004: Those of us who watched Tom DeLay during the three sessions he spent in the Texas Legislature, where he arrived in the late 1970s, never would have predicted it. No political oddsmaker in Austin would have put any money on Tom DeLay. Not even his colleagues saw in him any sign of great ambition—never mind great achievement. He was the back-bench ideologue, ridiculed when he stood up at the back mike to muddle through an argument about the over-regulated trucking industry. He was the right-wing crank from Sugar Land, hell-bent on making the case that government is bad because by its nature it limits individual freedom, yet completely lacking in the vocabulary to make his case. He was one of the many unremarkable legislators in a State House of 150, one of the guys who loved the Lege because it was the best, free 180-day party thrown in the Great State of Texas.

Everyone bet on George W. Bush—who lost his first election for a west Texas House seat the same year DeLay won his first one for a Southeast Texas State House seat—to make a comeback. Bush was what the State of Texas was about: oil, money, patrimonial power, and crony capitalism. No one was willing to wager much on Tom DeLay. DeLay was from the roughneck camps of the Texas oilpatch, home to the guys who drilled the wells and ran the casing for the bullies and bastards who owned the royalties and ran the state. His patrimony was the sort of dysfunction that is the psychological and biological inheritance of the children of alcoholics. Bush was an oilman. Not a very good one. But he had a never-ending source of family-related investment capital. DeLay was a bug man. Not a very good one. But he struggled to pay the bills and taxes at his small exterminating operation.

Men (and a few women) have risen from hardscrabble obscurity in Texas. Lyndon Johnson left an almost barren family farm in the Hill Country and carefully calculated every political move he made, even turning a student government office at Southwest Texas State Teachers College into a power center. Sam Rayburn won a seat in the same State House where Tom DeLay served without distinction. In exactly the same amount of time DeLay held office—Rayburn earned a law degree and was elected Speaker before moving on to Washington to become one of the most distinguished Speakers of the U.S. House. "Tom DeLay, well, he was amusing," said a woman who served with him in the Texas House.

How did Tom DeLay get from there to here? From a backbench position in the Texas House to the pinnacle of power in the U.S. House—without the blessing or backing of Bush political guru Karl Rove? What is his next goal, and what is he willing to do to achieve it? These are questions that anyone interested in American democracy ought to be asking. In the pages that follow, we have attempted to provide some of the answers.

"Dee-lay! Dee-lay! Dee-lay!" House Democrats would chant in unison, laughing as the state rep from Sugar Land stood up to speak on the floor of the State House.

Nobody is laughing at Tom DeLay anymore.

Lou Dubose and Jan Reid

ONE

Born in the USA

Tom DeLay was born in Laredo, Texas, on April 8, 1947, to a family of hard-luck Southerners who scrabbled their way out of the Great Depression by means of welding torch and ball peen hammer, not diploma and pedigree. They were frontiersmen who pushed on to the borderlands after the frontier had closed—believers in a Texas oil patch that dried up almost as soon as they got there. Consider other major American politicians born during World War II and the first years of the Cold War: Newt Gingrich and John Kerry, 1943; Rudolph Giuliani, 1944; Dan Quayle, Arnold Schwarzenegger, and Hillary Rodham Clinton, 1947; Al Gore, 1948; and by far the most nagging and confrontational of DeLay's personal measures, Bill Clinton and George W. Bush, 1946. (DeLay has much more in common with Clinton, whom he detests, than Bush, whose values and priorities he generally shares.) Those peers and rivals were positioned on the inside track by wealth, or families with connections and histories of performance in politics and government, or educations at Harvard and Yale and Oxford, and by ambition and self-importance that inflamed their hearts while still quite young. To their glowing résumés Tom DeLay's could only answer: college hellion, failed businessman in an un-prestigious line of work, backbencher in the Texas Legislature. Everything about DeLay set him out running far back in the pack. How could a man of such mediocre prospects and promise become one of the most powerful politicians in the country?

DeLay is heir to a hard edge of the American dream. His

father and uncles were of the generation who overcame the war might of Nazi Germany and the Japanese empire; having not much to settle down to after their military service, they roamed on in South America and Asia and on platform drilling rigs in the Gulf of Mexico, adventurers by necessity of making a living. They were a patriarchal bunch brought up to be God-fearing Baptists. They looked on college education as a means to an end—equipment that enabled sons to make a better living than their dads could—and as a rung up the ladder of social class. Through it all, a common trait bound them. They started out with a family business, an oilfield machine shop with everybody pitching in to keep it afloat, and wherever the sons and grandsons went, whatever they did, they meant to end up with a family business.

Family and business, family and business—those were the mantras of Tom DeLay's creed in politics. The ideals were widely shared, of course, but in his case they were ironic. By De-Lay's own account, the family he grew up within was exceptionally dysfunctional, and later his own performance as a husband and father tormented him with guilt—and his treatment of his mother and his siblings should have. He started making a reliable living and accumulating wealth only when a seat in Congress rescued him from his floundering small business, a pest control service. Gaining ground on the fast-running field of national politics required intellect, patience, and a mastery of process that in time astounded and cowed peers of both parties in the House. He plied the trade of rules and favors, lobbies and fundraising, with the precision of those machinists in the Rio Grande brush country. But the most important quality inherited from his elders was indomitability. Once DeLay made up his mind on a course of action, he believed that nothing or nobody could turn him back.

Laredo was Webb County's town with a hospital; DeLay came home with his parents to the outlying countryside, the chaparral. The Oxford English Dictionary paints a bleak picture of that terrain and term: "Dense tangled brushwood, composed of low thorny shrubs, brambles, briars, etc., such as abounds on poor soil in Mexico and Texas." Poor soil indeed. The brush can be handsome when the mesquites leaf out a delicate shimmering green in the spring, and a hint of moisture in the air triggers blooms of the cenizo, or purple sage. But the chaparral is dominated by tawny monotonous horizons and sweltering windblown heat. Its politics has always been defined by its proximity to the Rio Grande. The U.S.-Mexican War, which ended in 1848, certified the Americans' annexation of Texas, humiliated Mexico, and made the river the boundary, but the population and traditions of the brush country remained largely Hispanic. The U.S. political system was grafted onto the chaparral and became an eccentric hybrid. One dispute over an 1886 election in Laredo erupted in a gunfight that killed more than a dozen people. Local tradition has it that the Guaraches ("Sandals") and the Botas ("Boots") sent 5,000 bullets buzzing and whining across the town plaza that day. Outside Webb County, no one could say with certainty what the Sandals and Boots were so angry and exercised about—only that they were factions of the Democratic Party.

The discovery of oil brought dramatic change and the first large influx of non-Hispanics to the chaparral. In 1920 a lawyer turned wildcatter named Oliver Winfield Killam moved from Oklahoma to the borderlands and started convincing ranchers to lease him their mineral rights. Killam drilled two dry holes and was nearly broke in 1921 when he brought in a twenty-barrel-a-day well in Zapata County. The strike set off the first oil play in south Texas and ignited an economic boom. Before Killam was through he had brought in 150 wells, one of them a gusher that spewed out more than 300 barrels a day and was written about all over the country. On trains, buses, and in model T's the laborers, dreamers, and hustlers came pouring in. Killam did not want his workers living amid the sludge, moonshine, and whorehouses that sullied many oil boomtowns.

Thirty miles east of Laredo, he founded a company town named Mirando City. The houses were built with well-planed lumber, not adobe. Killam recruited a Texas Ranger as the town's policeman. Anyone who got out of hand spent the night chained to a tall pole at the town's center—the temporary jail. The town had an envied and respected system of public schools. Mirando City swarmed with roustabouts, roughnecks, and tool pushers but also engineers, chemists, and lab technicians. By 1930 the town's population exceeded 5,000.

One of the families answering the call of opportunity in Mirando City had an unusual name. Cajuns, the DeLays were called. Neighbors didn't know if that was ethnically correct—they just knew the DeLays came from Louisiana, and had a French-sounding name. Ray DeLay and his wife Grace had three sons; the oldest, Charlie, was born in 1923. Ray worked in the oilfields for a while after moving to Mirando City, but when Charlie was old enough to carry his weight, they opened and ran the machine shop catering to the drilling crews in the middle of town. The DeLay boys played high school football and prowled the town and dirt roads with Frank Stagg, whose family owned a hotel and boarding house.

The town's Community Church had a Baptist service one hour on Sunday, the Methodists another hour, and so on. A group of Mirando City women formed a gospel chorus called the Mother Singers; they performed in churches and town halls throughout the region. By the mid-twenties the Baptists had enough members, and dollars in their collection plates, that they were able to buy out the other denominations' interests in the Community Church. The DeLays and the Staggs were among the families who organized and led Mirando City's Baptist church.

"Mirando City was an interesting place," reminisced Frank Stagg, a career teacher, school administrator, and Webb County rancher. "It had a level of education and sophistication you don't find in many small towns, and it didn't have a lot of racial tension. The DeLays were as highly regarded as anyone who lived there. They were good people."

But the Depression brought an abrupt end to Webb County's oil boom. Trying to survive, the company founded by Killam pulled its headquarters out of Mirando City. The population plummeted to 1,800 by the start of World War II, and the town shrunk physically; the military commandeered lumber of the emptied houses to build barracks on bases in south Texas. Charlie DeLay served in the army air corps. He learned to fly planes and would have loved to be a combat pilot. But according to family lore, his knowledge of Spanish made him too valuable as an instructor. He spent the war in San Antonio, teaching pilots from Latin America. He picked up enough Portuguese to work with Brazilians.

Charlie married a young woman from Corpus Christi named Maxine Wimbish. Their first son, Ray, was born in 1944. Tom was three years younger than Ray; the third son, Randy, came three years after Tom. They had one sister named Tena. After the war Charlie DeLay returned to the border and business with his father, but Mirando City continued to fade. They moved the machine shop into Laredo in 1953. The DeLays owned some acreage in Arkansas, and they were tempted to try farming it. Old Ray and his sons Charlie and Billy went up to check it out. As Frank Stagg recalled sadly, "They were driving along some narrow road, and a truck veered right into them, head-on. Ray saw he couldn't do anything about it, and he threw himself in front of Billy. Ray was killed, but he saved his son's life." It was not the last time sudden tragedy and violent death would haunt the family of Tom DeLay.

The brush country continued to be a defining landscape of Tom's life. Long after his family quit the border, one of his most bitter political fights would be carried on with Hispanic Democrats in Webb and other counties along the Rio Grande. The brush country's politics still run heavily Democratic. The chaparral counties are the last bastion of the one-party rule that culminated with the machine of Lyndon Johnson and the local party chiefs who curried his favors and delivered the votes. The infamous Box 13, which enabled Johnson to steal the 1948 U.S. Senate election from another Democrat, Governor Coke Stevenson, was delivered by one such patrón, Duval County's George Parr. Half a century later, even GOP candidates named George Bush have never been able to carry the border brush country. Neither one of them. The brush country's defiance is more than a burr under the Republican Party's saddle. Hispanics are well on their way to becoming the most numerous ethnic group in Texas, and Republicans know that base must either be converted or dispirited. Despite rhetoric to the contrary, they have so far taken the latter tack.

If the native son cared to return to his first hometown, he might find its intactness eerie. Unlike many towns that came and went with the Texas oil booms, Mirando City is not fallen to rubble and strips of crumbling blacktop in the prickly pear and mesquite. It's just empty. Two or three hundred people live out there now. But apart from partisan animus, DeLay has demonstrated no sentiment toward the brush country he roamed as a boy. In a state that glorifies sense of place, DeLay is a fundamentally rootless man, drawn to company towns that were created whole cloth—like, for example, Washington, D.C.

DeLay once remarked that his father decided he'd better go work in the oilfields the day he realized he couldn't buy one of his sons a pair of shoes. Charlie DeLay knew the oil patch, and there was plenty of opportunity for an American driller who could speak Spanish. Huge fields were being discovered all over South America. In 1956 Charlie took a job in Venezuela as superintendent for a company called Hellmerich & Payne. He had a number of jobs over the next five years, and according to his wife, Maxine, they were constantly moving. Around the wells, camps for the rig crews were set up in trailers or cheap motel-like dorms smelling of beer and soiled men and socks. The work was dangerous, boring, and exhausting. But the wages were good, and—the perk that Americans always talked about—they were excused from paying federal income taxes. The tank farms and pipelines routed the oil through towns that looked like mestizo variations on Dodge City of the buffalo hunters or gold-rush towns in the Yukon. But companies like Atlantic Richfield, Texaco, Schlumberger, and Brown and Root (later Kellogg, Brown and Root, the Halliburton subsidiary charged with flagrant corruption during the second U.S.-Iraq war) built secure enclaves for the families of their high-ranking employees. They were company towns, like Mirando City. These island suburbs in the Third World had freshly painted stucco cottages, crisply mown St. Augustine lawns, schools, stores, churches, tennis courts.

At age fifty-six, while making a speech in honor of Winston Churchill in the context of defending Israel, and in the aftermath of the terrorist strikes on the World Trade Center and the Pentagon, DeLay told a remarkable story about that phase of his upbringing.

> Early in life, I saw the consequences of tyranny firsthand. When I was a boy, my family moved to South America. My father took a job as the general manager for an Oklahoma company's oil field operations in Venezuela in the 1950s.
>
> We lived in a small town near the center of the country. It was an incredible place to grow up. The countryside was beautiful. It was flowing ranchland separated by stretches of jungle.
>
> There were very few people living in our little town. It was basically the families of the oil field workers and the caballeros—the cowboys of Venezuela.
>
> My brothers and I rode horses and we would ride off to camp with the caballeros and explore the jungle. It was wild and new and exotic. There were amazing plants, animals, and insects to study. It was everything adventurous and curious young boys could have wanted.
>
> Out at their ranches, the caballeros practically had zoos.

They had pet monkeys and parrots and just about every animal that lived in the jungle. And they were friendly to us.

They showed us how to ride like real caballeros. And they taught us to crack whips and rope steers. Generally, they gave us free run of their cattle ranches.

Venezuela's rural heartland offered adventures that would be the envy of Huck Finn, and the DeLay brothers made the most of it. We rode and hiked and explored everything within miles around our little town. In the beginning, it was an innocent, idyllic childhood.

Unfortunately, Venezuela's political structure was unstable and chaotic. When I was only seven, I was exposed to my first revolution. The revolutionaries killed several local politicians and hung them in the town plaza. There were three revolutions in Venezuela during our years in South America.

The worst incident happened when I was eleven. At the time the revolution broke out, I was out visiting a ranch with a friend. My mother was frantic. She looked everywhere and couldn't find me.

When we finally made it home, we saw revolutionaries ransacking houses and rampaging through town. They destroyed my friend's house. Our own house was spared. But we had no idea how close to death we actually came.

Later, we learned that revolutionaries had arrived at the ranch just fifteen minutes after we left. They destroyed the ranch house. They killed all the people and every animal at the ranch. It was total chaos and complete destruction.

It was my introduction to the horrendous acts human beings are capable of when they operate with no regard for life. And it was the source of my passion for freedom and my hostility to unaccountable power.

This self-image of a horseback-riding, bullwhip-cracking Huck Finn losing his innocence in a cruel foreign world is plausible, if hyperbolic. DeLay also attributes his loathing of the

Castro regime and support of South Florida's Cuban community (there is no counterpart in his Texas constituency) to an experience in those years. He said that a plane carrying his family
stopped in Havana for refueling after Castro took power, that
his family was held three hours without explanation, and that he
was marched out on the tarmac "between these stinking soldiers with big German shepherds." He told NBC in 2000, "I
can still smell those soldiers."

Friends of the DeLays recall that the strain of that life was so
hard on the boys' mother that she returned to Corpus Christi
for extended stays with her family. Though the turmoil in
Venezuela in the fifties is not usually characterized as compris-
ing three revolutions, the politics were angry and anti-American
enough that a Caracas mob stoned the car of the visiting vice
president, Richard Nixon. But on another occasion, just four
years before his speech honoring Churchill, DeLay reportedly
painted that part of his upbringing in a quite different light. A
magazine writer quoted him recalling fondly that he first won
election as president of his English-language school in
Venezuela and caddied for pocket change on the golf courses
the oil companies built for the ex-pats.

"It was fabulous," DeLay allegedly said of his boyhood
abroad. "No telephones, no television, and a country club in
every camp."

Charlie DeLay was a charismatic man, something of a wild man,
and a difficult father. According to his children, he knocked
down a quart of scotch a night. He disciplined them with a belt
on occasion. DeLay, who as an adult would battle a nicotine
habit, said that when he was six his dad caught him puffing a
cigarette and made him smoke most of a carton. Charlie tried to
dictate the ambitions of his sons, and he was dead serious about
it; if they failed at those assignments, they were failing him. (At

least in the telling of that story, nothing was ever said about the expectations of his daughter, Tena.) Making fun of his father, Tom made a telling wisecrack about his younger brother, Randy. The old man, Tom chuckled, "wanted a doctor, a lawyer, and a veterinarian, and he got what he deserved—a lawyer."

Charlie moved the family back to Texas in 1960, when Tom was twelve, settling in a suburb of Corpus Christi. With partners he co-founded the Storm Drilling Company. Starting out with a few land rigs, over the next decade it became a multi-million-dollar producer of offshore wells in the Gulf of Mexico—the riskiest, costliest, loneliest, and most dangerous calling in the business. Tom DeLay likened him to the Jett Rink character played by James Dean in *Giant:* "My father was a wildcatter straight out of the movie *Giant*. He was a boisterous, domineering alcoholic."

Tom claimed his dad taught him to wield a thirty-six-inch pipe wrench by the time he was thirteen. He was fond of boasting: "I grew up on an oil rig." He said that hard work constituted most of what he learned from his dad. "He would put me on rigs and the roughnecks would give me a hard time. I wouldn't want to work anymore. But my father taught me in the oilfields early on that you never quit. You don't let 'em get you down. He would say, 'Too bad. Can't quit. You have to work out your own problems, son.'"

One close friend of Charlie's family, however, had trouble remembering when any of his sons would have been doing oilfield work. The matchup of years didn't seem quite right to him. When an interviewer asked Maxine DeLay if her son Tom ever worked on an oil rig, she left a long pause. "I think he did," she finally replied, "for a few weeks one summer. It was during high school. He quit after a couple of weeks and said, 'Mama, that work is too hard. I have to go to college.'"

Politicians, of course, are hardly the only people who edit their life stories, particularly their adolescent years. Tom went to Calallen High School, where he dominated student politics and played football. He was a five-foot-seven, 140-pound lineman, which limited his prowess, but he received the compliment often heard from Texans reminiscing about their days on the high school gridiron: "That little sonofabitch would knock the shit out of you." So he does still, on another field of endeavor.

He started going with Christine Furrh, a cheerleader who rode horses in small-town rodeos. "It was very sexy," she recalled of the first time she saw him. "He had on blue jeans and a big cowboy belt with a silver buckle, and a western shirt—a western shirt with sleeves rolled up. Tommy was just about the cutest thing I ever saw. He looked like a smart aleck, stuck up, full of himself. He acted cocky, but it was because he was nervous."

Charlie DeLay by then owned a house overlooking the Nueces River. He got himself elected to the Calallan school board, and when Tom graduated from high school in 1965 Charlie sent him to Baylor for pre-med. With respected faculty and professional schools, Baylor was the elite university of Southern Baptists, and in comparison with the state-supported colleges in Texas, an education at Baylor was costly. Waco, a prairie city of about 100,000 midway between Dallas and Austin, was known for Baylor more than anything. There were no dances on campus, but like other college towns in the sixties, it had its share of rowdies, even hippies and dope-smokers. Tom DeLay at Baylor was a hell-raiser of traditional vein. He continued to make good grades, but, he later admitted, he was called in and scolded on multiple occasions by the dean of students.

In athletics, Baylor competed with a measure of success against a nearby farmland school, Texas A&M. The history of friction between their male students ran deeper than football. Coeds had first been admitted to A&M in 1963 and were not yet rushing to enroll; Aggies were always swaggering over to court the Baptist girls of Baylor. Founded as a land grant college, A&M remained a defiant throwback even as Vietnam protests raged around the country and flower children ruled the streets of San Francisco. All Aggie underclassmen were still obliged to

belong to the ROTC Corps of Cadets and wear military uni-
forms and boot-camp haircuts. The Aggies were extremely
proud of their military heritage. Only the military academies
had contributed more officers to the nation's service, and the
campus's buildings, walls, and statues reflected that martial
mindset. Then one morning in 1966 Aggies found their treas-
ured citadel defaced by vandals—Baylor green spray paint, pro-
fanities, mocking insults.

Rumors spread quickly that the trail of the culprits led to
Waco. Baylor had always been a remarkably open campus, but
fear of retaliation pervaded Baylor's administration; students
gaped as suddenly a cordon of security guards ringed the campus. The administrators moved quickly to defuse the crisis.
Among others, Tom DeLay was once more called on the carpet.
According to a *George* magazine profile, DeLay ran with cronies
whom administrators called the Dirty Dozen; for his campus
social club, DeLay rented a beer joint outside Waco, and the academic teetotalers had it raided. DeLay was never formally ex-
pelled, but he was strongly urged to take some time off from
Baylor.

DeLay's dreams of medical school evaporated with his juvenile behavior at Baylor. He never returned to Waco as a student.
He and Christine got married, and he finished at the University
of Houston, a commuter school. He skirted military service and
Vietnam with student deferments. He was a standout in political science classes, but he received his degree in biology. After
graduation, he took a job at a Houston pest control company.
An exterminator recalled, "He worked the counter, and in the
back, making rat bait."

For Charlie DeLay, who wanted and demanded so much of
his sons, that must have seemed like a failure. There is no indi-
cation Tom ever made real peace with his dad, and his estrangement from the others in his family would get worse, not better.
DeLay would later reflect on his childhood in an oddly chilling
way. "My parents didn't participate in much of what I did. I

think I've been an adult my whole life." Maybe the humiliations and conflict hardened him toward the weaknesses and failures of others; maybe the upbringing produced a guarded loner. But Tom DeLay set out with the same grit that had brought his family to some of America's most desolate borderlands and made them gamblers on the long odds of oil. Bestowing authenticity and virility, at least in his mind, DeLay's origins were shown off like an old roughneck's faded tattoo. But really making it in that world meant that you escaped it. Even as a boy roaming the savannas of an alien continent, DeLay knew the kind of America that beckoned him. In order to live there, you gained admission to a country club, and the big new house where you lived was built next to a golf course where not just anyone could play.

Sugar Land

Tom DeLay arrived in politics as the Exterminator from Sugar Land. Neither credit was auspicious. The unfashionable service industry and the obsequious name of the town invited condescension. But DeLay was a political infighter who thrived at being taken lightly—it coaxed opponents to lower their guards while it bolstered his will and heightened his intensity. And the times were changing; new forces were gathering in American politics that made DeLay a man who could flourish in those times. He was a businessman, and by his lights, the *calling* to business was more important than the kind. His difficulties in the pest control business could enhance his credibility as a politician: people believed he knew first-hand how overregulation by government and burdensome taxes were holding him and everyone else back. He was the Republican as the new common man.

DeLay was also in the right place at the right time, though it took him a while to realize how opportune his footing and moment could be. Power in Texas had been rooted in a past of rural domination, a past that served the interests of the Democratic Party. For a century Texas was a one-party state. Elections were decided in the Democratic primary. But a massive population shift and the transformation of distinct small towns into interlocking suburbs would change all that with a rapidity that was breathtaking.

Thanks to an OPEC embargo of the United States, Western Europe, and Japan in the late seventies, oil prices soared. Texas enjoyed what was probably the last of its oil booms. Its cities mushroomed under the press of all the entrepreneurs and job seekers—utility poles in Houston were plastered with signs hawking business cards that could be printed and delivered in *one hour*. The cities swarmed with Texans who cut their ties with hometowns and countryside to get in on the action, and with migrants from other states, many of whom brought political outlooks and traditions that were sharply at odds with those they found. With young families they moved to the suburbs, drawn by affordable real estate and the hope of better schools and safer streets. The suburbanization of America raced along in other states, but in Texas the pace and effects of it were profound.

The oil boom of the seventies and eighties went bust, and the Texas economy had to be reconfigured. But when the dust had settled and the smoke had cleared, the politics of Texas had flipped; Texas was now poised to be a one-party state run by Republicans. The chemistry of the change was complex, rooted partly in scandals and infighting among the Democrats. There were national effects and counter-effects, such as civil rights breakthroughs and Richard Nixon's Southern strategy to claim disaffected whites for the GOP, and then Watergate and the presidency of Jimmy Carter, which shook out in Texas to the advantage of the GOP. And the Republicans had greater skill at harnessing a tidal wave of money in politics. Other mega-states—New York, California, Florida—staged lively races that could be won by candidates of either party, but dominance in Texas shifted to a suburban, middle-class Republicanism with inclinations toward the Christian right. GOP strategists saw in that Texas a mirror of the country: for the first time the Republicans had a chance to become a true majority party.

Sugar Land had been an ordinary little town with a spindly water tower jutting up through coastal haze; suddenly its subdivisions became the manifestation of the enormous changes driving Texas—and a harbinger of the nation's politics. In coming years voters in the United States would elect two presidents from Texas named George Bush; their triumphs would bolster GOP convictions about the transformed terrain. But Sugar Land had another champion who intends to still have a grip on national power when both Bushes are writing their memoirs and organizing their presidential libraries. That champion is Tom DeLay.

In 1974 American theaters were briefly graced by a movie called *The Sugarland Express*. Based on a true story, the film tells the adventures of a fugitive Texas convict and his spunky harebrained wife (played by Michael Sacks and Goldie Hawn), who kidnap a rookie state trooper in a desperate attempt to keep the state from putting their infant son in a foster home. Though the movie employs many action-picture clichés, the director had the good sense to slow it down; the chase across Texas is a comic foreshadowing of O. J. Simpson and the white Bronco. "I've been on the force eighteen years," drawls Ben Johnson, who plays a highway patrol captain trying to avert a disaster. "It's been my good fortune not to have killed anybody in that time. That's the way I'd like to keep it."

The town where the runaways mean to reclaim their baby is held off-camera, some sweet place where their family can be redeemed, always luring them on. When this fictional Sugar Land finally materializes onscreen, it is a Southern town with broad streets and swings on front porches and a sprawling junk car yard on the outskirts. *The Sugarland Express* is a minor classic, which is surprising only because the film is so little-known today. It was the first feature of a young director named Steven Spielberg.

Tom DeLay started doing business in Sugar Land during the time Spielberg was exploring the town as a metaphor, and De-

Lay later made his home there. But the Texas town that became his power base bore no resemblance to the one the filmmaker imagined.

In the 1820s the coastal prairie and savannah along the Brazos River, which empties into the Gulf of Mexico a few miles south of contemporary Houston, had lured the first settlers from the United States to the Texas colony of Stephen F. Austin, in what was then Mexico. Some residents of DeLay's congressional district still proudly claim heritage as descendants of "Austin's Three Hundred." The Brazos bottomlands get abundant rain—one legendary flood reached eight miles across—and the heavily silted, dark gumbo soil is extraordinarily fertile. Some of Texas's richest plantations sprawled across the valley in fields of cotton, corn, and sugar cane. The village of Sugar Land, which lay just west of the frenetic swamp town of Houston, grew around a raw sugar mill that two of the planters opened in 1843. Another thing the countryside nourished was prisons—a culture of dog boys and horseback-riding guards and convicts in white coveralls wielding ten-pound hoes. The Civil War killed off most of the original plantations, but sugar-cane farmers continued to thrive with unpaid labor leased from the prisons. De facto slavery was alive and well, legal and brutal. The convicts suffered malaria and tuberculosis and all kinds of infective fevers. Texas convicts called Sugar Land "the Hell Hole on the Brazos."

Though the hamlet became a depot on a fourteen-mile railroad, its population was just 500 in the early 1890s. But in the first decade of the new century a group of investors bought two of the old plantations. They named their enterprise the Imperial Sugar Company, and one of Imperial's founders devoted himself to re-creating Sugar Land as a company town. Ethnic Germans and Czechs moved in and gave the town a stable population, but outside town, the planters' labor pool and the convicts' bitterness went unchanged. In 1914 the company sold one of the sugar plantations to the Texas prison system, which continued to run it the same way. The pioneering blues singer Lead-belly—better known to wardens as the Dallas murderer Huddie Ledbetter—composed a version of a classic song called "Midnight Special." The Midnight Special was a train that each night passed right beside the Sugar Land prison. Leadbelly said that the inmates considered it good luck to inhabit a cell in which the headlight from the locomotive shone through the bars as the train passed. One verse goes:

> If you ever go to Houston, boy, you better walk right
> *and you better not gamble, and you better not fight*
> 'Cuz Benson Crocker will arrest you
> *and Jimmy Boone will take you down*
> And you better bet your bottom dollar
> *that you're Sugar Land bound*

Imports of raw sugar sent the cane the way of antebellum king cotton in the country of the Brazos. Farmers moved on to other crops, especially rice. By 1932 Imperial was the last sugar manufacturer in Texas. The company diversified into vinegar and pickles, mattresses and warehousing, and the plant held on by refining Cuban sugar. After Cold War politics eliminated that supply, the refinery endured a long slow death, though Imperial retained its headquarters in Sugar Land. Until Spielberg came along, the most fame ever bestowed on the town was the blessing and curse of a 1950s high school running back named Ken Hall. Many of his records still stand, but his college coach, Bear Bryant, rarely let him off the bench at Texas A&M because he couldn't play defense, and the can't-miss All-American abruptly quit and wound up back in Sugar Land, pumping gas.

A small cluster of dignified homes and tall trees is the last vestige of the Czech and German community. But Sugar Land's destiny was hardly that of a slowly wasting small town. The coastal plain had lavish mineral wealth—oil, gas, sulfur. Houston had become a major seaport, and sprawling outward from the city was an industrial goliath of oil refineries and petro-chemical plants. Sugar Land was just west of Houston and was built on or near major highways—Texas 90, U.S. 59, and U.S. Interstate 10—that moved that commerce overland: it was a suburb waiting to happen, and the catalyst of its transformation was the oil boom of the seventies. Son of an oilman, Tom DeLay didn't follow his dad into that business, but he subscribed to the boom mentality and understood the ground rules. From pest control to advertising agencies to fleets of dump trucks, everything in the coastal economy was riding on a flood of oil money. Office towers and balloon-note mortgages shot up; real estate speculators were flipping raw land like burgers. Almost overnight, metropolitan Houston spilled out the highways to Sugar Land and engulfed it, endowing it with fast food, vast shopping centers, and upscale brick subdivisions crowded right up to the fences of the prisons. The gated-entry homes were jammed close together and had a numbing sameness, but to the commuters they seemed so far, so secure from the intimidating ethnicities and crime of Houston. With dozens of churches, reborn Sugar Land transformed murky bayous into high-spurting fountains, golf courses were its public parks, and the malls along the highways made the town look like the world capital of Bed Bath & Beyond.

Tom DeLay might have remained a frustrated conservative fighting off tax liens in a sugar mill town that today is a Houston suburb if not for a sea change in Texas politics. The forces roiling the sea had never been entirely insular. After the Civil War, Texas paid dearly for its secession from the Union; carpetbaggers and scalawags, who claimed the government's offices through restrictions on who could vote, carried out the vengeance of Republican radicals. The Reconstruction Republicans trampled individual liberties and all but looted the state.

When Reconstruction ended, in the 1870s, Texas enacted one of the most restrictive state constitutions in the country—its purpose was to ensure that such abuses by government could not recur. Definitions of what constituted a Democrat or Republican would change vastly, of course, but historically those abuses were identified with the GOP.

The ideological tilt in Texas had always been rightward, but the state was swayed by national trends. The Depression—and the blame for it that Democrats successfully laid on Herbert Hoover—further strengthened the Democrats' grip in Texas. The aristocratic New Yorker Franklin D. Roosevelt was popular enough in Texas to carry the state handily four times; a number of Texas politicians won high office while voicing their commitment to carry out the New Deal. Roosevelt mentored several young Texans in Congress, among them a tall, rawboned, ambitious ex-schoolteacher from the Hill Country, Lyndon Baines Johnson. During the Truman and Eisenhower presidencies, Johnson rose to power in the Senate while performing a nimble high-wire act over liberal and conservative camps in Texas. As things turned out, his inability to control those factions helped the Republicans slip inside the tent.

Johnson accepted John Fitzgerald Kennedy's offer of the vice presidential nomination in 1960, but LBJ was always one to cover his rear. By then he was the Senate majority leader, a position of great power, and he was up for reelection the same year. His allies in the Texas Legislature graciously allowed him to file for both offices on the ballot. A diminutive political science professor named John Tower offered himself as the Republicans' sacrificial lamb in the Senate race. Johnson delivered Kennedy the White House—JFK would not have squeaked by in Texas and defeated Nixon without him. But in the Senate race John Tower's numbers were surprising; he gained his first traction among voters who were annoyed by Johnson's strategy of keeping all of his bases covered. Later, in the 1961 special election to fill the Senate seat vacated when Johnson became vice president, Tower had the good fortune of an opponent named Bill Blakly, the interim appointee and choice of conservative Democrats. Liberals came up with the idea that because party and state convention rules were stacked against them, they could succeed only by encouraging conservatives to leave the party and become Republicans. They pitched in to help make the Republican Party more viable. Liberal Democrats stayed home in the 1961 Senate election, or else they voted for Tower. The liberal Machiavellians thought they could easily get rid of him later. They were wrong.

Texas's other Senate seat was held by Ralph Yarborough, a liberal and populist. Yarborough's nemesis was the governor, John Connally, an LBJ protégé and a darling of the conservative lawyers and businessmen who financed the Johnson machine. Yarborough had gotten his start as an assistant attorney general suing oil companies for bilking public schools out of royalties. Connally was a lawyer for oilmen. The two disagreed about labor unions, the rights of farmworkers, drilling for oil and gas in natural areas—they despised each other. Yarborough, who had been tarred by the right-wingers as a communist sympathizer, was paranoid about Johnson and his crowd; Connally was a moderate in many ways, but he was indeed working with those same right-wingers to line up a primary opponent against Yarborough. Texas opinion polls for the 1964 presidential election had Kennedy trailing Barry Goldwater in the state by a substantial margin. Exasperated that Johnson couldn't bring the feuding leaders into line for the ticket—and wanting to raise some Texas money—Kennedy decided to force them to behave by scheduling a high-profile swing through Texas that took him to Dallas in November 1963.

The Great Society legislation that Johnson bullied through Congress as president, with considerable help from Yarborough, was more a fulfillment of Roosevelt's vision than Kennedy's. Johnson's career proved to be both the apotheosis and end of the Democrats' hegemony in Texas. The one-party rule of the Democrats had a rotten spine—a long tradition of financial corruption, electoral fraud, and racial prejudice and exclusion. The contradictions of LBJ were captured in the glory and gloom that accompanied his engineering and signature of the U.S. Voting Rights Act in 1964. In rebuking his segregationist past he knew his finest hour—his greatest act of conscience. Yet he confided to an aide his fears that he had just signed over the South to the Republicans for a generation. That may have been a typically egocentric interpretation of cause and effect, but Johnson's vision of the future was accurate.

George Bush the elder, a war hero and Connecticut scion who had made a dashing fortune as a west Texas wildcatter, was projected as the next champion of the Republican takeover of the state. It didn't happen. The patrician Bush lost Senate races to Yarborough in 1964 and then to a conservative Democrat, Lloyd Bentsen, who knocked off Yarborough in a nasty primary race in 1970. Bush had to rely on the largesse of the national Republican Party to extend his career.

The coup de grace to the Texas Democratic machine was instead applied by a cranky Dallas oilman named Bill Clements. In the 1978 Democratic primary, the incumbent governor Dolph Briscoe was upset by a business-oriented attorney general named John Hill. Everyone thought the old ways would hold—the election of the next governor had been decided. But national politics was again a factor. Clements, who favored garish sport coats and swore like a roughneck, kicked off the general election campaign by flinging a rubber chicken across a banquet table and telling the astonished Hill that he was going to hang Jimmy Carter around his neck in the way that country people cured chicken-killing dogs. Clements attracted a cadre of ideologically charged and self-assured young Republicans that included one Karl Rove. They used direct mail and phone banks in ways that were brand-new to Texas politics. Clements won the election in the last hours and rescued John Tower in his closest call.

The Republicans did take some casualties. In west Texas George W. Bush was doing all he could to live up to the example of his dad, but his oil wells were dry holes, and in an impulsive race for Congress that year he campaigned poorly and was spanked by a clever conservative Democrat. Except for governor, the Democrats held every statewide office, and they dominated the Legislature. Still, with that election a century of one-party rule in Texas began to crumble like the loose banks of a flooding Brazos River. After 1978 a phrase in political news coverage became a cliché: "the first Republican _____ since Reconstruction." It wasn't just a governor and a senator. Fill in the blank. Though it was little noted at the time, one of the politicians who caught a ride on that wave was an exterminator named Tom DeLay.

Across the Brazos from Sugar Land is a small town that retains the air and flavor celebrated in Steven Spielberg's movie. One of the first communities chartered by the Republic of Texas, Richmond has little in common with the posh suburb that Sugar Land became. A cattle rancher named Hilmar Moore, whose family was among Austin's Three Hundred, has been Richmond's mayor since 1950. Once a prominent Democrat, now an independent, Moore reminisced in an interview, "Tom had a pest control operation when he first came here, but he's a wealthy man now. Back then he was a Democrat." The mayor laughed at the surprise provoked by his remark (and a DeLay press aide would dismiss that proposition with an indignant snort). "What else would he have been?" the mayor persisted. "Around here in those days, it was like, 'Look, there's a Republican.' Like a freak in a circus."

When his hopes of getting into medical school faded, DeLay had thought about engineering. But after graduating from the University of Houston in 1970, he had gone to work for Redwood

Chemical, which sold rat bait. He and Christine had a daughter, Danielle, in 1972. After a couple of years of working for wages, DeLay believed he saw enough opportunity to go into business for himself; the warm and muggy lowlands of Texas always have a surfeit of pest insects. With a wry and mocking nod to a growing and fashionable political movement, he christened his start-up enterprise Environmental Services. Months later he bought a larger and more established service, Albo Pest Control. He didn't much like the name, he once said, but he kept it in hopes that clients might associate it with the big Alpo dog food company. DeLay schmoozed with suppliers and competitors in the Greater Houston Pest Control Association and other trade groups, looking for leads and an edge. In the boom climate he picked up accounts in west Houston and suburban Stafford, Rosenberg, Missouri City, and Sugar Land. He was a good salesman, but his dream of running a small business was troubled from the start.

DeLay surfaced in public life at thirty-one looking much different than he does today. He had a full head of black hair, sideburns to his earlobes, and a thick mustache—in some photos he resembled the movie star Cliff Robertson. DeLay and his wife and daughter had been living in Simonton, a rodeo town evolving into a bedroom community near Sugar Land. DeLay went to a Republican precinct meeting in Fort Bend County one night and come away their elected chairman. A Democrat was vacating the legislative House seat that embraced Fort Bend and parts of Harris and Brazoria counties. DeLay had been meeting with a small group of Republicans who were handicapping elections and cultivating candidates, and they decided it was his time to run. DeLay read a how-to book on running campaigns and paid his filing fee for the GOP unopposed. Two young attorneys and an optometrist named Larry Wilkinson fought it out gently in the Democratic primary. A *Houston Post* reporter watched the candidates together at a rally and wrote a story headlined, "Four 'Nice Guys' in the Running." The reporter, who seemed charmed by the Republican, ended his piece: "'Give me your support,' [DeLay] urged the crowd. 'Give me your money,' he said with a smile. 'Give me your vote.'"

Ah, yes, money. DeLay was out front on that from the start. But he was less forthright about his party affiliation. He kept his inclinations vague when he courted the favor of Richmond mayor Hilmar Moore, the dean of politicians in Fort Bend County, and early in the race DeLay tried to hide the ball, just as he had in naming an exterminating company Environmental Services. Years later, at a local chamber of commerce luncheon, he would recall the 1978 race:

> I didn't tell anybody I was a Republican. . . . Because I would run into business people, quite frankly, and they would say, "I'm going to support you, Tom, but don't tell anybody, because if they find out that I'm supporting a Republican, they won't do business with me."
>
> True. I ran into that all across the district.
>
> Back then, if you remember, the Democrat primary was the election, and if you won the Democrat nomination, you were elected. So it was pretty difficult. In fact, I'll never forget, three weeks after the primary I was standing in front of Howard's cafeteria in downtown Rosenberg, Texas, in the middle of the week at lunch. That was the best place to politic back then because that was where all the business people ate lunch, and ranchers and farmers from Fort Bend and Brazoria [counties] ate lunch there. It was about two-fifty or three dollars for all you could eat. Wonderful home cooking. I'd stand out there any chance I'd get and work the crowds. . . .
>
> I found out very quickly that you waited until they came out. Going in, they were hungry and mean, so you always waited until they came out. You aspiring politicians out there, you should take that to heart. But I'll never forget this particular day. I was standing out there and this huge, tall Czech rice farmer came walking out. Now, I knew he was a rice farmer because in Fort

Bend County, all the rice farmers wear a uniform. They wear brown cowboy boots, brown khaki pants, and a brown khaki shirt. I knew he was of Czech descent, because he had on the Czech small-crown cowboy hat, and he must have been at least six-six or six-seven, and weighed at least two hundred eighty pounds, if he weighed a pound, all muscle.

I mean, this was a big dude, and he came walking out and I said, "Hi, I'm Tom DeLay. I'm running for state representative, I'd like to talk to you about your vote." And he looked down at me and he said, "Now, wait a minute, wasn't that election about three weeks ago? And Larry Wilkinson won that."

I said, "No, no, I'm the Republican in the race. My name is Tom DeLay, and I'm running for the general election in November."

Well, that did take him aback. He'd never seen a Republican before. Much less some idiot in Fort Bend County that would admit he was a Republican.

But finally, well, I waited him out, and he said, "I want to tell you something, boy. It'll be a cold day in hell when a Republican wins in this county."

Tom DeLay had no trouble coming off as a hometown good old boy, but his speeches delivered bland clichés. "It's time for the common citizen to get involved in our government." "We need a state representative who will ask us what we want instead of telling us what we need." Still, he made it clear that what people needed from Austin was less. "Government has become a monster," DeLay proclaimed. "Texas government is becoming too big and powerful."

The Texas monster always ranked near the bottom in teacher salaries, overall spending for education, and social services, a front-runner only in toxic pollution. But thanks to the oil boom, state government was running a billion-dollar surplus (which would not occur again until the tech boom of the nineties, when Governor George W. Bush returned a $3 billion surplus to tax-

payers, leaving the state a huge deficit after he moved on). De-
Lay advocated giving that money back by repealing the state
sales tax and reforming property taxes, especially estate taxes.
He had only one spending priority: more roads. The biggest issue to him was clogged highways. DeLay promised he would
take on transportation bureaucrats from the county seats to
Washington, D.C. To DeLay, transportation meant only cars
and trucks, not public transit. "I want to make the highway dollar worth a dollar," he shouted.

In content, his campaign was unexceptional, but he subscribed to ideas that were working for Republicans. He sent out
26,000 well-aimed "legislative questionnaires"— direct-mail
pleas for contributions and turnout. Many of his supporters
were women. They felt empowered by advances gained in the
name of women's rights, but also that their suburban priorities
and middle-class way of life were being ignored, and the Democrats represented the status quo. A vote for Republicans was a
vote for change. After the traffic jams let go of their husbands
and the kids were fed, they worked phone banks and walked
blocks for Bill Clements, John Tower, and Tom DeLay. The
folksy Democratic optometrist Larry Wilkinson was favored to
win the general election. But the Republican vote in the suburbs
came in strong, and their candidate won the race handily, 13,012
to 10,905, or 54 percent of the vote. So it was that Tom DeLay
became the first Republican elected to the Texas Legislature in
Fort Bend County since Reconstruction.

A. R. "Babe" Schwartz is an Austin lobbyist who for many
years was a charismatic state senator from Galveston. He is a
Democrat. Schwartz's district included Fort Bend County; one
would think he had some opportunity to take the measure of his
peer in the House chamber. But Schwartz professes to be
stumped when he tries to dredge up much impression or even
memory of DeLay's work in the Legislature. "It was totally nondescript," Schwartz describes the performance. "You wouldn't
have known he was there except that he was elected. I would say

he gave Fort Bend County the kind of representation it expected and deserved. The only time I recall working with him was on a deregulation bill. I was always the liberal against regulation. I cosponsored a bill that proposed to deregulate trucking; Tom carried a companion bill on the House side that was going to deregulate use of agricultural vehicles on the road. But that's all, in my experience. He didn't appear to have any ambition."

That's not quite accurate or fair. DeLay authored or co-authored twenty other bills that spring of 1979, and nearly a hundred more in sessions of 1981 and 1983. But none reflecting his Republican values passed. The bulk of DeLay's freshman measures were attempts to reform elective procedures. They dealt with the transmission of election results, distribution of filing fees to state party chairmen, the duties of poll watchers, and the like. Texas legislators serve two-year terms; DeLay won twice more against token Democratic opposition. In his terms he showed some glimmers of a social conscience. With Wilhelmina Delco, a liberal black educator from Austin, he cosponsored proposals to create a pilot program for parent education, to prohibit racial discrimination by the state's alcoholic beverage commission, to make school lunches available to senior citizens, and to grant special parking permits to disabled persons.

DeLay also got on well with Craig Washington, a black legislator and future congressman who was cut from the mold of his Houston predecessors Barbara Jordan and Mickey Leland. Washington said that in the 1980s, "DeLay blossomed, I think, because he's smart and he's good at consensus-building. We would meet in the back and talk through issues sometimes, and he would come to me on a sticking point between Democrats and Republicans, and if he thought I could help, he would ask me to intercede. He's a good guy, as far as I know."

DeLay's voting record was emphatically conservative. He was against extending workmen's compensation benefits to farmworkers. He was for allowing loan sharks to charge borrowers interest rates of up to 90 percent for loans of under $300. He voted to weaken a consumer protection and deceptive trade practices act. With so many prisons in his district, he naturally tried to assert himself in that realm of policy making. He was against granting conjugal visits to state inmates. He was against restoring voting rights to felons who had been pardoned (though he later accepted a great deal of money and policy advice from one such person in Sugar Land). He was against allowing nonviolent offenders to do their time in community corrections centers. He was against allowing inmates furloughs to attend family funerals or visit terminally ill relatives. Back in the wider world, he was against providing public education to children of illegal aliens, and against bringing state laws into agreement with the federal civil rights acts of 1964 and 1968, but he was for allowing storage of radioactive waste within fifty miles of the state's cities.

DeLay later said, "It took me two years to change my reputation from a fire-breathing right-winger to a guy you can work with." His colleagues may have encouraged him to regulate the burners, too. "It's not correct to say he played no role," said veteran capitol observer Sam Kinch, then with the *Dallas Morning News*. "He was way over on the right—you didn't have any trouble recognizing that. And he was not such a backbencher that he was invisible. He'd dress down people testifying before committees. But when he'd take the mike on the floor, he just wasn't very good at it. I think other Republicans gently told him that." When he tried to make a speech on the floor, Democrats raised an amiable jeer—"Dee-lay, Dee-lay!" The reference was to the time it required him to frame his thoughts and sentences. Despite his fervent conservatism and belief that the rules were wrongly jiggered to keep the other side in eternal power, he was then the kind of Republican who would call it a day and go out and raise a glass with Democrats. He hit it off with John Sharp, a Democratic senator from Victoria of much promise and backing but who would only rise as high in statewide office as comptroller. "He was one of the most fun, humorous guys I hung around with," Sharp said, trying to balance those perceptions against the fierce partisan who later emerged in Congress. "We carried bills together, we laughed, we joked. The stuff you read now . . . it's like 180 degrees different." Sharp's rival for higher office, Garry Mauro, was the land commissioner and a close friend of an Arkansas couple named Bill and Hillary Clinton. Mauro was never a friend of DeLay, but he remembered him as a legislator who would listen and might be persuaded. "This guy was no radical. He was a pragmatist."

Kinch said: "DeLay wasn't an easy guy to get to know, or to like. But toward the end of his time it became apparent that he could count votes. Both sides, Democrats and Republicans, and not just how people were going to vote—how they would probably vote. That's a valuable gift to have in legislating. Which is how he caught on in Congress, and he had the skill even then. I noticed he had become the leadership's go-to guy when they had a close vote on the floor. So I started going to him, too."

But DeLay is remembered most in Austin as a party animal. His wife and daughter were 250 miles away, and he didn't have the air of someone pining for home and hearth. The Speaker was a folksy conservative Democrat from west Texas named Billy Clayton. Clayton seemed to like DeLay, though he never entrusted him with a committee chairmanship, and he made other Republicans part of his leadership team. Clayton organized a morale builder called Speaker's Night at the Broken Spoke, an old beery dance hall with low ceilings, red tablecloths, country-western music, and chicken-fried steak. DeLay was almost always there. "And you know what?" recalled Shelia Cheany, an attorney and lobbyist whose employers have included the American Civil Liberties Union. "He was a terrific dancer."

DeLay and several House colleagues—of both parties— spent the sessions in a rental that came to be known as Macho Manor. "They had the wildest parties in town," said Debra Danburg, a liberal Democrat who plunged right into the festivities.

Near the Capitol were two saloons favored by the legislative crowd. In an office building, the Quorum looked down on a ground-floor joint called the Cedar Door. A short walk from the Cedar Door was a massage parlor. He had a nickname around the Legislature and its pleasure-seeking camp followers. With no particular malice they called him Hot Tub Tom.

Carl Parker was a senator and trial lawyer who came out of Gulf Coast refinery towns and was renowned for his legislative skills and withering sarcasm; those attributes didn't keep him from being swept from power in a strategy that DeLay would help fund and engineer. "I see DeLay around now and he carries on like we're old long-lost buddies," Parker said from his perch in private life. "In those days he was just good-time Tom, partying and drinking that lobby whiskey. I don't remember him having any effect on legislation."

Sour grapes, one can say. But Democrats aren't the only ones who remember Sugar Land's champion as a hedonistic backbencher; Republicans and capitol reporters as well blink and shake their heads when they try to align those memories with his thundering prowess in national politics today. It is an extraordinarily common refrain: he would have been the last one you ever figured.

THREE

Freshman Year:
The Exterminator Finds Jesus

The Texas Legislature meets for six months every other year, with occasional special sessions. This schedule, according to a past Speaker of its lower house, is designed to make it almost impossible to pass legislation. Also by design of the authors of the anti-carpetbagger, anti-scalawag constitution of 1876, Texans with little money are discouraged from thinking they might fashion a career in politics. Texas legislators are paid $7,200 a year, an amount fixed by the state constitution. The result is a Legislature made up of those wealthy enough to serve and those who live off the largesse of the business lobby—or those who fall into both categories. This governing body, hostile to the notion of government and subservient to the business lobby, was a perfect training ground for the Republican Congress Tom De-Lay would dominate three decades later.

If the experience was instructive, the honorarium he earned as a Texas state rep wasn't enough to steer him past the chug-holes that constantly rattled his finances and business life. Depending on his audience, DeLay might say he stayed in the pest control business for either six or eighteen years after he was elected in 1978 (hostile attorneys the former, friendly Lions Clubs and Rotarians the latter). However long it lasted, his life as an exterminator was a never-ending struggle.

According to company tax returns and minutes of stockholder meetings, Albo Pest Control reached and maintained gross receipts of about $250,000, though a net operating loss was carried forward each year. One year the company reported sales of $394,000, and the accountant whittled the taxable income down to zero—no taxes owed. But the cost of insurance and chemicals kept going up, and there was a limit to what people would pay for his service. Killing roaches and rats was no way to get rich.

Though DeLay was a state legislator, the most significant act of government to personally touch him came with little fanfare out of Washington. It was a federal regulation—the very sort of regulation he believed was strangling small businesses—of one specific pesticide. The imported fire ant is an exotic species that first arrived in the U.S. in Mobile, Alabama, hitching a ride on steamships from South America. One fire ant is not a prepossessing creature. But its venom far exceeds its size—hence the name. Fire ants are aggressive. And they swarm. They kill game birds and even newborn livestock. Floods have sent clumps of ants the size of basketballs bobbing downstream. They thrive where the air is warm, direct sun is plentiful, and the ground is wet. Cold winters have blocked their spread northward from the Gulf states, but they've ranged north into the Carolinas and westward into Texas along irrigation ditches and well-watered golf courses. God help California, entomologists say, if fire ants ever jump from Texas west across the desert.

But the prime habitat of fire ants is pastures and suburban lawns in places like Sugar Land. Fire ants defy pesticides. Spray an anthill and the ants will move a few meters to avoid any noxious liquid drainage. Unless the queen ant is killed, the mound keeps growing. And the queen is one tough bug. DeLay and other exterminators on the Gulf Coast used Mirex, one of very few pesticides that could kill fire ants. But Mirex also had the potential to kill more than fire ants. It is a persistent bioaccumulative toxin. That is, it doesn't break down in the environment, but builds up in body tissue, increasing in concentration as it moves up the food chain. When it settles in at the top of the food chain, it potentially causes cancer—and certainly damage to the kidney, liver, intestinal system, central nervous system, and reproductive organs. Humans are at the top of the food chain. In 1978, after six years of hearings, the Environmental Protection Agency banned the product as unsafe. That, DeLay said, was when he decided that the EPA was an evil empire. That was when he decided he was going to stop simply complaining about the federal government. He would run for Congress, and start fixing the problem.

"Christ," a beleaguered EPA official would later mutter on hearing that story. "We could have lived with Mirex."

By 1984 Senator John Tower had enjoyed enough pioneering for his party and Texas. To critics he was furniture—someone who took up floor space and never passed a bill. To Texas Republicans he was a hero. Though Tower probably could have held the seat as long as he wanted, Texas Democrats considered him a pompous lightweight who could be defeated. They believed if they raised enough money and recruited the right young, energetic candidate, eventually they would take him down. The 1978 election had led them to believe they were right, and worried Republicans; Hill Country Congressman Bob Krueger came close to defeating Tower, losing by 12,000 votes out of 2.3 million cast. So as his second term was winding down, before the '84 elections, Tower retired from the Senate, continuing to serve the Reagan administration as an arms negotiator, and he headed the commission that investigated the Iran-Contra scandal. In 1989, Reagan's successor, George H. W. Bush, nominated Tower as his secretary of defense, but Tower was forced to withdraw after a prolonged and vicious confirmation fight. Senate Democrats shredded Tower's reputation, portraying him as a drunk and fanny-grabber—though he'd been one of their colleagues a few months earlier. A bitter man, he later died (with a daughter) in a small-plane crash, a sad end for such an historic figure.

Following Tower's retirement, Republicans had scrambled to hold his Senate seat. Ron Paul was the congressman from the twenty-second district, which included Fort Bend County. Paul, a doctor and quirky conservative, decided to give up his House seat to run for the Senate. He lost the primary to Phil Gramm, an economics professor from Texas A&M who had left the Democratic Party when he held a seat in the U.S. House. Gramm played an important role in the Republican takeover of Texas—he proved that a party-switcher with enough energy and money could overcome the blue bloods and ideologues who had always voted in the GOP primary. (After the loss Paul declared himself a Libertarian, though he eventually returned to Congress as a Republican.)

There was more going on here than the end of the elitist Republican Party that had put down its roots along the fairways of the state's country clubs, weekend ranches, or all-white fin-and-feather lodges like the Koon Kreek Klub. (The racist pun that brought together coons and the KKK was what passed for humor among some white Texans. It certainly wasn't sufficiently offensive to keep old Dallas money—including Governor Bill Clements and the ownership of the *Dallas Morning News*—from joining the exclusive East Texas hunt club. Unable to get in because there were no more lots or memberships available, George W. Bush joined the adjacent, less prestigious, but equally white Rainbo Club.) Texas, like the rest of the South, was heading precisely where Lyndon Johnson had predicted it would go. The tectonic plates of American electoral politics were shifting and once again, race was the fault line. The first civil rights movement, led by Lincoln, had made the Republican Party anathema in Texas and the rest of the South, leaving the region in the hands of conservative Democrats. Tory Democrats, they called them in Texas. Lacking a viable Republican Party, they made their home in the right wing of the Democratic Party. When King, the Kennedy brothers, and Johnson began to complete the civil rights movement that Douglass and Lincoln had begun a hundred years earlier, that party was over. In 1961 John Tower was a very early bellwether. He sneaked into the U.S. Senate after every Democratic politician who could get it up ran for the seat vacated by LBJ, dividing the party and producing a candidate more conservative and less charismatic than Tower. Twenty-two years later, the next Republican to win a Senate race in Texas was a man of the political moment. Phil Gramm didn't quietly walk away from the Democratic Party in 1983; he gave it a kick in its moldering ass and strutted into history. Gramm had been a leader of the Boll Weevils — Southern congressional Democrats who supported the tax cuts, savaging of social services, and expansion of the military that were Ronald Reagan's core program. First Gramm resigned from his seat in the U.S. House and filed as a Republican in the special election called to fill the seat he had just given up. George W. Bush's career-long political adviser Karl Rove had talked Gramm into making the switch to the Republican Party. Then Gramm entered the Senate race and with Rove's help defeated a liberal opponent, wrapping up a three-step process that included Gramm's departure from the Democratic Party, Tower's decision not to run a fifth time for the Senate, and Gramm's 1984 ride into the Senate.

The down-ballot seats that opened up with Tower's departure from the Senate were gifts to whoever could win the Republican nominations, and the twenty-second district seat Ron Paul abandoned for his failed race against Gramm held real appeal for Republican candidates. With each redistricting the twenty-second district was nudged away from ethnic and blue-collar neighborhoods in southwest Houston into the outlying suburbs, which were shaped by white flight. Each bump out into the burbs made it more difficult for a Democrat to win in the twenty-second.

DeLay had never achieved much in the Texas State House, but that didn't discourage him from running for the seat that opened up when Paul and Gramm scrambled to run for the Senate seat Tower left. DeLay even seemed cut in the mold of John Tower. A major donor in Houston told DeLay that his mustache would turn off GOP voters, so he shaved it; without the mustache, DeLay resembled Tower. DeLay was never going to affect the senator's hauteur and airs as an intellectual. But he was short, a natty dresser, and his black hair, no longer fluffy, was combed to the side, away from a part sprayed on so straight it looked like a bullet had skimmed his head. Like Tower, DeLay was perceived to be too much a man of the world to be an extremist. In those days nobody talked about a mean streak.

The race for a congressional seat looked easier than his first run for the Texas Legislature. DeLay was certain he could catch a big ride at the top of the ballot; Reagan was running for reelection against Walter Mondale and certain to carry Texas. In September 1983 DeLay announced his candidacy at a Holiday Inn in west Houston. "I want to help President Reagan stay the course, and I hope you do too," he told a couple of hundred supporters. He described himself as "a consistent, conscientious conservative" and promised to vote against every spending bill he could in Congress. He declared sternly, "We have to teach the federal government how to live within its means."

DeLay had directed his own campaigns for the Legislature, but this time he hired a firm called Southern Political Consulting (SPC), which had close ties to another first-time congressional candidate, Dick Armey, an economics professor from the Dallas suburbs. The race was the start of a close alliance and friendship between DeLay and Armey that in time would go terribly awry. DeLay ran on deregulation—and on his support of a bill that had been passed but vetoed by the Democratic governor, Mark White, who had ousted Republican Bill Clements in 1982. The bill DeLay ran on would have blocked the city of Houston from sucking the groundwater out from under DeLay's suburban district in Fort Bend County. There wasn't much more for him to run on. DeLay could hardly stand on a record of

passing resolutions honoring the retirement of beloved constituents, the centennial of the city of Rosenberg, and the
Willowridge high school football team. His principal accomplishment in the 1983 session had been a bill designating a Big
Brothers/Big Sisters Day in Texas.

DeLay was confident, but he had several GOP opponents,
and they didn't roll over for him. They knew DeLay had compiled a thin résumé in his three terms in the Texas House. And
they weren't going to let him pad that résumé by running as a
small businessman who paid his bills, met his payroll, and did
his part to sustain the local economy. A developer in the race
disclosed that the IRS had filed liens against DeLay and Albo in
1979, 1980, and 1983. DeLay had consistently failed to pay income and Social Security taxes that he had withheld from the
paychecks of employees. DeLay quickly ran radio spots to con-
tain the damage, claiming that everything about his relationship
with the IRS was on the up-and-up now. "Times were hard," he
explained to the *Houston Chronicle*. "The pest control business is
seasonal, and it was a choice of paying off employees or post-
poning the taxes and paying off the penalties and interest. I
chose to keep the employees."

He overcame that embarrassment and won the primary without a runoff. In the general election, incumbent President
Ronald Reagan carried 69 percent of the vote in Texas, and like
a Pinto tailgating an eighteen-wheeler, DeLay cruised along in
the president's slipstream, dispatching his Democratic opponent with ease. One political attribute he never lacked was luck.
"My opponent called me an extremist, a right-wing extremist,"
DeLay crowed. "I just thanked him for it." (In the hothouse political culture of suburban Texas, "right-wing" was hardly a pejo-
rative.) In Dallas, SPC's other client, Dick Armey, won his race
as well. DeLay's history of winning elections and Armey's
supreme self-assurance made them leaders of the largest class of
Texas Republicans elected to Congress since the rigged elections of Reconstruction. Nationwide the Republicans picked up

fourteen House seats, not as many as handicappers thought would be carried into office by Reagan's resounding defeat of Mondale. In Texas, the balance of power in the House shifted from twenty-one Democrats and six Republicans to seventeen Democrats and ten Republicans. Six of the Texas Republicans were freshmen; they were soon touted as the "Texas Six-Pack." DeLay told one writer, "We are all what you would consider the new young right."

But they still were in the minority. Democrats controlled the House by a comfortable 253–182 margin. DeLay had to find some way to make his mark as a member of the minority—just as he had in Austin. So along with Armey and another Dallas freshman from the suburbs, Steve Bartlett, he found an issue certain to attract the attention of the media. Half the Texas six-pack decided to take on the National Endowment for the Arts.

After arriving in Washington DeLay called a press conference and apologized to reporters for asking them to read poems that included profanity and passages meant to be erotic. "Smut!" he condemned the selected verses, written by people who had won NEA grants. "Even *Penthouse* wouldn't print them," he carried on, deleting certain offensive vowels from his dramatic reading. (In fact, they had been printed in *Policy Review,* the magazine published by the conservative Heritage Foundation, where De-Lay found them.) "I feel that many people would never believe the grossness of the writing." He spotted easy pickings in NEA-approved visual and pop arts, too: $25,000 for a documentary about an elephant roundup in Thailand, $10,000 to research new shapes of bathtubs, $5,000 for design of clothing using sheet metal, $3,000 for a study of people's relationships with their cars. DeLay was no prude or censor, he assured the reporters, but he had not come to Congress to stand for taxpayer dollars being spent on pornography and banalities.

The performance was vintage DeLay, full of sound and fury, signifying a little—and desperately trying to get somebody's attention. Under the Reagan administration and the Democrats' congressional leadership, the government was running up $200 billion deficits—then an astounding figure—and the NEA was just getting used to the idea that it was not a sacred cow. DeLay wanted to cut $16 million, a full tenth, from the arts agency's budget. He set off a hot-tempered debate that resulted in a proposed $8 million cut before the measure moved on to conference with the Senate and numbers crunchers at the White House, where the real budgets are worked out. The chairman of the NEA growled, "What does he want us to be? An official art agency where you only fund things that are acceptable to everybody? That's just like they have in the Soviet Union."

In fact, that wasn't far off the mark from what he wanted. The NEA and its beneficiaries were learning that arts were a low priority of the new young right, as DeLay described himself; if the curators and elitists wanted any public funding, they had better start falling in line, and it wasn't long before they did. DeLay accomplished exactly what he set out to do with his stunt about poetry, and then moved on in search of more publicity and exposure.

The arts community in Houston was stunned, then incensed. Who the hell was Tom DeLay? A board member of the Houston Ballet and prestigious Alley Theater said, "I really am very outraged that any congressman would take a morality march against the arts." Cynthia Macdonald, a poet of national reputation and a professor in the budding writing program at DeLay's alma mater, the University of Houston, proclaimed, "This reminds me of what happened to D. H. Lawrence and James Joyce." DeLay was pleased, and he fired back in the *Houston Chronicle*. "I don't know of one dollar in this whole budget that feeds anybody or clothes anybody or helps anybody but a bunch of rich people in Houston."

Rich people in Houston. For Tom DeLay in 1985 true conservatism was a class issue, a fight against those elitists who were always looking down their noses at him and his constituents. Those natural enemies were not just liberal snobs who voted for

Democrats. If they crossed him and lived in mansions in Tangle-
wood or River Oaks and their names happened to be Bush or
Baker, then to hell with them, too.

As is often the case, DeLay was in the right place at precisely
the right time—and agile enough to take advantage of it. The
election of Ronald Reagan had divided the nation in two: conservatives in the central southern and southern states, moderates and liberals in the coastal states—or clustered in redoubts
of decadence like Houston. The Republican Party was becoming the party of suburban America, and Tom DeLay lived in and
represented suburban America.

Among the Republican Congressmen to carry Reagan's torch
in the House were three suburban conservatives who would lead
the party when it gained control of the House. From suburban
Atlanta, Newt Gingrich stood out because he was an ideologue
and gadfly who defined himself as an intellectual; he was an his-
torian of Congress and a social theorist, a cyber-visionary before
that became a fad. Dick Armey was initially a lone wolf and the
big loud aggressor of the new young right. Armey had defeated a
Democratic incumbent of some repute in the Dallas suburbs,
after losing out in an academic catfight at North Texas State
University in Denton. Denied tenure, he embarked on a career
change in telling manner: cleaning out his office, he yanked a
window open and repeatedly sent blaring across the campus
Johnny Paycheck's redneck country anthem, "Take This Job and
Shove It."

Gingrich and Armey were in the big leagues of ego and talent,
but DeLay would outlast both of them. In the infighting of
their revolution, they came out the losers; a former rat poisoner
would end up King of the Hill. The outcome was all the more
remarkable because DeLay was such a rube when he arrived in
Washington. He had plenty of reason to be insecure. He knew
that to succeed he would have to figure out the system and
make it work for him. Yet he was far from certain he was up to
the task. That first session in Congress in 1985, the aging party

animal from the Texas Legislature was riven with guilt and falling asleep drunk most nights. Tom DeLay was having himself a full-blown midlife crisis.

Then he found religion. Or more accurately, religion found him. Because of the enormous effect on the way this country is governed—and perhaps because of its effect on the history of the world—the come-to-Jesus experiences of two Texans born within a few months of each other were arguably the most important conversions of their generation. But the contrast between George W. Bush's epiphany and that of Tom DeLay could not be greater. Bush lived in Texas long enough to pick up the drawl and love of cowboy boots, but his family provided him with the finishing of an East Coast preppie: a bachelor's degree from Yale, an MBA from Harvard. He was the grandson of a U.S. senator and son of a vice president and president, but his dad's friends had to bail him out of several business failures, and he had failed when he tried to use his name to get elected to Congress in 1978. In 1985, the prodigal son came home to the family compound in Maine. Bush in his crisis of the spirit was afforded the benefit of a personal mission by his dad's friend, the legendary evangelist, the Reverend Billy Graham. If there was no single conversion moment, Graham's visit to Kennebunkport began the process. Graham and Bush prayed together, Graham counseled him, and the two men walked the grounds of Walker Point, the Bush family estate on the coast. One can imagine Bush in button-down shirt, chinos, and tasseled loafers as he walked and prayed with Graham and surrendered himself to Jesus. After his meeting with Graham, Bush returned home to Midland to join a men's Bible Study group at the church he and his wife, Laura, attended. It took him a while to quit drinking. He woke up with a bad hangover after his fortieth-birthday party, agreed with Laura's urging, and just quit. Prayer and strength of character were how he explained his conquest of addiction. He commended the approach to everyone. It didn't take twelve steps to quit drinking and make his life right.

DeLay had come up harder in all ways, all his life. He had absorbed enough Baptist teaching and upbringing to call himself a Christian, yet as he neared forty he knew he was a sinner. His road to Damascus was plebeian, and he choked in the dust of patricians like George Bush.

DeLay has inspired a number of fascinating profiles by journalists, but the most provocative assessment of his character and personality was written in 2001 by the *Washington Post*'s Peter Perl. DeLay told the reporter that when he got to Washington in 1985 and plunged into Congress, he was knocking down ten to twelve martinis a night (more hyperbole, unless his capacity for alcohol was superhuman). "I would stay out all night drinking till the bars closed," he said. "I just did it, then I got up sober and went to work." A Republican colleague, Frank Wolf, observed DeLay's stress level and urged him to watch a video of the conservative evangelist James Dobson. George W. Bush was reborn in a private audience with the most iconic preacher in the world, arm-in-arm at Kennebunkport with a man who had preached to millions and ministered to presidents. DeLay, the quintessential suburbanite, found God while staring at a TV screen.

Dobson is a pediatrician and former professor at the medical school of the University of Southern California. He loved to tell the stories of his own personal epiphanies and had written a best-selling book directed at parents and teachers called *Dare to Discipline*. He would be hailed for his work on family issues and charged with governmental tasks and power by Jimmy Carter, Ronald Reagan, Edwin Meese, George Bush the elder, Bob Dole, and Trent Lott. By 1978 he was on the road speaking six or seven days a month. He had two children, aged nine and five, and feared that in all his bookselling and racing around on planes to tell people about their families and children, he was neglecting his own. Several San Antonio congregations had pitched in to bring Dobson to speak at Trinity University, which was founded by Presbyterians but is largely secular. (Dobson was most often described as a Nazarene.) As Dobson tells it, while he was praying one night, as he always did, the Lord told him he was going to redirect his primary focus; Dobson could no longer be an itinerant preacher. He wouldn't stand up those folks at Trinity, but he would honor no other commitments after that one. "Because the Lord just spoke to me and told me to stop speaking," he told the man who booked his many appearances. "For Pete's sake," said the friend, who abruptly came up with the idea of videotaping his sermons. Hastily arranged, the production at Trinity flew around the world as the program *Where's Dad?* The pilot was a sensation and launched the series *Focus on the Family*. The Reverend Dobson would both stay at home with his children and, through his videotaped sermons, reach out to multitudes. Seven years after *Focus on the Family* broadened the world of televangelism, Congressman Tom DeLay punched the tape of the series' first installment into his VCR.

Dobson's form of address was not exactly a sermon. He began that day in San Antonio by asking everybody who had failed their families in the prior twenty-four hours to please stand up: if they had yelled at their kids, stand up; failed to put the meat out to thaw, stand up; and so on. The audience responded to the game, and Dobson observed that hardly anyone was sitting down. They laughed. The folksy pediatrician then told them about driving with his children past an X-rated movie theater. The feature on the marquee was *Flesh Gordon*. His little girl asked, "Is that a dirty movie, Daddy?"

"Yes, honey, I guess that is a dirty movie."

Dobson said he didn't know the songwriter Harry Chapin, couldn't say if Chapin personally knew the Lord or not, but he read the lyrics of "Cat's in the Cradle" (written by Chapin's wife Sandra, actually—he wrote the tune). In any case, the song recorded by Chapin was about a father and son who were always saying to each other, *"We're gonna have a good time then,"* but never lived up to their promises, they were too busy. Dobson cited a survey on how much time middle-class fathers spent with their kids each day—the average was 377 seconds.

"Then tell me," Dobson said, raising his voice, *"where the values are coming from?"* Too often, he went on, they came from peers and dirty movies, the filth rampant in the culture. Precept by precept, a system of values is constructed in the minds of children, but too many parents, especially fathers, are absent without leave, lying down on the job. Dobson said that he and his wife prayed and fasted all of one day each week to help the Lord help them maintain their vigilance.

Dobson was more restrained in his use of Scripture than most evangelical preachers—just two mentions of Old Testament patriarchs and prophets who followed the path of God but lost their children along the way. "Fathers have in their hands the power to save the family," he reasoned, "because most women will follow." The peril of failing to wield that power was dire: "If America is going to make it . . . it will be because husbands and fathers begin to put their families first."

Power, redemption, relief of guilt, the true man's man: the James Dobson videotape *Where's Dad?* changed Tom DeLay's life. "I started crying," he told the *Washington Post*'s Peter Perl, "because I had missed my daughter's whole childhood. It was awful. My daughter in third grade asked her mother 'if somebody adopted Daddy,' because he was never around." The conversations with Perl took place sixteen years after his viewing of the Dobson tape, but DeLay continued to berate himself. "I was totally self-centered. It was me, me, me, me. It was golf or my business or politics that came first. It told me what a jerk I really was. You cannot throw off your self-centeredness. That's the problem of our culture. You can't love someone unless you are loved, and being loved by the Lord changes that."

Psychologists could devote entire seminars to weighing that language against DeLay's claim that he was unloved and his descriptions of what it was like to grow up in a dysfunctional family tormented by alcoholism. Was DeLay attempting to live up to the expectations of his father, whom he failed when he didn't go to medical school? Was he trying to prove himself to his wife, Christine, who had been left behind in Sugar Land while Hot Tub Tom was drinking his way through the Texas Legislature? Was he setting out to create the complete Christian family he never had as a child or a young man on the make? Whatever the interior motivation, DeLay became a stronger person when he embraced Christ. And his faith made him a vastly more effective politician. Call it providence. Or be redundant and call it Divine Providence. DeLay's timing was again nothing less than extraordinary. Tom DeLay was both defining and riding a demographic wave in American politics. For as he converted to fundamentalist Christianity, the country was converting with him, in a second Great Awakening of evangelical fervor. Christians were flocking to new, often non-denominational churches. And they were taking their convictions to the voting booth in a religious political movement without precedent in this country. At the time DeLay fell to his knees in Frank Wolf's congressional office, the Moral Majority—the first nationally organized Christian political group, founded by Jerry Falwell in 1979—was at the peak of its power, with Falwell claiming 17 to 28 million viewers (Arbitron reported a more modest 1.6 million). Across the country, and particularly in the South, sixty-six major electronic ministries commanded an audience of twenty million viewers and listeners. Four years later, Pat Robertson would retool the political organization he built around his failed presidential campaign, creating the Christian Coalition—a nominally nonpartisan organization that embraced (because it could not legally "endorse") Republican candidates from thousands of pulpits across the nation.

The Dobson tape and conversion experience returned DeLay to a brick-and-mortar congregation of the Southern Baptist affiliation that was part of his upbringing. At Sugar Land's First Baptist Church DeLay frequently called out *A-A-men!* in the old Southern style when the preacher's sermon moved him. But it

was not the kind of Baptist service he would have known as a
child in Mirando City. An amplified worship band boogied down
in Christian rock. Pastor Scott Rambo, young, trim, strikingly
handsome with a neat goatee and a casual Eddie Bauer wardrobe,
roamed about with a cordless mike—as charismatic and engag-
ing as Bill Clinton at a town hall meeting. The DeLays sat or
stood side by side sharing a hymnal, and unlike some brethren
who grew self-conscious and subdued in the music service, the
congressman threw back his head and made a joyful noise unto
the Lord, as singers are admonished to do in Psalms. He knew
many of the hymns by heart. DeLay would approach the altar
and kneel in prayer, a ritual of faith and contrition. After worship
service on Sunday, the congressman and his wife regularly joined
another assembly to pray for the sick and suffering.

At home among his fellow Baptists, Tom DeLay demonstrated an astonishing ability to bare his soul. For two consecutive years, he joined Pastor Rambo, a physician, and two owners
of small businesses in a "men's accountability group." The *Post*'s
Peter Perl got inside the organization and DeLay's religious
experience:

> It is here that DeLay often reconciles the contradictions be-
> tween the gut-punching political fighter and the man of God
> and family that he aspires to be.
>
> In often-emotional sessions, the five men ask and explore
> deeply personal questions. Have you followed the teachings of
> Christ? Are you spending enough time with your family? Are
> you behaving honorably toward your wife? Have you been hon-
> est in all your financial dealings? Are there problems you want
> to share? Have you looked at a woman in an improper way?
> Have you been an effective minister in spreading the Gospel?
> And finally—have you lied to us in answering any of these ques-
> tions?
>
> "It keeps me honest," DeLay says of the hour-long talks,
> which were inspired by the Promise Keepers evangelical

movement. "You can't lie. You can't look your brother-in-Christ in the eye and lie to him . . . and you go through the week and think about having to face them on Saturday, and it makes you reassess."

"God is perfect, so he could not make something imperfect," DeLay said, providing the perfect disproof of evolution. In a speech DeLay once said: "Christianity offers the only viable, reasonable, definitive answer to the questions of 'Where did I come from?' 'Why am I here?' 'Where am I going?' 'Does life have any meaningful purpose?'" The United States, he believed, came into being as the perfect country, its constitution inspired by the Ten Commandments. Turning away from God could destroy the country. "Our entire system is built on the Judeo-Christian ethic, but it fell apart when we started denying God." It was painful and dangerous to have to admit that truth about America. "When faced with the truth, the truth hurts. It is human nature not to face that . . . People hate the messenger. That's why they killed Christ." DeLay's mission is "to bring us back to the Constitution and to Absolute Truth that has been manipulated and destroyed by a liberal worldview."

Sunday nights at First Baptist in Sugar Land, he taught a class based on the premise that only Christianity can heal the wounds of humanity and save America's system of government and reform its lascivious culture. He designed the course by drawing on the best-selling book *How Now Shall We Live?* The book's author —designer of the faith-based anti-recidivism program commissioned by Governor George W. Bush at Sugar Land's Beauford Jester prison, the historic Hell Hole on the Brazos—was the one-time Watergate hatchet man Charles Colson.

When Tom DeLay fell to his knees before a video clip of James Dobson, he was not only born again in Christ, he was born again in Republican electoral politics. This is not to suggest that his motives were anything less than spiritual, but the result was political. Not only did his return to the church provide him the focus and discipline he lacked when he had been Hot Tub Tom of Macho Manor in Austin, DeLay immediately became part of a religious community that is also a political community. As a high-profile evangelical Christian, Tom DeLay connected to the Christian base without which the Republican Party cannot win national elections—and many state elections. Like George W. Bush, DeLay found Jesus at the precise moment in American political history when Jesus became a political asset. The timing was so perfect that the nonbeliever is left to wonder if it just might have been God's Plan.

Finding religion in the office of Virginia Congressman Frank Wolf was also DeLay's greatest accomplishment of his first two years in Congress. He got some public attention with his fight against the NEA. And he defined himself as a member of the hard right, as one of eight congressmen to receive a 100 percent voting record from the American Conservative Union. Among the eight were three of his colleagues from the Texas six-pack and Wyoming Representative Dick Cheney—perhaps the only House member farther to the right than DeLay. DeLay also set a new House personnel standard by requiring applicants for staff positions in his office to complete a questionnaire in which they were asked about their positions on gun control, mining of Nicaraguan harbors, returning the country to the gold standard, school prayer, allowing homosexuals to teach in public schools, the bailout of Chrysler, recognition of the PLO, and Arab-Israeli relations. Applicants for staff positions tend to self-select by party, and at the time most members of Congress didn't even inquire about party affiliation.

One achievement involving internal institutional politics suggested that DeLay was determined to become a player. He fought to become the freshman representative on the Republican Committee on Committees, which accepts requests for committee assignments and allocates committee seats. There he was perfectly placed to begin cultivating the favor of his colleagues. After defeating a Democrat drafted to run against him in 1986 by a 71-39 percent margin, DeLay returned to Washington and called in the political chits he had earned as a freshman on the committee on committees. He won a position on the Appropriations Committee. "He never was an appropriator," a committee staffer said when asked about DeLay. "He was in it for purely political purposes."

He would never be seriously challenged in his district again. All his energy would be focused on building the party and acquiring personal power within the House of Representatives.

FOUR

Solidifying the Base

Tom DeLay had known the back bench too well in the Texas Legislature, and he worked diligently to escape that obscurity in Congress. In just his second term, seated on the prestigious and powerful Appropriations Committee, DeLay was making connections and gaining an understanding of how to turn those connections and their wealth into power. In his district he lavished care on large constituents—including NASA's Johnson Space Center and a dense line of refineries and petrochemical plants owned by corporate giants like Monsanto and Dow—and he possessed an astute sense of how the political winds were blowing in Texas. Pro-choice Republican women who had worked phone banks for him in the early days were startled to hear him attacking abortion rights now. After his born-again experience, DeLay left no doubt that he wanted to be identified with the Christian Right. The evangelical Republicans shared his convictions, and he was solidifying his base.

Ronald Reagan was president—a conservative's dream—and though the Democrats still had an eighty-seat majority in the House, the Congressman from Sugar Land was on the way up in an energized GOP. But as he moved to the right and wielded his power, the nice guy from the Texas Legislature began to inspire comment, even among Republicans, about a petty and vindictive mean streak.

He also had a penchant for shooting from the hip, and was still not the smoothest orator. Nearing the end of his second term in 1988, he knew that a national convention was audition time for up-and-comers in the party, and in New Orleans that year he nominated himself to help rescue Dan Quayle. George Bush the elder had plucked the handsome but bland and intellectually unimpressive Quayle off the back bench of the Senate to be his running mate. Pundits jumped on Bush and his nominee—a story spread that advisers had speculated that women voters might be swayed by Quayle's resemblance to Robert Redford. In the scramble for stories reporters discovered that Quayle—like Bush's oldest son, George W.—had leaped in suspicious fashion to the head of an enlistment waiting list of the National Guard in the 1960s. Lyndon Johnson and Richard Nixon both refused to call up the reserves in the Vietnam War, though at one point in Johnson's term the Joint Chiefs asked for several hundred thousand of them, but opted instead for a strategy built on the draft. Families of draftees did not tend to have as much visibility and clout as those whose sons could get in reserve units. A spot in the six-month reserves was a deliverance for those who wanted to avoid the war without burning draft cards, expatriating to Canada, and generally turning their lives upside down.

Born the same year as Quayle, DeLay had skirted military service during the war with student and marriage deferments. One day at the convention he called a press conference and explained that so many blacks and members of other ethnic minorities had rushed to claim the handsome paychecks in the regular armed forces that patriotic whites such as Quayle and himself had no choice but to loyally support the war in the reserves or as civilians. A television journalist watched this event unfold, and when it was over he turned and memorably asked a colleague: "Who was that idiot?"

It was not the first or last time DeLay made a fool of himself, but he was no idiot. A more telling footnote of the 1988 GOP convention was that Wyoming's Dick Cheney, then the House minority whip, observed that DeLay possessed the rare and indispensable gift for counting votes, a gift DeLay had first begun to show in the Texas Legislature. It was a skill of intelligence gathering—knowing whose votes were certain and whose might change and why. Cheney told DeLay he wanted to make him a deputy whip. One of the big leaguers in the GOP had spotted him as someone who might be a player.

The election of George Herbert Walker Bush was not an unambiguous victory for conservatives such as Tom DeLay. Bush wasn't Ronald Reagan but rather a throwback to the old Republican Party that young radicals in the House despised—a pragmatic internationalist whose "Read My Lips: No New Taxes" promise sounded hollow when he made it. His politics didn't square with the growing resentment, restiveness, and talk of revolution by the junior members or the Republican Conference in the House. And Bush eliminated the one House leader who had taken an interest in DeLay. When Bush appointed Dick Cheney his secretary of defense, DeLay was hung out to dry: there would be a new minority whip and DeLay's small position of power would probably go.

DeLay also made one tactical error that seemed to seal his fate. He backed the losing candidate in the race to replace Cheney—betting with the odds in the whip horse race.

The tectonic plates were moving again in the Republican Party and the epicenter of any potential earthquake was the floor of the House chamber. Or the ornate House caucus chamber, where the Republican Conference would meet to select its leadership. There were two factions fighting for power within the Republican House delegation in 1989. One was led by the minority leader, Illinois Congressman Bob Michel, a conventional and congenial institutionalist who cut deals with the leadership of the Democratic majority. As a Republican with an eighty-vote deficit, he got what concessions he could. He also was a shrewd and calculating party politician who undercut his potential challengers and controlled who was elected to lead what seemed like a permanent Republican minority party in the House.

Bob Michel was "getting the crumbs" that the Democrats would leave for him, said the leader of the House's younger power faction. Since he had been elected to Congress in 1978 to represent an Atlanta suburb, Newt Gingrich had been fomenting two revolts: one against the Democrats and another against the timid Old Guard Republicans in the House. With Minnesota rep Vin Weber and Pennsylvanian Bob Walker, he formed the Conservative Opportunity Society, a small cabal of angry conservatives eager for change. They seized on the idea of giving after-hour speeches to an empty House floor, a tactic that had previously been the almost exclusive realm of quixotic San Antonio Democrat Henry B. González, which courtesy of C-SPAN provided them an instant audience of 300,000 to 500,000 television viewers. The revolution would be televised. They confronted the Democrats, with Weber strategizing, Walker patrolling the floor exploiting any opportunity he found, and Gingrich doing the big thinking and providing a public face—often in the after-hours "special orders speeches." Together, they became the vanguard of the hard-ass new Republicans who came into the House after Ronald Reagan's first victory and who now feared the party was losing Reagan's crusade for low taxes, limited government, traditional values, and military spending on big-ticket items such as the star wars initiative. They began to meet weekly, in the mediocre restaurants on Capitol Hill, and came to be known as the jihadists. (It was an ironic term, considering the Republicans' loathing of the jihadists in the Middle East.)

They didn't include Tom DeLay. He had been warned off them by advisers and colleagues who were chary of their backbench bomb throwing. An aide to a Republican House member, looking back on DeLay's career after he was elected majority leader, insists that DeLay's refusal to join the radicals in the small rump caucus is very telling: "DeLay goes with winners. If he had been born in the Soviet Union and elected to the Duma in 1984, he would be a Marxist. Until it became obvious the reformers were going to win. What he cared about was the shortest route to power."

The day Cheney resigned to move on to the Department of Defense, Bob Walker called Gingrich and told him he had no choice. "Of course you're going to run," Walker said. It was their moment. Gingrich was the leader of the Conservative Opportunity Society and of the back-bench revolt. Gingrich announced, and Walker, who had worked the floor for the COS, helped count votes. DeLay managed the campaign for Ed Madigan—the safe choice and Bob Michel's handpicked candidate. Like Michel, Madigan was from Illinois. He was also a compromiser, rather colorless, and nothing like the fire-breathing Gingrich. "Ed Madigan is a nice guy," said one of the Gingrich revolutionaries. "And nice guys aren't what we were looking for." Gingrich won 87-85, a harbinger of the end of the go-along-to-get-along politics of Michel. In the months to come, Gingrich would not forget that DeLay had not been on his team.

On another occasion DeLay started out trying to help Bush's Houston benefactors but wound up in a fight with one of the president's bureaucrats. On the outskirts of Sugar Land is a tony development called Cinco Ranch. A Houston oligarch named Bob Mosbacher had been Bush's finance chairman in the campaign and was now secretary of commerce. In personal commerce, Mosbacher and other big-name investors had bought 5,400 acres of scrubby pasture in the seventies and designated them as the future Cinco Ranch; the development stalled because there was no convenient way for commuters to reach it. The proposed solution was an outer loop called the Grand Parkway that was supposed to connect major highways and eventually encircle greater Houston. It would tie in Interstate 10 with the major state highways that went through Sugar Land. But the Grand Parkway had slipped off the Texas Department of Transportation's list of priorities because it would be so expensive to build. Then in the early eighties developers came up with an idea that was eagerly embraced by the commission's chairman, a

conservative Democrat and future Houston mayor named Bob
Lanier. Landowners would get together and privatize the right-
of-way acquisition. The state would be spared the unpleasant-
ness and huge expense of condemning land for its most desired
highways. All it had to do was contract for the surveying and
paving. Developers saw the value of raw land multiply exponen-
tially, for the highways made it accessible. That revolution in
road-building finance revived the Grand Parkway, which was a
top priority for Lanier. While sitting on the board of the State
Department of Transportation, Lanier oversaw an authoriza-
tion that neatly mapped the route through 1,700 acres that he
owned with partners. The money grab was aired thoroughly by
the Houston press when Lanier ran for mayor, but he won the
race in a landslide. He was a popular man, and evidently the voters who kept reelecting him thought politicians were supposed
to behave like that.

Thirty miles from downtown Houston, the completed seg-
ment of the parkway ran from Interstate 10 through Cinco
Ranch to the prisons and subdivisions of Sugar Land. In the
early seventies, Mosbacher had bought into the project for less
than $5 million. It's not clear exactly how much he profited
from construction of the six-mile highway, but the sale in 1984
of the development property for $84 million, was trumpeted as
the largest in Houston's real estate history. The Mosbacher family shared those proceeds, and after the parkway was green-
lighted, they sold a second tract for $12.9 million more.

There is no evidence that Tom DeLay benefited financially
from the real estate scam. He and his wife were not exactly
swinging in that crowd of investors. But he had first gotten
elected to political office promising to fight for more unclogged
highways to the suburbs, and in Congress he now had a seat on
the Transportation Committee. Roads were one of his abiding
passions; he considered himself an expert on the issue. Also, he
got on extremely well with Bob Lanier. They wanted the Grand
Parkway to fulfill its destiny and keep going all around Houston,

but it ran into a barricade of federal environmental regulations. If the freeway continued on its projected track it would cross a remnant prairie, knock down parts of a unique oak forest, and foul wetlands along the sensitive Galveston Bay. Another politician might have surveyed the landscape of that battle and found it unpromising. But the battle raged for years. If there was any way to get Tom DeLay's goat, this was it. A project that he badly wanted was being thwarted by the *Environmental Protection Agency* — and by a federal bureaucrat who was a prominent country club Republican!

Buck Wynne was a well-liked comer in the Texas GOP. Governor Bill Clements had appointed him chair of the state's water commission — the administration's highest ranking environmental official. But then Ann Richards was elected governor in 1990, and Wynne left state government; a short time later, the first President Bush appointed him director of the EPA's southwest region. In the dispute over the Grand Parkway, Wynne agreed with environmentalists that the law required that construction would have to be cleared first by an environmental impact study for the entire road. Highway engineers and developers knew it would be easier to overcome the problematic prairie, hardwoods, and marshes if each of nine different segments of the road received a low-profile study. In April 1992 Wynne received a letter, copied to Vice President Quayle, from Congressman DeLay.

Dear Buck:

I am very disappointed to learn that the EPA Region VI office is making every effort to prevent the implementation of President Bush's program to restore the economic health of the United States.

President Bush has clearly stated that rebuilding our infrastructure and highways is important to restoring a vigorous economy. The proposed Grand Parkway in Houston, Texas has complied with every State and Federal government mandate

and regulation. . . . Clearly the general public wants to see the
Grand Parkway built without endless bureaucratic foot-drag-
ging. I was extremely disappointed to read a quote from an EPA
official in the *Houston Chronicle* on March 26, 1992 stating, "It's
clear that the general public really wants to see a comprehensive environmental impact statement.". . .

I want a detailed report on how many people in the "general
public" had officially told the EPA by that date that they demanded construction of the Grand Parkway be shelved while a
massive environmental impact statement of the entire parkway,
including routes that may change in the future or never even be
built, is conducted.

I want to know on what authority does the EPA have the
right to misrepresent the views of special interest groups as
those of the general public. . . . I appreciate your attention to
this public matter and look forward to your swift response.

Wynne wrote back and stood his ground. He observed that
several federal laws, including the Clean Air Act, required the
EPA to review and evaluate environmental impact statements
and report its findings publicly, in writing. He acknowledged
that the EPA had met with the Sierra Club, the Houston
Audubon Society, and the Galveston-Houston Association for
Smog Prevention at the hearing that angered DeLay. "Please
note that the EPA considers the organizations represented at
the scoping hearing 'public interest groups' as opposed to 'special interest groups' (inasmuch as the latter term connotes a financial interest in the outcome of an issue)."

DeLay fired off a livid reply:

Regarding my letter being one of only three opposing such
environmental considerations, please remember that as an
elected official *I,* not the EPA, represent the general public.
The general public has voted to keep me in office as their U.S.
Representative. The general public has voted in a majority in

support of my views. Please, as a reminder, my letter is not just one voice but rather the voice of thousands. The representatives of the Sierra Club and the Audubon Society are not elected by the public and are not accountable to the public. If the public does not agree with their views, the public has no way to vote them out of power. They do not represent the desires of the general public.

In your letter, you draw the line between public and special interest groups as those that have financial interests in the outcome of an issue. I cannot see the accuracy in defining public interest groups in this manner. The Ku Klux Klan, for example, is a special interest group that has no financial stake in the outcome of any particular issue, yet, I think we can safely say that the KKK is not representative of the general public. Obviously, financial gain is irrelevant in this case and is immaterial in defining special interest groups.

The Grand Parkway would remain a strange-looking boulevard on the outskirts of Sugar Land because of a dearth of funds in Texas coffers, not because of obstruction by a George Bush loyalist and the EPA. DeLay always had difficulty maintaining his composure on any matter related to the EPA. But did he have to try to bully someone as affable and popular among Republicans as the late Buck Wynne? Did he really believe that a financial return of about $10 million a mile—to Mosbacher and other right-of-way donors to the parkway—was irrelevant and immaterial? Did he really think the Texas Ornithological Society was the equivalent of the Ku Klux Klan?

DeLay's growing power and his opinion of his importance did not make him immune to vicissitudes of family and business. Charlie DeLay must have come around to being proud of his oldest son; the Sugar Land congressman's stature in the Houston area was unquestioned. But old wounds in their bond left deep scars. Following his retirement from the offshore drilling company in 1972, Charlie built a hillside home at Canyon Lake, between Austin and San Antonio. He had a boat dock at the foot of his steep property, and ever the mechanic and amateur engineer, he built a cog train that would hoist him and a passenger up and down from house to water and back. One winter day in 1988 Charlie and his brother Jerry started down, as happy and thrilled as the adventurous boys they once had been. Then, something went terribly wrong: chains broke loose, and they hurtled seventy feet down the precipice. Jerry was seriously injured but recovered. Charlie crashed head-first into a juniper tree. He died of the massive injuries on December 14, 1988. The DeLay family hired a trial lawyer (anathema to Tom) and sued the manufacturer of a part Charlie had used in his homemade train.

Horrendous events can draw survivors together, but in this case the father's death seemed to accelerate Tom DeLay's estrangement from his family. When the accident occurred, the first husband of his sister, Tena DeLay Neislar, was dying of cancer. "I expected Tommy to be the backbone of the family, and he wasn't," she later told the *Washington Post.* She partly blamed the estrangement on his career obsession and politics: "The power that these people have or think they have. I think they get screwed up and paranoid, and their priorities get messed up." It was a startling public rebuke, but they were, as Tom put it in *Rolling Stone,* "not exactly an ideal family." Maybe he just wanted some emotional distance and a shred of the privacy that is torn from politicians. All of Charlie DeLay's sons also tussled with demon booze. Ray DeLay—the one charged with becoming a veterinarian—told the *New Yorker* that their father "enforced his values with a belt." The oldest son drifted in and out of trouble. He got off with probation after his first larceny conviction, but the second would put him in a South Dakota prison for several months in the early nineties. After that he would come back to Houston and offer himself as a storefront preacher and counselor. He described his ministry on a website: "We preach the healing message of deliverance through Jesus Christ to those with life controlling problems including drug addiction and the incarcerated. We believe that only through Jesus can we find identity, belonging, and security that will deliver us from the bondage of alcoholism, drug addiction, immorality, depression, and all other life controlling problems. . . . If you have a problem, we have the answer—Jesus." One night the Houston police arrested and charged Ray with aggravated assault on a woman friend who worked in the ministry, and, identifying the assailant as the brother of the congressman, the *Houston Chronicle* ran a story about how Ray DeLay had beaten her with a walking stick. The woman told officers they had been drinking. Ray De-Lay told them that the devil made him do it. Earlier, in 1999, Tom DeLay had described him cruelly in the press as "a real skid-row type."

After a while the congressman stopped going to family gatherings. The only time that he publicly addressed the family's dissolution, he told the *Washington Post*'s Peter Perl that his dad's alcoholism was just part of the family's dysfunction, and he strongly hinted that he had given up. "I am certainly nowhere near where I would like to be in my walk. But at some point in time you just have to move on and try to create those relationships with other people, and keep moving forward. It's the way it goes." His way of dealing with that conflict was characteristic; friends of DeLay in Sugar Land said they knew that if they ever crossed him, they would be banished. Still, DeLay's break with his elderly mother was mystifying. DeLay's sister claimed he would not speak to her unless his wife Christine was present. And when their daughter Danielle married, they hosted a wedding and gala; DeLay's mother was not invited, nor was her existence even mentioned in the newspaper announcements. That shunning was "like a dagger in my heart," she told her youngest son, Randy. "It was like I never existed." As Randy DeLay elaborated in the *Washington Post,* "Eventually, I know Tom will be sorry for this, what he is doing to Mom. My mother watches C-SPAN just to watch him walk across the floor." A quiet person, Maxine DeLay lives just a few miles from Sugar Land. She said of her famous son, "I get to see him. I see him on TV, and it helps. I keep all the tapes."

Randy was the only one who maintained a relationship with Tom. One couldn't miss that the two men were brothers. Randy was stockier, but he had the same intense eyes, wide-bridged nose, and immovable crown of thick, short black hair. Randy had lived up to their father's expectations for a while. After receiving a law degree in Houston, he had returned to the Corpus Christi area. Randy was an extrovert, active in the Kiwanis Club, and he served as a board member of a charity children's hospital. He had a hunting retreat in the brush country near Corpus and decorated his office with trophy heads from African safaris. He owned a popular Mexican restaurant and nightspot called Josie's. And in 1987 he helped his Uncle Bill set up a business that delivered drilling mud to oil well sites in Texas. Relying on the expertise of his father, Randy also invested in an oil exploration venture called Well Drillers Inc. But then the price of oil plummeted, and Charlie DeLay was killed. That same year, shareholders in the drilling company sued Randy for failing to pay a $65,000 note to a shareholders' trust. He counter-sued, and the settlement enabled him to buy the company's drilling equipment, using the resources of the other mud delivery company.

Despite the bust of the oil boom and nosedive of the Texas economy, Randy was hanging on, making $120,000 as the president and CEO of the company, whose assets he used to get out of the failed drilling venture. But that commingling of finances angered his Uncle Bill and the other partners of the drilling mud company. They sold the company out from under him, and the new owners fired him in 1990. Then they sued him over his management of the company's insurance, payroll, and benefits. One of the new owners accused him of conduct that was "willful, wanton, intentional, malicious, reckless, and grossly negligent." In 1992 the parties to the oilfield services suit tried to settle, but Randy couldn't come up with his share of the mediator's fees. A Corpus Christi bank also sued him for defaulting on a $131,000 loan to his Mexican restaurant. Both suits against him were dropped that year after he filed for bankruptcy, according to the *Houston Press*. At some point during that downward spiral Randy decided he had better do something about his drinking problem. He dried up, moved to Houston, and started over. He offered to do some work for his older brother. Tom DeLay might be a big shot in Congress, but he still had a hand in Albo Pest Control, and like hundreds of other Texas businessman in that boom gone bust, he needed help from a lawyer whose fees wouldn't make a bad situation worse.

After his election to Congress in 1984, Tom DeLay had realized that a seat in Congress, unlike a seat in the Texas House, was not a part-time gig. He began to worry about managing a business in Texas and a political career in Washington simultaneously and brought in a pest control colleague, Darrell Hutto, to manage Albo. Like DeLay, Hutto had attended the University of Houston in the 1960s and put in more than a dozen years in pest control. He had sold his business, End-O-Pest, and gone into the sign business in East Texas. But he still conducted training seminars for exterminators and produced videos on termites, weeds, and commodity fumigation (gassing insects in bulk food stored in grain bins, railroad cars, and holds of ships). A month before the election, at his wife Christine's urging, DeLay incorporated Albo and closed the deal with Hutto. The manager would make $36,000 a year and still continue in his training and video sideline. He would also serve as vice president of the corporation. The two partners agreed that Hutto could buy half the company—1,000 shares of stock, valued at $50,000—and pay for it out of the profits—though at the time there were no profits. Hutto wrote his partner company checks totaling $7,000 the year after DeLay was elected to Congress. After that, DeLay received no more payments on the note. Albo struggled on, its losses mounting. When DeLay had gone into business, he enjoyed the luxury of a thriving economy, but in 1986 OPEC flooded the world with oil. Three hundred thousand Texans lost their jobs. For small businesses and homeowners, a pest control service was one of the most expendable items.

In 1986 Hutto mentioned to DeLay that a competitor, Robert Hicks, who later changed his name to Blankenship, was going through the same hard times, and they might be able to persuade him to merge his company, A-Abco Pest Control, with Albo. Blankenship said that DeLay told him that in agreeing to merge the companies, he would be cutting himself "a bigger piece of the pie." They agreed on the merger, retaining the Albo name. In the new arrangement they each owned a third of the company stock. DeLay was the director, Hutto the president, Blankenship the vice president. Blankenship assumed some of Albo's debts. A new company brochure pictured Congressman DeLay, chairman of the board, with his fellow "Residential Experts," all of them in suits, spiffy and well-groomed, smiling. "We're protecting your health and your environment," the brochure said.

The arrangement started coming apart about five years after the partnership began in 1986, according to Blankenship: a competing exterminator told him that he had encountered DeLay and Hutto on a golf course one day where the duffers began talking about selling Albo, without clearing it with their third partner. Over a period of several months, Albo entertained a number of inquiries and some real interest in buying the company. In mid-1991 one man offered them $200,000, but that deal didn't close. Blankenship considered another offer only to be told by a business consultant that Albo's books were a mess, the company was carrying substantial debt and totals that didn't add up. That buyout deal also fell through. But not before Blankenship learned that his medical insurance policy had been canceled for some time, though his wife was ill and Albo had continued to deduct the premium from his paycheck. He assumed that his standing as the company vice president, his one-third share of the stock, and his $44,000 salary made him an owner of the company, not an employee, and he began to wonder why he hadn't been consulted. Hutto maintained that, with DeLay's approval from Washington, he made Blankenship a fair offer for his interest in Albo. Blankenship, in turn, ordered the company secretary to print out a master list of Albo's customers. She refused, and he left in a huff with an outdated list. Hutto deemed that a hostile act, and, after informing DeLay of his intentions, in December of 1993 he changed the office locks and posted a notice on the front door telling Blankenship he was fired. Blankenship filed suit.

Politics in Washington consumed DeLay's time and interest now. He obviously considered *Robert Blankenship, Plaintiff, vs. Thomas D. DeLay et al.* an imposition and affront. Accompanying him at the February 1994 deposition was his brother Randy, who would introduce himself as a corporate lawyer—a bit of a stretch. The *Houston Press* concluded that he was a pro bono lawyer in that case and received no payment for helping his brother out. Whether he was paid or not, on pertinent issues of law—management of employee insurance, commingling of personal debt and corporate funds, attempted sale of a company without a partner's consent—Randy DeLay was in a position to offer his big brother some seasoned advice.

The congressman was deposed in Houston in February 1994. He was feisty and contemptuous responding to Blankenship's attorney. DeLay said he had effectively taken himself out of Albo's affairs after his election to Congress in 1984. He had talked to Hutto when necessary and made perhaps fifty calls from Washington, trying to help him drum up business. That was all. He said that he had resigned his official duties in an agreement with Darrell Hutto some years prior. It was a verbal agreement, never written. DeLay's statement contradicted IRS tax returns and congressional financial disclosure forms that listed him as a financial officer of the corporation through 1993. And his role in the company while he was serving in Congress was central to what Blankenship and his attorney were trying to prove.

The lawyer asked him, "At the time that you began serving as a congressman in January of '85, do you remember whether or not Albo Pest Control was making a profit?"

"I knew we weren't making a profit," DeLay replied.

"Okay. In fact, was the company in pretty bad financial condition?"

"Well, it had—" he began, then started over. "It was a bad economy. It had a poor cash flow. But it was sustaining and making payroll in the economic climate. I think it was doing fairly well."

In the course of an exchange over a tax return, the DeLay brothers, lawyer and client, started giggling. Randy interrupted Blankenship's attorney: "Why don't we for clarity—what is the question and what is the answer . . . ?"

"The answer is on Schedule E. If this is funny to you guys—"

Randy DeLay: "I'm just—"

Tom DeLay: "It's funny to me."

The lawyer: "I'm glad it's funny to you."

"This is ridiculous and stupid," said DeLay.

Bob Blankenship watched his adversary being deposed. It is altogether natural for a defendant in a lawsuit to take the matter personally, and to DeLay this was clearly an insult. His remarks about Blankenship that day were frosty with disdain. At one point the plaintiff's attorney asked if Blankenship should have known that Hutto was sending DeLay company checks to pay for his shares of stock.

"There was no reason for him to know," DeLay shot back.

Why was that? the lawyer asked.

"Well, Bob Blankenship works for Albo Pest Control. He has no, no management standing. He has no standing to make any decisions for Albo or the operation of Albo, and he never has."

The lawyer: "He was the vice president of the corporation pursuant to the merger—was he not?"

"Name only."

Blankenship's attorney was incredulous: "You're telling me that he merged his company with you, knowing that he wasn't going to have a management say in what happened to his company?"

"You'll have to ask him that."

"Is that your position?"

"That's always been my position, yes."

"Okay. What did Mr. Blankenship, as vice president, do for Albo Pest Control?"

"From my understanding, I never saw him perform anything," DeLay said. "I hardly ever talked to him during the time he worked for Albo. He serviced accounts and sales."

As the congressman saw it, he was being sued by a loser and a chump.

The central question posed by the lawsuit was whether the corporation had absorbed $48,000 in debt from DeLay's first campaign for Congress. If true, it was a serious violation of federal law. In his deposition, Blankenship told a potentially explosive story. He said that a few weeks after he merged his company with Albo, he was going over the financial records with Darrell Hutto. "When I first saw the [profit and loss] statement," Blankenship claimed, "I looked at the money owed to these banks; and Darrell and I were looking at it together; and I said, 'Darrell, what is all this money owed for—what is this?'

"And he said, 'This is money'—quote—'that Tom DeLay borrowed to run his campaign; and we're stuck with paying it back.'"

When deposed, Hutto hotly and repeatedly denied that he ever said such a thing. He said that DeLay had amassed the personal debt keeping Albo afloat before it was incorporated, and that the discrepancy was the fault of a stubborn tax account-ant who insisted on characterizing the debt as stockholder loans on a 1986 corporate return. Finally, tired of arguing with the ac-countants, Hutto just let it go.

Blankenship's lawyer wanted to go to trial right away, but Randy DeLay said he wasn't ready, that several more witnesses had to be deposed. The trial date kept getting pushed back. The plaintiff did obtain one injunction against the other partners' sale of the company. Then in November 1994 DeLay and Hutto received a serious overture to buy the company from Roger's Pest Control in nearby Stafford. A state district judge listened to the account of the buyout offer and advised the attorneys to negotiate a settlement, so the sale could proceed. The terms of the agreement they reached were to be confidential, and all par-ties but the buyer walked away from Albo Pest Control.

After twenty-three years, DeLay was an exterminator and small businessman in name only. Blankenship at least got a share of the proceeds; a year earlier, he had been staring at a termina-tion noticed taped to a locked door twelve days before Christ-mas. He didn't know the fight wasn't over. He had embarrassed and angered Tom DeLay, who considers business and politics contact sports, like Texas high school football.

Congressional politics are often described as "tribal." De-Lay's campaign against his former business partner was tribal and vindictive in the most primitive way. Once wronged, the exterminator-turned-congressman set out to settle the score— with his former partner, his partner's wife, and his partner's friends. House Democrats (and Republicans) who would get crossways with Tom DeLay would be advised to pay careful at-tention to his fight with Bob and Jacqueline Blankenship. Tom DeLay didn't just follow the political imperative: "Don't get mad, get even." He got mad and got even—and then he got even some more, and some more after that. "He doesn't just want to defeat you," said a Texas Democrat who served in the House with DeLay. "He wants to defeat you then kill you."

The closest Bob Blankenship and his trial lawyer came to corroborating his account of campaign finance misconduct was in the deposition of Lyn Colby, the tax accountant. Colby had grown up across the street from Hutto, who may have thought he was doing an old friend a favor in steering him the business. The lawyer asked Colby if he recalled, in his discussions with Hutto, any mention of political debts paid by corporate funds. "There could have been," said the accountant. "You know, when he said a personal debt, he could have told me that it had something to do with the campaign. That, I can't recall exactly."

DeLay had dodged a bullet, and in the name of political prudence he should have walked away from the mundane episode of rancor and litigiousness all too common in the American business world. He didn't. Over a pissant Texas lawsuit and an extinct pest control outfit, he was going to shake the skies to get even.

Despite the confidentiality agreement that was part of the settlement, the day after the case was settled DeLay called together a group of Fort Bend County Republicans and spun them the story, making them sit through a videotape of Blankenship's long deposition. He sniggered as his brother Randy went at the Blankenships over Victorian Cottage, a failed restaurant Blankenship's wife Jacqueline had run for a few months in 1992.

"You were not an owner?" said Randy.

"I was not an owner," Blankenship confirmed.

"Okay. Who did own it?"

"I'm not—see, I really don't think it was ever owned. It was just a venture that was tried out."

"Okay. Who was behind the venture?"

"Well . . . Jacqueline."

"Did you just look over at Jacqueline and get permission from her to answer that question?"

Blankenship's lawyer objected and when the wrangling ended, Randy obliged the plaintiff to look at a document he had signed to get the lights turned on at the restaurant. "And over on the right," said the loyal brother, "who is listed as the guarantor?"

"Well—"

"Answer, please."

"Tom DeLay," Blankenship muttered.

"Thomas DeLay. Is that correct?"

"That's correct."

"Did you get permission from Thomas DeLay to guarantee this account for Jacqueline Blankenship as Victorian Cottage?"

"No, I did not," he had to reply.

The chairman of the Fort Bend County Republicans was among those summoned to the viewing. He told the *Houston Press* that he believed the congressman was just trying to tell his side of the story. But others were queasy and anxious to get out of that room. DeLay "must have watched that deposition a hundred times," said one Republican, "because he could quote things in it verbatim." Another said of DeLay: "I think he enjoyed himself. He was like a kid, laughing, saying, 'Now listen to this, now listen to this.' It was a nauseating performance."

DeLay's vindictiveness was by no means spent. In the weeks leading up to the 1998 GOP primary, he set out to punish Jacqueline Blankenship, a dedicated Republican Party activist who had done years of volunteer work to elect Republican candidates. The wife of DeLay's former business partner was a paralegal and mediator who had managed local phone banks in the presidential races of George Bush the elder and his son's 1994 upset of popular Democratic Governor Ann Richards. During the Albo lawsuit, she had resigned as manager of the local state representative's campaign, and DeLay pressured Fort Bend Republicans to take her off the phone banks of Governor Bush's re-election campaign. The volunteer appointment she was awaiting on the Texas Structural Pest Control Board went instead to Darrell Hutto. She had some idea Tom DeLay was going to be a problem. He had warned her, she claimed, the last time he spoke to her. "You don't want me as an enemy," he said in a phone call. "I'll destroy you." It was intimidating, but she had no idea of the extremes to which the congressman would go. DeLay spokesman Tony Rudy said he doubted that DeLay had made the threat because "It doesn't sound like Tom."

DeLay was using his political muscle to blackball Blankenship from any involvement in local politics. His bullying angered *Fort Bend Star* publisher Bev Carter. "I don't like to see somebody picked on," Carter said, "and Jacqueline's being picked on. Who's going to hire her if they know Tom DeLay is going to come down on them like an avenging angel?" As energetic as he was vindictive, Tom DeLay began investing much of his money and effort in this protracted local fight while he was funding thirty or more House races, working on the Contract, and organizing his own race for House whip.

One man wasn't intimidated. Jacqueline Blankenship found work in the office of the Fort Bend County sheriff, an ex-Texas Ranger named Milton Wright. DeLay sent word to the sheriff that he wanted her fired. Wright said a local Republican came to his house one night and indicated that if he got rid of Blankenship, DeLay wouldn't endorse the sheriff's principal opponent, a former deputy. Wright refused. DeLay said that he happened to be a good friend of Wright's opponent in the sheriff's race; his support of the man had nothing to do with Jacqueline Blankenship. But he did finance a telephone poll designed to discredit Wright and made radio and television spots endorsing the challenger. "What scares me," said Blankenship at the time, "is that I just want to get a job. If I can't get a volunteer job, how am I going to get a regular job? This is a congressman, and all he wants to do is go after me. Doesn't he have better things to do?"

Richmond Mayor Hilmar Moore was also bothered by DeLay's conduct. "A lot of people around here didn't appreciate him raising $70,000 from them and then spending it on a local race. What business has a congressman got telling people who ought to be their sheriff? A good number of folks liked the one we had." Seventy thousand dollars was a big deal in a sheriff's race and unprecedented as a contribution from an incumbent congressman.

Funding and organizing a campaign of a candidate running against someone who crossed you is a tactic DeLay would use with greater frequency after the Republicans took control of the House and he won a place in the leadership. Sometimes, the threat "to primary" someone was sufficient. Usually he got his way. With Wright he wasn't so lucky.

Wright said that one night his wife received a call from someone conducting a push poll—a questionable campaign practice that uses what appears to be a standard opinion survey to attack or discredit an opponent. Would she be willing to change her vote in the sheriff's race if she knew the challenger had eighteen years of experience in law enforcement while the incumbent had none? A Texas Ranger who had spent fourteen years being called in to investigate major crimes by the local district attorney had no experience! It was amateurish, cornball politics, but DeLay was not easily shamed. His campaign manager admitted that DeLay had commissioned the push poll and said the question was technically accurate. Wright had been Texas Ranger; he had not been on the sheriff's payroll.

Milton Wright refused to fire Jacqueline Blankenship and won the election with 59 percent of the vote. "Five-foot-seven, if he's wearing high heels," the former Texas Ranger said. "Tom DeLay can kiss my ass."

Now the Revolution

"George has always had good timing," said Laura Bush of a husband who upset a popular incumbent governor in Texas, claimed the Republication presidential nomination as if it were his own, and took the presidency away from Vice President Al Gore. In truth, Karl Rove and a cabal of Republican donors created George W. Bush's timing. Tom DeLay created his own. He had no patrons. He had to make his own opportunities. Karl Rove never directed one of his races. And DeLay rarely missed. If he "made a mistake" in 1989, when he supported Ed Madigan in the Speaker's race against Newt Gingrich, he got it right in 1994. And 1994 was a good year for Republican members of the House to get things right. It was the year Ronald Reagan's revolution finally took hold in the Congress. Republicans picked up fifty-two seats in the House (and eight in the Senate) in 1994—a year when no single Republican incumbent lost a House seat. The collapse of the Democratic House marked the end of forty years of domination.

The Republican class of '94 ran against a president they considered an usurper. In his State of the Union address that year Bill Clinton had made a show of whacking a fountain pen against the podium and ordering Congress to send him a health care reform bill that would pass his muster. It may have been dramatically adept, but the political blowback was ruinous. Clinton's health care reform bill, drafted by a working group directed by his wife Hillary, not only failed to pass the Congress. The medical and insurance lobby combine that set out to bury it was so successful with its nationwide media buys that the president and the first lady came to be seen as subversive agents of socialized medicine—even if the complex plan Hillary finally delivered was an accommodation of the insurance industry. On another front, House Democrats who took a big risk by voting for the assault weapons ban in Clinton's anti-crime legislation incurred the wrath of the National Rifle Association. Clinton had also opened a new front in the cultural wars, by advocating allowing gays in the military.

Rarely has a party paid so dearly for supporting public policy designed to provide for and protect the general public. Bill Clinton would have time to recover before he faced the voters in 1996. The Democratic House members associated with him did not. The NRA spent $70 million on political activities in 1994. Seven million moved through its political action committee (PAC), most of it aimed at Democrats who voted for the assault rifle ban. In a Southeast Texas district close to DeLay's, Jack Brooks, the dean of the Texas House delegation, chair of the Judiciary Committee, and an ardent NRA supporter who had held his seat since 1954, lost to Steve Stockman, a loopy right-winger even by Texas standards, who would embarrass his party and haplessly entertain the public during the two terms he served in Congress. Brooks had made the mistake of sponsoring a compromise measure that would have allowed the sale of assault weapons with smaller magazines that held fewer rounds. While he been told by a moderate NRA lobbyist that his provision was okay, the hardliners who controlled the organization's political money came after him in the election. In fact, the hard-asses in the NRA lobby wanted the assault ban passed—so they could mobilize their core voters and turn the Democrats out of the House. In the state of Washington, the NRA defeated Tom Foley, the sitting Speaker who had served in Congress for thirty years. Foley lost to George Nethercutt, a lawyer making his first run for public office. "The NRA is the reason the Republicans control the House," Clinton said at the time.

It wasn't the only reason. Evangelical Christians offended by Clinton's position on gays in the military and his support for women's reproductive rights also turned out to defeat the Democratic Congress. The Christian Coalition distributed thirty-three million voter guides in the two weeks before the election and religious conservatives made up 35 percent of the vote, up from 24 percent two years earlier. One poll found that people most likely to vote in the off-year election came from evangelical Christian households where there were two guns. The Republican Class of '94 was put in office by the God and gun lobby.

The repudiation of Clinton and the Democrats wasn't limited to Congress; also washed out that election night were two of the Democrats' stars—Governor Mario Cuomo in New York and Governor Ann Richards in Texas. DeLay saw the blowout coming, and it fueled his ambition. The prospect of serving in the leadership of the first Republican majority in forty years set DeLay on fire. He had begun climbing out of the hole he had dug himself in the '89 whip race. He won the chairmanship of the Republican Study Group—a House policy shop founded by conservatives who thought Nixon too liberal, then backslid into moderation. (DeLay would turn that around.) But his options were limited. He served on Appropriations but never was considered an "appropriator" and would never be a star on the most challenging and labor-intensive committee in the Congress. Even if he had, it was not likely that Gingrich would ever make him chair. Dick Armey—DeLay's colleague who had arrived with him ten years earlier as part of the celebrated "Texas Six Pack" of right-wing Republican novitiates—was the consensus choice for the majority leader position, and DeLay knew better than to challenge him. The only way to advance was to run for the whip office Gingrich was vacating. The race was a challenge. DeLay had not been part of Gingrich's back-bench revolt. His support of Gingrich's opponent in the '89 whip race alienated him from the Gingrich revolutionaries. And Newt had his own candidate for the position, his closest friend and confidant,

Pennsylvania Congressman Bob Walker. Walker had been with Gingrich since the early eighties, when they founded the Conservative Opportunity Society and began the guerrilla tactics by which they would tear the House down to save it. Gingrich was the big idea guy. Walker was the pit bull, working the floor and looking for opportunities to undermine or embarrass the Democrats, using parliamentary procedure to make their lives difficult. (On one occasion he called for a teller vote, a protracted and archaic procedure in which each member of the House has to walk down the center aisle and declare his vote to a teller.) Walker was such an effective parliamentary obstructionist that Gingrich had him both directing mock sessions Republicans held to prepare for their debut as a majority and playing the role of minority leader Dick Gephardt. Walker also shared the C-SPAN special orders forum with Gingrich, blistering the Democrats and laying out the agenda of the Republican right. Gingrich endorsed Walker—over DeLay and Florida Republican Bill McCollum. Walker was clearly the candidate of the Gingrich right. The *Washington Times,* the odd and perennially unprofitable newspaper owned by Reverend Sung Myung Moon, served as the house organ for the Gingrich revolution. When its reporters referred to DeLay as "a moderate," it was a clear signal that he was not close enough to Newt to be part of the team.

The whip race was the only game in town when the House selected its leaders in January 1995. The Democrats were history. Gingrich and Dick Armey were running unopposed. Absent contested races for Speaker and majority leader, money and media attention focused on the whip race. Inside-the-Beltway handicappers had Newt's chosen candidate winning the race. After all, Gingrich had led his party out of forty years in the desert; he had earned the right to select the whip who would make his agenda happen on the House floor. Yet DeLay (and McCollum to a lesser extent) understood something Bob Walker didn't: money. DeLay had watched Gingrich use his political action committee to buy the loyalty of members by contributing to their races. He did the same, and though he was outspent by Gingrich—a fault he would correct later—he did more than spend. DeLay hired an experienced political consultant to direct his giving and advise the candidates he was backing. Mildred Webber was DeLay's handicapper and bag woman, picking the races where he could get the most bang for his buck and delivering checks to candidates. Working with Webber, DeLay set up a candidate school to complement his political giving. They provided candidates with tapes, talking points, even a video that demonstrated the effective use of yard signs. "Tom knew it wasn't just going to be money that got us the majority or won him the whip race," Webber said. "It was going to be a full-service operation and that's what we became." There was even a slush fund bigger than DeLay's leadership PAC. When one of the eighty candidates DeLay supported would call for help, Webber would phone one of the lobbyists on DeLay's rolodex. "We'd rustle up checks for the guy and make sure Tom got the credit," beer lobbyist David Rher told the *Washington Post*. DeLay was running an ancillary funding operation, moving other people's money to the candidates of his choice. After the election, he admitted he lost count of the lobby money he had moved on to his preferred candidates—when it surpassed $2 million. DeLay couldn't rewrite history and write himself into the Gingrich revolution. But he could write enough checks to win the support of newly elected House members.

He also traveled to twenty-five states, showing up for (and setting up) fundraisers for candidates. "I wanted them to think of me as their brother," DeLay said of the candidates he backed. DeLay also paid attention to a lesson he had learned in the Texas Legislature. There, almost all power is held by the leadership, so Speaker's races are protracted, organized, and often bitter. (When one East Texas state rep discovered that a colleague who was a double amputee had committed to his opponent he threatened to "take one of those peg legs and beat your fucking brains out." That wasn't ancient legislative history; the candidate the remarkably able disabled legislator supported was Speaker while DeLay was in office.) Candidates begin well ahead of the race, collecting pledge cards from members. DeLay wasn't using any prosthetic aid to win the race, but he got a leg up on Walker and McCollum by working the freshman class he'd helped elect. Before the vote was cast, DeLay had the commitment of fifty-three of the seventy freshmen elected in the class of 1994. It was a class that would change the character of Congress and DeLay was its leader. Only half had ever held elective office, three-fourths had no previous legislative experience, and almost all of them were conservative ideologues. They made up almost a third of the Republican House Conference and most of them were signed on with DeLay before the session began. Walker, Gingrich, and McCollum didn't know it, but the race was over before it had begun. Bob Walker was a good revolutionary, vote counter, and soldier. But he was a lousy candidate for leadership in a House in which money is power. He mailed one $1,000 check to a member of the freshman class elected in 1994. That was it. Only Gingrich could have saved him, by openly working on his behalf. But Gingrich was wary of taking on DeLay, because of the mean streak for which he was known, because of his ruthlessness, and because of the loyalty DeLay was cultivating among candidates who would be around for a while if they won. DeLay selected a former wrestling coach from Illinois, Dennis Hastert, to work with Webber on the campaign. Hastert, then relatively unknown, put together a twenty-member team to work the House Republican Conference.

It wasn't even close. DeLay prevailed, with 119 votes, to Walker's 80 and McCollum's 28. He immediately named Denny Hastert his chief deputy whip. Gingrich talked of creating a special leadership position for Walker—which never happened, though he included him in leadership meetings. Gingrich also took a swipe at DeLay by slashing a quarter of the whip's budget. But Newt had let down a friend and collaborator when he avoided a direct challenge of DeLay.

"He knew I'd make a terrible enemy," DeLay said—an observation that squared with his warning to Jacqueline Blankenship.

"Look, they needed each other and Newt was pragmatic," said a former Gingrich associate. If the two men weren't the closest of friends, DeLay had moved closer to Gingrich, even if not as close as Bob Walker. Nor was DeLay the "moderate" described by the *Washington Times*—a characterization that was almost libelous. He had been an open and often angry critic of President Bush—in particular of the tax increase that had contradicted his "Read my lips: no new taxes" promise. When Bush proposed new taxes in 1990, DeLay and Armey tried to persuade all House Republicans to sign a resolution requiring the president to recommit himself to the pledge he had made in 1988. DeLay led the right-wing mugging of Bush's budget director, Richard Darman, whose budget projections and tax plan made him the target of conservatives led by anti-tax agitator Grover Norquist. He moved the Republican Study Committee to the right and used his position there to attack the Bush budget and propose an economic reform package modeled on tax cuts pushed through at the beginning of Reagan's first term. The DeLay-Wallop bill (co-sponsored by Wyoming Senator Malcolm Wallop) set out to lower the Social Security tax, cut the top rate on capital gains to 15 percent, make depreciation schedules more favorable to business, and set up "IRA-plus" accounts that provided a mechanism for contributors to evade taxes on what was at the time taxable income. And DeLay was present at the creation of Gingrich's ten-point Contract with America—along with Armey and Walker.

Armey directed the preparation of the Contract, which began with focus groups, proceeded to polling then moved from issue questionnaires to a list that Gingrich insisted be pared down to ten—because he believed the number ten had near mythical qualities. The plan was to be implemented in 100 days—again, a number that held special appeal to Gingrich, in part because he associated it with Napoleon's 100 days after his return from exile. And because Gingrich saw himself as a transformative figure like FDR, who laid out his own celebrated One Hundred Days Agenda. To accommodate Gingrich's numbers fetish, the twenty issues that were squeezed into the ten points included:

- a vote on a balanced-budget amendment;
- more punitive and less preventative crime legislation;
- welfare reform that would impose limits on young unwed mothers and reductions in Aid to Families With Dependent Children funding;
- child support enforcement and tax incentives for adoption;
- increased tax credits for children and the repeal of the marriage tax penalty;
- stronger child pornography laws;
- tax incentives for elder care insurance;
- a prohibition of U.S. troops serving under UN Command and increased national defense spending;
- an increase to the amount of money retirees can earn while receiving Social Security;
- tort reform that would lower punitive damage awards;
- a vote on term limits;
- reduction in capital gains tax;
- business incentives and regulatory reduction;
- repeal of the 1993 tax increase on Social Security benefits

After Mildred Webber helped make DeLay whip, she moved on to another office to help implement part of the revolution. One freshman DeLay and Webber helped elect was David McIntosh, who had worked for Vice President Dan Quayle's Council on Competitiveness—an office established to eliminate government regulation. Gingrich appointed McIntosh to chair the House Regulatory Affairs Subcommittee, and McIntosh hired Webber to work on the committee. As soon as she was set up in her office in Regulatory Affairs, Webber began faxing Republican members to request their lists of "dumb regulations" to be stricken from the books on "Corrections Day."

While the Republican Conference attended to the homework Webber assigned, a smaller caucus was meeting in the Capitol. It was a gathering so historic that it might someday be memorialized by a plaque. The so-called K Street Project, designed to discipline the business lobby and capture its political contributions, traced its beginning to the day before the 104th Congress convened on January 4, 1995. On the day before the first Republican majority to hold the House of Representatives in forty years began its official business, the majority whip turned his offices over to something called Project Relief. It was not, despite what its title suggests, a humanitarian operation—unless freeing business from government regulation and cutting corporate taxes can be considered humanitarian. DeLay's office suite was filled with lobbyists drafting legislation to do precisely that.

Before Speaker Gingrich called the new House to order, it was evident that the populist revolution he had sold to voters was no more than a changing of the guard. Taking the place of Democratic lobbyists representing construction, entertainment, and trial lawyer interests were Republican lobbyists representing oil and gas, timber, pharmaceuticals, and insurance interests. Only one development might be called revolutionary: lobbyists had thrown off their shackles, moved out of their K Street office suites, and set up shop in the Capitol office of the new majority whip. They arrived for work before DeLay had time to unpack. It was an unprecedented private occupation of the public places where the nation's laws are made. Any reporter who has ever covered the legislative process knows that lobbyists sometimes write bills, or sit in legislators' offices during floor debates and write amendments and talking points. But never had the corporate lobby so brazenly occupied the office of a member of the House leadership. It was more revolting than revolutionary.

The "concerned citizens" working in the whip's office wasted little time. Gordon Gooch, an amiable and permanent presence in the lobby, where he had represented energy and petrochemical interests since Dick Nixon was president, presided over the meetings. Gooch was coordinating the work of lobbyists for the 350 companies signed on with Project Relief. And he was writing the big deregulation bill—one of the set pieces for the House floor theatrics of the Gingrich Revolution. To see that it would pass, the corporate interests represented in the room put up a half million dollars, a modest investment considering that the PACs associated with Project Relief had contributed $10.3 million to House campaigns in 1994.

The committee staffers who usually provide the expertise for the arcane work of drafting legislation were irrelevant now. Gooch took their place. Because the task was a large one, he wasn't the only legislative ghostwriter working in the whip's office. When Gooch's first draft of a bill that would impose a 100-day moratorium on new government regulations didn't satisfy the real carnivores in the anti-regulation feeding frenzy, it was passed on to others, who trimmed flabby language and included their add-ons: provisions protecting motor fleets in California, industrial consumers of natural gas, and Union Carbide (in its fight with the Labor Department).

New to leadership, DeLay made the mistake of allowing the *Washington Post*'s Michael Weisskopf and David Maraniss in to watch some of the process. Readers of their reporting could almost feel the writers' jaws dropping as they witnessed the business lobby literally taking over the office of the number three man in the House. By the time floor debate on the regulation moratorium approached, the pack of lobbyists had outgrown DeLay's suite and moved on to a committee room, where De-

Lay joined them on the eve of the floor vote to deliver a keynote address. He did not want only Republicans voting for the bill, he said. He wanted enough Democrats to make it veto-proof.

DeLay would prevail in the House, 276-147, but short of his veto-proof margin. Ultimately, the moratorium bill failed, foundering in the more reasonable Senate. But Project Relief changed the relationship between Congress and the business lobby. Lobbyists were being asked to take the lead in passing the leadership's bills. Many of the same Project Relief lobbyists, who had worked with both Democrats and Republicans, suddenly realized they had a permanent home in the Republican Party. Lobbyists were even assigned individual members to work, often based on the presence of an industry in a member's district. Suddenly, New Jersey Democrat Frank Pallone was lobbied by a Johnson & Johnson lobbyist from Project Relief, because Johnson & Johnson had a plant in Pallone's Jersey district. Federal Express, which operated out of Memphis, worked on Tennessee Republican Congressman John Tanner. Retail farm outlets were assigned to west Texas Democrat Charlie Stenholm.

When the bill moved to the floor, amendments were written by lobbyists who took their laptops to the Capitol. "They did everything but allow these guys to walk onto the floor with drafts of their amendments," said a House staff member of the push to pass the regulatory reform bill. Lobbyists were writing the legislation, DeLay said at the time, "because they have the expertise."

Equally remarkable was the reversal of the lobbyist-legislator roles, as the House leadership made the lobbyists do their bidding. "I've had members pull me aside and ask me to talk to another member of Congress about a bill or an amendment," a lobbyist said in an interview. "But I've never been asked to work on a bill—at least like they are asking us to whip bills now." It was a paradigm shift that began in one month early in 1995. And it represents a greater threat to the legislative process than having lobbyists draft bills, which had been done in a more discreet fashion for years. For the first time in history, the vast resources of the business lobby were placed in the service of the House leadership.

At the same time, lobbyists were being pressed to make additional contributions, or to address their deficiencies in contributions to Republican candidates. DeLay began calling lobbyists into his office and showing them his ledger of those contributions, with "friendly" and "unfriendly" columns for lobbyists contributing to Republicans or Democrats.

Maraniss and Weisskopf wrote: "It didn't take long for the word to spread around town about [DeLay's] book. By some accounts—apocryphal it turns out—DeLay even made lobbyists turn to their contribution totals and initial them, like a report card." Such stories actually make DeLay's job easier. When an aide once asked whether efforts should be made to quell the legend, DeLay leaned back in his chair and said, "No, let it get bigger."

Dick Armey had assigned DeLay to draft and work the deregulation section of the Contract, and there was no one in the House more dedicated to the subject than the whip who had first made a name in the Texas Legislature as Hot Tub Tom but left as Tom DeReg. The moratorium on regulations failed, in part because it was a free-standing bill, easier to defeat than a rider in a larger piece of legislation.

Much of the Contract would not appear as single bills. To avoid protracted and public committee hearings or a veto by the president, Gingrich decided to legislate through the budget and appropriations process. Attaching riders to appropriations bills is faster and more efficient than drafting, marking up, and holding committee votes on free-standing bills. And with no line item veto (it only existed as a Republican policy proposal), the president would have to kill an entire appropriations bill to stop a particular policy grafted on to it. In "Approps," DeLay went after the agency he always believed was most in need of deregulation—if not complete dismantling. He attached seventeen EPA riders to a bill that came out of the appropriations subcommittee where he served. The riders would cut EPA funding by a third and cut funds for the agency's enforcement division by a half. They would block agency policies related to oil refinery pollution and toxic waste, stop the EPA from spending money to enforce wetland protections, end vehicle emissions tests required under the Clean Air Act, and impede EPA regulation of cement kilns that burned hazardous waste classified as "fuel" (to evade higher public health standards imposed on the incineration of hazardous waste when it is properly classified as "hazardous waste"). The rider pertaining to cement kiln regulation included language lifted from a Cement Kiln Recycling Association position paper.

Because Gingrich decided to cut *$200 billion* from the federal budget as a down payment on his Contract, the central confrontation of the 104th Congress involved the budget process—and the House radicals dragging their more reasonable Senate colleagues into a showdown with Bill Clinton. Clinton negotiated, compromised, but refused to surrender. Much of the federal government was shut down for weeks. Finally, Bob Dole prevailed on Gingrich to do a deal with a president who was using the electronic bully pulpit to remind the public that the national parks were closed and unemployment checks weren't in the mail because House Republicans wouldn't produce a realistic budget.

The EPA riders were Tom DeLay's personal crusade. They were a stunning assault. "The Contract with America didn't mention the environment," said Clinton's EPA director, Carol Browner. "I looked at the [appropriations] bill and said this is all about us. He intended to shut the agency down." She lobbied the president to use the issue, the shutdown of the government, and the threats to dismantle the EPA to fight back on the Contract. The EPA, she told Clinton, had to be sold to the people as a public service and not a regulatory agency. Gradually, Clinton came around. "Any daylight between the president and Browner disappeared," said a lobbyist who had worked at the EPA at the time. "Browner started making speeches, writing op-ed pieces, warning that the environmental cop was being taken off the beat. About the prospect of Superfund sites in your backyard. She turned the attack against the EPA against DeLay and he never forgot it."

According to Browner, the hero was Sherwood Boehlert, a moderate Republican from upstate New York. "Sherry Boehlert and a group of moderate Republicans worked very hard to block the riders," Browner said. "He convinced enough Republicans that this was not good policy." Boehlert was getting in the way of the leadership and taking on an adversary bigger than DeLay and Hastert. DeLay had been working with industry lobbyists. "You've got to understand," DeLay said. "We are ideologues. We have an agenda. We have a philosophy. I want to repeal the Clean Air Act. No one came to me and said 'please repeal the Clean Air Act.' We say to the lobbyists 'help us.' We know what we want to do and we find the people to help us do that. We go to the lobbyists and say 'help us get this into the appropriations bill.'" It was an approach that DeLay would later master: making the lobbyists part of the whip's team.

DeLay's understanding of the lobby was better than his understanding of the evolving dynamics of the 104th Congress. Since 1995 DeLay has mastered the art of bringing a bill to the floor when the margin of support is very narrow—or when a few wavering members of the Republican Conference can be brought on board with promises or threats. On a Friday afternoon in July during his first session as majority whip, he learned something about rolling the dice on a critical vote. He ordered no formal whip count on the Boehlert amendment. And he was unaware that Sherry Boehlert had secured the votes of fifty-one Republicans. They joined the Democratic minority to kill all seventeen of DeLay's EPA riders, by a vote of 212-206. (Thirty-one Democrats voted for DeLay's plan to gut the EPA.) A bewildered and angry DeLay didn't realize how badly he had misread public opinion and the will of his own colleagues in the House. "The critical promise we made to the American people was to get the government off their backs," he said, "and the EPA, the Gestapo of government, pure and simply has been one of the major claw hooks that the government has maintained on the backs of our constituents." With Democrats cheering, Gingrich shut down the House for the remainder of the afternoon because he feared the Republican moderates would bolt on other votes critical to the Contract. "I was just livid," DeLay later said in an interview with Washington journalist Elizabeth Drew, "because the Boehlert amendment gutted all my regulatory reform that I had been working on all year."

DeLay would try again, and again miscalculate on his floor count. On the Monday following the defeat of the amendments, his deputy whips tipped him off that more than a dozen Democrats hadn't appeared on the floor and apparently hadn't made it back to the District after the weekend. Armey and DeLay hastily scheduled a vote, after informing Boehlert it was coming. Boehlert had his own list of lobbyists and he called upon them for help. Sixteen environmental groups co-signed a letter that was faxed to every member of the House. Boehlert also attacked the process. Re-votes almost never occurred; Boehlert knew he had defeated the riders once and believed the leadership wasn't playing fair. "They're assuming that people are voting one way or the other that has nothing to do with principle, that people are like clay that can be molded," he said. "For forty years we were in the minority and we complained about Democratic high-handed tactics. Now we're in power and we're doing the same thing." Nonetheless, DeLay and Armey gave the go-ahead on an 8 P.M. vote and Boehlert's amendment lost on a vote of 210-210. (An amendment must have a majority to pass.) In the end, however, Boehlert prevailed. Though he was one of the most liberal members of the Republican Conference, he was also a friend of Gingrich, who was out of town on the day of the tie vote. In the 1989 whip contest Boehlert had provided one of the two votes by which Gingrich defeated Ed Madigan. If the two men shared almost nothing in terms of philosophy, they shared a deep mutual respect. When the Republicans stormed the House in 1994, Gingrich appointed Boehlert to direct a task force on the environment. The DeLay amendments, despite the second vote, were ultimately stripped from the appropriations bill. Boehlert had the last word: "Washington doesn't change major policy on tie votes."

It was one of very few defeats DeLay would suffer during his first session as whip. Tony Blankley, currently editor of the *Washington Times* editorial page, who at that time was working for Gingrich, said the Republican leadership seemed capable of pulling anything off at the time. "They had an extraordinary record passing bills," Blankley said. He added that it would be worthwhile to go back and look at the win-loss record on the bills DeLay whipped. It is indeed worthwhile for anyone who would ever underestimate Tom DeLay. He got thirty bills through during the first 100 days. And over the session he went 300-3, an almost unprecedented batting average on the House floor.

But DeLay and the Gingrich revolutionaries won the pennant and lost the series. Much of what they passed was neutered by the Senate, which was controlled by Republicans but not banshee-caucus Republicans. DeLay would never forgive the Senate, later telling *Texas Monthly* political editor Paul Burka that he was grilling steaks for a half dozen members gathered at his condo when he turned on the television and saw Gingrich and Dole at the White House—negotiating a settlement to the budget impasse that had shut down the government. He held Dole responsible. "Ever since then he's thought the Republicans in the Senate are a bunch of pussies," said a veteran House staffer. It was figurative language that fit DeLay. "Screw the Senate," he famously shouted when Gingrich decided to negotiate. He believed he'd been betrayed by moderate senators who were far too eager to cut deals with Democrats. "Our biggest mistake was backing off from the government shutdown," DeLay would say a year later. "We should have stuck it out."

Bill Clinton didn't exactly win by using his veto and threats of veto to hold back the Republican revolution. But he stopped the most extreme measures of the Gingrich revolution.

Batting average on the House floor was one thing. Getting bills signed into law another. In the end, the Contract with America was a dud. Only three minor pieces of the Contract made it into law. In fact, the procedural changes the leadership put in place in 1995 were far more important and far-reaching than what came out of the Contract. Like true putschists, they did it in one day—the first day of the 104th Congress. Gingrich and his leadership team eliminated the seniority system by which committee chairs had always been selected. In a dramatic fashion he did so by reaching around four senior members of the most important committee in the House, Appropriations, to select Bob Livingston, who was younger, more dynamic, and inclined to adhere to the tenets of the new regime. They imposed a six-year limit on committee chairs—just about the length of time it takes to understand and begin to master the workings of a complex committee. They appointed freshmen to subcommittee chairs and sent a powerful message regarding independence of chairs, demanding letters promising they would support the Contract. They cut committee staffs by a third. And they eliminated the parties' study groups, which published newsletters that included brief summaries of complex pieces of legislation that most members had no time to read. Every measure put in place limited the power of committees, where legislation was shaped, while increasing the power of the Speaker and his leadership team. Even their admirable measure imposing limits on gifts members could accept from lobbyists tended to concentrate power with the leadership—making it more difficult for lobbyists to cultivate the support of a large bloc of House members.

The changes imposed upon the House would be the genuine

legacy of the Gingrich revolution. The revolutionaries reformed the institution, even if they failed to pass their Contract and re-make the government. DeLay was disappointed that many measures, like his EPA riders, never even made it through the House. If he had had a clear mandate from the House, pushing the Senate to action, he would have gotten more. "We don't have 218 hard-right votes. It may be the vast majority of the party, 190 out of 232 wants to do those things but another forty or fifty don't," he said. Sherry Boehlert had pulled together that fifty—the moderates from the Tuesday Lunch Bunch—to block DeLay's attempt to dismantle the EPA. DeLay lost on the issue most important to him because he didn't have a governing ma-jority. He lost because the moderates didn't understand "the revolution" and party loyalty. He would work relentlessly to build a governing majority, marginalizing the moderates and en-couraging (and funding) conservative challengers in Republican primaries.

He would also build the largest, most elaborate, and most ef-ficient whip organization ever seen in the United States House of Representatives.

SIX

Everything Is Deregulated

By 1995 Walter Cronkite must have thought he'd seen and heard it all. But at the end of an interview Cronkite conducted for a report called "Environment Beware," which ran that fall on the Discovery channel, DeLay had the old man frowning and pursing his lips. Cronkite was almost speechless. "DDT," DeLay assured him, "is a very viable pesticide, and in fact, the stoppage of usage of DDT around the world is now costing about two million people their lives a year—because of malaria."

Cronkite blinked. The frightful toll of malaria on people in developing and undeveloped countries in the tropics is generally attributed to unsanitary water and anything else that facilitates breeding mosquitoes. A team of international scientists had attributed a reported spike in malaria cases to massive clearcutting of rain forest—more standing water, more mosquitoes. But few besides the majority whip in the U.S. House could be heard beating a drum to bring back DDT.

"You in effect deny," Cronkite said, "the general assumption —by a lot of scientists at any rate—that the bald eagle was saved, the osprey was saved—many birds were saved by banning DDT?"

DeLay nodded. "There is scientific fact, by many scientific studies, that show the claims made by Rachel Carson in her book *Silent Spring* indeed had no scientific basis—it was all based on emotion."

Apart from its softening of fertile eggshells in the wild, killing chicks before they could be born, and sending bald eagles, ospreys, brown pelicans, and many other species in a free fall toward extinction, DDT is a probable human carcinogen that does not break down in the environment. Nearly thirty years after it was banned in the United States trace amounts were still being found in soil and in food grown in that dirt. But as Cronkite sputtered about DDT, DeLay forged ahead, making the most of his airtime. "There is no crisis of acid rain in the Northeast. In fact, instead of spending the billions of dollars that have been imposed on industry . . . we could have simply spent $500,000 on lime, and put it in the lakes in the Northeast and corrected the acid problem." He laughed. "Now, that's what I'm talking about. You need good science, reasonableness, and common sense in this debate."

DeLay was dead wrong about the damage being caused by acid rain in northern states and Canada. And it was always hard to be certain that DeLay believed everything he spouted. Playing at the edges of his smile that day was a knowing smirk. He clearly got a kick out of shocking this icon of the media. He informed Cronkite that the wing of the Republican Party he represented, and which was now running the House, had no fundamental interest in any real debate on this or any other issue. "We have a strategy," he crowed, "of using every tool available—every vehicle available to us—to make sure our positions prevail."

Despite the strong public sentiment against gutting the EPA and eliminating government regulation in general, DeLay was not going to abandon his cause. A reporter asked him in 1995 if there were any federal regulation he would keep intact. After a moment DeLay replied, "Not that I can think of."

As outrageous as that answer was, Tom DeLay seemed to mean it. He certainly wasn't going to be discouraged by public opinion or the votes cast by his colleagues. For example, after the moderate House Republicans joined Democrats to defeat his anti-EPA riders, DeLay never ceased to use the small bully pulpit provided him by the Appropriations Committee he served on to attack EPA director Carol Browner. Any time

Browner was scheduled to testify before the Veterans Affairs, Housing and Urban Development and Independent Agencies Subcommittee, DeLay would appear at hearings that began to look like political Kabuki. Browner had led the fight to defeat his appropriations riders and DeLay was nothing if not vindictive. The majority whip would show up angry and eager to tear into a list of questions directed at the unflappable Browner, who always responded to him idiomatically and literally: "With all due respect." Browner's remarkable self-control would inflame DeLay and his line of questioning would grow more outrageous as his face grew redder. In a small hearing room, he was often literally in Browner's face. The entertainment possibilities in watching a squat, perspiring, frustrated congressman attempt to take down an intellectually and physically elegant woman almost a foot taller than him made the subcommittee hearings one of the hottest tickets on the Hill.

"Look at the data," Browner told DeLay on one occasion, when he was disputing scientific findings that suspended particulates in the air are a public health risk because they become entrapped in lung tissue.

"I understand that. I'm a scientist myself, Ms. Browner," DeLay said, then pointed to the statistical risks related to breathing dirty air. "Did you know that the relative risk factor of getting mouth cancer by using mouth wash regularly is what that is?" (Browner had not read the mouthwash study.)

The EPA's attempt to regulate PM, or particulate matter in the air, was regulation. And regulation was bad for business. DeLay claimed the EPA was cooking its books on the number of premature deaths that could be prevented by lowering the level of PM, and he insisted that Browner tell him precisely how many lives could be saved each year by imposing a regulation on business.

Rep. DeLay: What is your number now?
Ms. Browner: It is very, very clear.

Rep. DeLay: What is your number now. What is your number?

Ms. Browner: The total number of people affected?

Rep . DeLay: No, total numbers of deaths that is your number.

Ms. Browner: Premature deaths. They range based on the best
available science and the range is between 30 [thousand] and
55 [thousand].

Rep . DeLay: Carol, I don't want to go back and review that
again, but I got to tell you. You're trying to—I don't know
what you're trying to do, but 19 of 21 [scientists, rather than a
unanimous panel] said PM 2.5 ought to be, something ought
to be done with.

Ms. Browner: That's not insignificant.

Rep . DeLay: What, that but, you're trying to equate that to the
standard. The standard's only two people said there was
enough data—well, I'm not going to argue the fact, it is the
case, and we can prove it.

Though DeLay was so angry and hostile that he was utterly
inarticulate, Browner never considered his attacks personal.
Nor did she sense DeLay was browbeating her because she is a
woman. He wasn't, by her assessment, nearly as good at using
the hearing process as many of his colleagues. He wasn't that
well prepared. Nor that agile. And he was predictable. Yet despite his shortcomings, he was doing what he was doing because
he believed in it. In fact it was at the core of his beliefs about
government: Regulation is bad, and the Environmental Protection Agency is one of the greatest abusers of the regulatory
process.

The majority whip felt that government regulation was so
bad that, although he was preoccupied with building his own
center of power in the House and passing legislation, he would
still take the time to attend a series of subcommittee hearings to
harass the director of the EPA. Such dedication to the fight
against all forms of government regulation is what Tom DeLay
is all about. He had been at it since he arrived in Washington in

1985. During his freshman session in Congress he had opposed amendments to a Superfund reauthorization that required companies to disclose emissions of chemicals known or suspected to cause cancer, birth defects, and other chronic illness. The amendments were adopted 212-211. Early in his career in the House, DeLay vented his frustration and attracted the attention of the media by making outrageous statements. In 1987 California Democrat Henry Waxman introduced a bill to ban a chemical called chlordane. Its use had been prohibited as a farming pesticide since the mid-seventies, but it was still widely used in homes. Chlordane was alleged to have caused up to 300,000 cancer deaths in the United States during the seven decades of its use, but in the debate DeLay championed the Illinois manufacturer and offered his expertise in the pest control industry. He said he had been "doused in this terrible chemical, bathed in it" during his time as an exterminator. Chlordane was dangerous only when it was misapplied: "Aspirin is a health problem when it's misapplied." Waxman's bill died in the House, but the next year the EPA, citing evidence that three out of 1,000 Americans exposed to the chemical developed cancer, banned it from domestic use.

The deregulation issue for DeLay was larger than the EPA, and in 1995 he at last had the power to make some changes. The moratorium bill DeLay, Webber, and the lobbyists from Project Relief had failed to pass was aimed at *all* government regulation. If DeLay couldn't block all government regulations with one big dereg bill, he would go at them one at a time. DeLay had referred to the EPA as the Gestapo. But he also loved to hang the Nazi metaphor on the Occupational Safety and Health Administration. He would use the same simple anecdotes President Ronald Reagan typically had employed to make his case. "OSHA just recently fined a business $2,000 because they filled in line 18 instead of line 17," DeLay claimed, characterizing the agency's rampant bureaucratic horrors. "OSHA has fined a roofing company because it caught the roofers on top of a house chewing gum. Another company was fined because they didn't put up a piece of paper on the wall showing how many accidents they've had in the last five years, when they haven't even had an accident in five years. Those kinds of things sort of are like Gestapo tactics of our federal government and our agencies," he told Fox News.

OSHA was a perennial target of the small business community and the big corporate lobby who were determined to dismantle an agency already so strapped for funds and constrained in authority that a lighting strike was more likely than a workplace visit by an OSHA inspector. The business lobby feared the laissez-faire regulation would end if OSHA completed the slow process of writing specific rules and standards protecting workers. So the same lobbyists who joined with DeLay to create Project Relief went to Congress to try to block OSHA's development of an ergonomic rule, or more correctly, a set of standards to provide protection against workplace injuries. (The rule had been proposed and the hearing process started by Elizabeth Dole when she was Bush the elder's secretary of labor.) DeLay used an appropriations rider to block the process, winning a 254-168 vote. He cut $3.5 million out of OSHA's budget, the approximate amount it would cost to continue working on the worker-protection rule. He also used his position on House Appropriations and the extra authority he acquired when he was selected as majority whip to help cut OSHA's enforcement budget by a third. There was not, it seemed, any government regulation he would leave standing.

Critics looking for behavior that suggests DeLay has used his position in leadership to enrich himself have found nothing. His home next to the golf course in Sugar Land is appraised at $392,510, which while not a Texas double-wide is hardly excessive for a congressman who cashed out on his small business.

When in Washington, he lives in an unremarkable high-rise condo on a greenbelt just off the freeway—in an Alexandria neighborhood so suburban it's hard to distinguish from Sugar Land. But the condo is appraised at $99,000, almost substandard housing for the Washington area. Tom DeLay "wants to acquire power more than anything else," said one Republican congressional aide. "That's what he's about."

DeLay didn't seem to mind, however, helping a family member acquire real wealth. Deregulation is not only profitable for business; it can mean big profits for lobbyists and consultants. When DeLay made it to the leadership of the majority party in the House, deregulation (and lobbying in general) became profitable for his brother Randy. In the summer of 1995, Majority Whip DeLay prevailed on a group of his House colleagues to sign on to a letter to Clinton's Secretary of Commerce Ron Brown and U.S. Trade Representative Mickey Kantor, protesting duties imposed on a Mexican concrete monopoly called Cemex. The company had been "dumping," or selling cement at an unjustifiably low cost in the United States. In response, the Commerce Department imposed a tariff. In a *Houston Chronicle* op-ed DeLay complained that the victims of the tariff were not Mexicans:

> It turns out that the real harm has been done to cement consumers: small contractors, ready mixers, and home builders across the United States. . . . Mexico, our close neighbor and North American Free Trade Agreement partner, would like to provide the United States with the cement it needs using the same competitive price structure as all other countries, but the federal government won't let it. The Commerce Department says Mexican cement must cost $30 to $40 more per ton than the same cement from any other country. This logic eludes me; it apparently makes perfect sense to the government lawyers who spend time figuring out complicated formulas. But tell that to a hard-pressed foreman who needs cement to finish a project

or the consumer who must pay higher prices for homes or higher taxes to build roads and bridges.

DeLay didn't mention the name of the company. Nor that his brother was lobbying on its behalf.

DeLay was also looking out for the interests of road builders. Cemex had gotten support from the National Association of Homebuilders and three large lobbying firms, among them Fulbright & Jaworski, which rented Randy DeLay his Houston office space. Working with lobbyists of the Texas mega-law firm, the younger DeLay rounded up support for the measure, though he said he asked another man to place the call to his brother. During his first three months' work as a Washington lobbyist, Randy DeLay was paid $176,000. It was just a start, but this was a man who had gone broke three years earlier—before he began a second career as a lobbyist.

(Randy DeLay suddenly found his services were also needed by the city of Houston, which was trying to keep the National Football League from allowing owner Bud Adams to move his Houston Oilers. The Oilers had been a team cursed by years of mediocrity and spurts of flash and promise that always broke the hearts of its fans in the playoffs. When Adams demanded a new city-financed stadium, long-suffering Houston fans gave up and welcomed a fresh start with a new team, the Texans. Despite the efforts of the DeLay brothers, Adams's team ended up in Tennessee, where they became the Titans, a respectable franchise, as if they had shaken off a bad marriage and fled a house of ghosts.)

"I am a free-market nut," Tom DeLay explained his usual position to stop government regulation of international trade. Were the DeLays the formidable tag team they appeared to be, working in the interest of the older brother's constituents? Or was Randy following his brother around, feeding off crumbs from his table?

Whatever the nature of their collaboration, it was most successful in two huge issues. In the summer of 1995, the federal Surface Transportation Board ruled to allow a $5.4 billion merger between the Union Pacific and Southern Pacific railroads. The board's decision came despite fierce opposition to the merger from state and federal agencies, elected officials, and industry trade groups. An assistant U.S. attorney for antitrust called the decision "the most anti-competitive rail merger in history." The Justice Department said it would drive up consumer costs $800 million a year. A conservative Republican elected to the Texas Railroad Commission said the merger would "have a stranglehold over Houston," throttling eleven of thirteen rail lines connecting the city and the Gulf coast's petrochemical plants. Despite industry opposition in his state and congressional district, DeLay and five House colleagues urged the board to approve the merger. "Texas shippers . . . should benefit from extensive capital improvements, expanded facilities, and track upgrades. . . . Competition could also be much stronger." But one railroad giant would now control all tracks west of the Mississippi. Hardly strangled was Union Pacific, whose political action committee had given $98,000 in soft money to the Republican Party that year—or Southern Pacific's largest shareholder, Denver billionaire Philip Anschutz, who stood to make hundreds of millions from the merger and ponied up $300,000 for the GOP in the weeks right before the board made its ruling. On retainer at Union Pacific was Randy DeLay. His duties, according to his disclosure forms, were the "Merger Application pending before Surface Transportation Board . . . and edification of Texas congressional delegation."

But for both brothers the biggest bacon haul was I-69, an interstate highway that would start in the Rio Grande Valley and, if they got their wish, would follow the route of the old U.S. 59 through Sugar Land and the heart of smog-stricken Houston; then angle northeastward through Arkansas and the Mississippi River valley to Indiana. Co-chair of the Congressional I-69 caucus in the House and Senate, DeLay inserted language in the 1995 National Highway System bill that would officially designate the part of U.S. 59 that crossed Fort Bend County as the route of the interstate. It could only add to the woes of Sugar Land commuters, but it would be a bonanza for cement companies, highway engineers, road contractors, and real estate developers of the right-of-way. "Interstates bring with them economic growth and development," DeLay's statement enthused. "The construction of I-69 through Houston brings these opportunities to 5.5 million people living and working in Texas." Making at least $15,000 a month from multiple I-69 clients was Randy DeLay. For both brothers, I-69 was the truly grand parkway.

For the younger DeLay brother it was a stirring run while it lasted. In less than a year Randy DeLay made a reported $750,000 from clients who shared the legislative priorities of the House majority whip. (He also contributed $25,000 to his brother's PAC, as any other workaday lobbyist would.) But in 1996 the press would excoriate the DeLay brothers for their behavior. "Be assured there is no conflict of interest," the congressman would say in a prepared statement. "I have taken steps to make Randy's access to my office more difficult than any other registered lobbyist or constituent, except for purely personal visits. I have also instructed my staff to take every step possible to avoid any actions that may be taken the wrong way by outside observers."

Though an ethics investigation would clear DeLay of wrongdoing, the applicable rules said more about the prevailing mores of both parties in Congress than the particulars of the brothers' collusion. It would have been wrong, according to House rules drawn up by its members, only if DeLay had himself been enriched by his brother's profiteering. But to DeLay, the damage had been done. Randy DeLay's lobbying career withered as quickly as it had flowered. As for the personal visits to his brother's office, there would be no opportunity. When he cut

Randy loose, Tom DeLay completed the long process of total estrangement from his family. The separation was brutal and total; they would no longer speak. Though the brothers have reportedly reconciled again, Randy then said that the congressman informed him, "I can't afford you as a brother right now. You chose lobbying over me."

Among interests seeking to avoid liability for toxic cleanups, DeLay was the favorite congressman, receiving $106,000 in contributions in 1995. Shortly after the Republicans gained control of the House, he raked in $105,000 more from contributors who hoped to weaken clean air and clean water regulations. In just a year his campaign committee and political action committees took in $623,000 from the energy industry. But his obsession with environmental protection was becoming a liability—in part because he hadn't yet learned that some things are best achieved beyond the reach of reporters who always found him so quotable. When a group of scientists won a Nobel Prize for research on ozone depletion in 1995, DeLay sneered, "The Nobel *appeasement* prize." He explained his contempt: "The Nobel Prize is liberal and extremist, to the extent that these people are super-liberal and have a political agenda." Emissions from human activities had little to do with global warming. "It's the arrogance of man to think that man can change the climate of the world," he assured the House Science committee. "Only nature can change the climate—a volcano, for instance."

In the end he got hammered on the environment. In legislation, he grabbed for too much and delivered almost nothing. It had been unwise to pop off to Walter Cronkite. "Tom was way off the deep end on environmental issues," one of his supporters on K Street told Peter Stone of the *National Journal* in 1996, in a message obviously directed at DeLay. "Republicans are getting slaughtered on environmental issues." DeLay grumbled, "We

flat-out lost the debate. The mistake we've made is not to answer the lies that have been put out about us. A lie unanswered
becomes a fact." A chief lobbyist for the Chemical Manufacturers Association said, "With all due respect for Tom DeLay, I
don't think he's the poster child for regulatory relief anymore.
DeLay will have to moderate his message."

Of course he didn't. He was furious when Bill Clinton negoti-
ated a compromise on environmental requirements with corporations that included Dow Chemical, the giant on the south
edge of DeLay's district. And he went after Dow, one of his
biggest constituents and a big political donor. "They have some
strange leadership at the top," he said of Dow. "I think they're
backsliding."

The verb "backslide" is a term used often by evangelical
Christians to describe brothers and sisters who have lost their
religious fervor. On issues of deregulation, there would be no
backsliding for DeLay. In future years he would vote to weaken
local control over land-use decisions and prohibit the government from designating any tract larger than 50,000 acres as a
national monument. He would lead the fight to drill for oil in
the Arctic National Wildlife Refuge (ANWR), in the Great
Lakes, and off the coast of Florida. He would vote against protecting water from pollution by mining companies, against
stricter standards for arsenic in drinking water.

DeLay would have to wait six years after his Appropriations
Committee assault on OSHA to finally achieve what he wanted
with the agency charged with protecting American workers. In
1995 he had only slowed OSHA's process of developing ergonomic protections. No matter how hard you hit Bill Clinton,
he always got up and kept coming at you—which was precisely
what Clinton and his secretary of labor did with the ergonomics
rule. Clinton decided that the process started during the presidency of Bush the elder was too important to be derailed by
Tom DeLay and the Revolution. Even after the woman Clinton
had brought in to direct the rulemaking process packed up and

quit in response to DeLay's cutting $3.5 million out of the 1995 OSHA appropriation bill, Clinton persisted. He ordered the Department of Labor to continue work on ergonomic rules that would protect workers from strained backs, torn tendons, carpal tunnel injuries associated with repetitive motion, and a broad range of workplace MSDs or musculoskeletal disorders.

As Clinton saw it, Department of Labor administrative law judges had already heard thousands of hours of testimony from business, labor, medical experts, and the insurance industry and he was not going to abandon the process. But the same business coalition that had worked with DeLay on his Project Relief slowed the OSHA rulemaking process to a crawl, demanding more hearings and presenting more evidence. The comprehensive rule was not ready until the final months of Clinton's second term. On the eve of his departure from office, after the Supreme Court had declared George Bush the next president, Bill Clinton ordered the rules posted in the Federal Registry, making them the new worker protection law in the American workplace. Clinton Labor Department officials justified the midnight posting, citing the twelve-year process involved in developing a rule that would help prevent the 1.8 million workplace injuries that occur each year.

But the U.S. Chamber of Commerce, the National Federation of Independent Businesses, UPS, the beef and chicken processing industry, all opposed the rule, which they claimed would cost business $100 billion a year to implement. (OSHA had calculated only a $4.5 billion annual cost to business.)

Bush chief of staff Andrew Card and senior advisor Karl Rove put holds on many unimplemented federal rules, but the ergo rule was a done deal when the new Federal Registry was published in January 2001.

For DeLay, it was 1995 all over, but this time he had an anti-regulation ally in the White House. Project Relief had devolved into a Wednesday morning meeting of lobbyists in DeLay's office—the gathering of a group he sometimes referred to as his "kitchen cabinet." "DeLay really wanted to kill the ergo rule," said a staffer on the Senate Labor Committee. "But he didn't have a way to do it." Because it was literally on the books, it seemed as if it was beyond his reach. Then a lobbyist at one of DeLay's Wednesday meetings realized there was a mechanism that could be used to kill the entire worker protection package. Everyone had been missing the most obvious solution. The Congressional Review Act allowed Congress to rescind any rule that had not been posted in the Federal Register for more than sixty days. The solution to the problem was so evident it was almost embarrassing: a Newt Gingrich law pushed through the House by DeLay in 1995. Any attempt to rescind the rules would be blocked by a filibuster in the Senate. But the CRA, the lobbyist said, was the perfect solution. It limited debate to ten hours in each House, allowed no amendments, and required only a simple majority to rescind a law.

Once again, the business lobbyists returned to DeLay's office suite, where they met every day for a week until 6 P.M. to work on a strategy, talk with House members, and count votes. (Snacks were provided by Entemanns and Krispy Kreme, courtesy of the American Bakers Association, which was fighting the ergo rule.) DeLay's staff and the lobbyists also set up a war room on the other side of Independence Ave. in the Longworth Building.

An aide to the late Senator Paul Wellstone described the move to rescind the worker safety protections as a "House deal cooked up in Tom DeLay's office." "We heard there was a bill drafted before we convened," she said in an interview. The CRA resolution had to clear the Senate first, because with the 50-50 partisan division (before Jim Jeffords bolted the Republican Party), passage there was not as certain as it was in the House. Once six Senate Democrats joined Republicans voting for the bill, it moved to the House, where DeLay and his deputy whips, Denny Hastert and Roy Blunt, helped the boys in the business lobby lock up the vote. Twenty-four hours after the CRA resolution cleared the Senate, it passed the House 223-206. What De-Lay started in 1995, he completed in 2001. The victory over worker protections was total and absolute. The CRA prohibited Congress or any federal department from rewriting a similar rule. The whole package was dead.

When President Bush called to congratulate DeLay for a stunning victory on behalf of the business lobby, DeLay thanked the president for his help. Bush seemed bewildered. He said he hadn't called a single member of Congress, DeLay told *New York Times* reporter Adam Clymer. The president, in office for fewer than ninety days, didn't quite understand that the bill had passed because of "the very fact that he was in the White House," said DeLay. Without a Republican in the White House, senators with large labor constituencies would never have risked such a vote. (It also helped to have Karl Rove letting the Department of Labor and the Congress know that the president wanted the ergonomics rule undone.)

Democrats complained that ten years of work, $1.5 million of Labor Department funds spent on public hearings and drafting the rule, tens of thousands of pages of testimony, and thousands of hours of hearings were discarded in twenty hours of debate and two fifteen-minute roll call votes. At the end of the ten hours allocated to debate in the Senate, Paul Wellstone, the Minnesota senator who would die in a plane crash while campaigning a year later, knew the rule was dead:

> I believe, once again, the message of passing this resolution tonight is to say to many citizens in our country, who are not the big players and the heavy hitters—and they are not powerful, and they are not high income, and they do not have a lot of lobbyists—I think the message to them is: You are expendable.

"I can't get this grin off my face," DeLay told the *Washington Times* after the ergonomics resolution passed. "I go to sleep and wake up with it."

SEVEN

DeLay Inc.:
The Man and His Political Money

Peter Cloeren was a virgin. At least when it came to politics. He had never participated in a political campaign. He had never written a check to a candidate for elected office. He lived in a beat-to-shit Texas Gulf Coast town abandoned first by the shipping industry and more recently by big oil.

He was CEO and majority owner of one of the remaining successful and growing businesses in Orange, Texas. Cloeren Inc. was built on the inventive genius of Peter Cloeren Sr. and expanded by Pete Cloeren's hard work and market savvy. The company, which does more than $40 million in annual sales, designs, manufactures, and markets extrusion dies, coextrusion dies, and feedblocks. In the English we speak in Texas: tools that inject color into colorless plastic.

Until he was seduced by Tom DeLay—a seduction that would cost him $37,000 in political contributions, $400,000 in fines, a two-year probated sentence, and a hundred hours in community service—politics to Pete Cloeren meant showing up to vote for conservative candidates. After his brief involvement with Tom DeLay and an East Texas dentist he was trying to get elected to Congress, Cloeren was done with politics. If Brian Babin lost the 1996 race for the second congressional district in East Texas, Pete Cloeren lost a lot more. And DeLay walked away unscathed. Actually, he flew. Cloeren picked up the $1,320 tab for the executive jet service that made the 180-mile round-trip from Sugar Land to Orange less of a burden for the congressman.

Texas songwriter James McMurtry once said he writes about small towns because they're easier to figure out than big cities. The $37,000 contribution scheme that got Pete Cloeren crossways with the FBI used the same devices to hide and move tens of thousands of dollars that DeLay and his political PACs use to move millions. It was just done on a small-town scale. Babin needed to raise a lot of money to compete for an open seat in a district that was more Democratic than Republican. In order to circumvent federal campaign finance laws, which then limited individual contributions to $1,000 per candidate and placed restrictions on corporate contributions, he needed "vehicles." That is, fresh names to attach to money from donors willing to donate more than the $1,000 federal max. Or the cover provided by organizations that were not corporations and could legally contribute to campaigns for federal office. That's why he needed Cloeren, who had both the money and, as Babin and DeLay would explain to him, the "vehicles."

Cloeren's story (told in detail in a sworn affidavit) begins with one of his employees introducing him to Babin, a candidate in the Republican congressional primary. Cloeren was flattered. And impressed. Babin wanted his help and told him that businessmen like him were essential to expanding a conservative Republican majority in Congress. And Babin was the kind of candidate Cloeren could get excited about. A small businessman with Main Street values. A Christian. A candidate who promised less government regulation and lower taxes. A Republican running for a House seat that had been the private property of larger-than-life Democrat Charlie Wilson. When Babin asked him to help raise $50,000, Cloeren said that it was impossible to do in a rural county peopled by blue-collar Democrats. He offered to write Babin a check for $20,000 or $25,000—a clear sign he was utterly out of touch with federal campaign finance law. Babin advised him there was a $1,000 per-person limit and suggested Cloeren "work with loyal employees."

In other words, Cloeren should make contributions in his workers' names, or have them make the contributions and reimburse them. Before long, Cloeren was sending his employees home on their lunch breaks to pick up their checkbooks. And Babin was swinging by Cloeren's plant parking lot to pick up his checks. The same way Paulie Walnuts picks up the *tributo* payments that Jersey businessmen owe Tony Soprano. In a charmingly naïve line in his congressional affidavit, Cloeren says: "Since I had never raised funds for a political candidate before, I didn't know whether it was unusual for the candidate to pick up the checks in person." (He would later learn why Babin avoided the mail.) When Babin made the runoff, he was back again, asking Cloeren to find more employees through which company money could be funneled to the campaign. (Like the wisecracking boys at Tony Soprano's Bada Bing Club, Babin knew that once you get your hand into somebody's pocket, you gotta work to keep it there.) Babin's fundraising consultant even devised a scheme by which Cloeren Inc. employees would get bonuses from the boss—precisely the amount they were contributing to the campaign. After Babin won the runoff, House Majority Whip Tom DeLay got behind his candidacy. And Babin, who had served as mayor of the tiny East Texas town of Woodville, began to show real growth as a candidate. For example, he called Cloeren to ask if he would pick up the tab to fly the congressman in for a fundraiser.

DeLay was the talent at Babin's campaign event at the Ramada Inn, where the congressman made his standard stump speech: conservative, family values, small government, running against a liberal professional politician. After the speech, DeLay invited Cloeren to a private lunch at the local country club. Cloeren later provided Congressman Henry Waxman's investigator on the House Committee on Government Reform a detailed account of the lunch:

Congressman DeLay turned to me and told me that Mr. Babin's campaign needed more money because Mr. Babin was being out-spent by his Democratic opponent.

Congressman DeLay told me that the Democratic candidate was receiving a lot of money from liberal interest groups like labor unions and trial lawyers. I told Congressman DeLay that I could not help Mr. Babin raise more money because I had run out of vehicles. Congressman DeLay specifically told me that it would not be a problem for him to find, in his words, "additional vehicles," since he knew some organizations and campaigns which could serve as these vehicles. Mr. DeLay turned to his aide, Mr. [Robert] Mills and stated that money could be funneled to the Babin campaign through both Triad [a corporation that ran two nonprofit foundations] and other congressional campaigns. Congressman DeLay then specifically told me that Mr. Mills would follow up with me on the details of how to funnel additional monies to Mr. Babin's campaign.

After lunch DeLay and Babin held a press conference at the Cloeren Inc. plant. And Pete Cloeren was an instant political player. On the ride to the airport, DeLay told Cloeren that Babin could win if he could raise enough money. He urged Cloeren to do all he could. It was here that fundraising became more sophisticated. As Cloeren listened, DeLay explained how the money could be moved.

DeLay campaign manager Robert Mills suggested that Cloeren contribute to Strom Thurmond's Senate campaign in South Carolina and Stephen Gill's House campaign in Tennessee. They would, in turn, donate money to Babin's campaign. Babin also made the "Triad connection" and Cloeren began writing checks to organizations he had never heard of: $5,000 to the Citizens United Political Victory Fund PAC, which would run issue ads supporting Babin; $20,000 to Citizens for Reform, yet another Triad operation. He also wrote checks to the Thurmond and Gill campaigns, though he had never heard of Gill.

Money was moving in circles: Cloeren wrote a $5,000 check to Citizens United and the PAC wrote a $5,000 check to Babin's congressional campaign. And the campaign committees of a South Carolina senator and a House candidate from Tennessee were suddenly contributing to a congressional campaign committee in Texas. If the requests were unusual, Cloeren at least had convinced himself he was doing nothing wrong. "I assumed that if a senior member of Congress said to do something that it would be legal, proper, and ethical to do it," he would later say.

According to Cloeren, Babin and his consultant Walter Whetsell used Triad, Citizens for Reform, and Citizens United interchangeably. Their comments led Cloeren "to believe that Triad might be composed of all these different groups." It was. Triad Management Services Inc. was a queer political animal, a for-profit corporation that earned no profits, sold no goods or services, and operated two nonprofit organizations: Citizens for Reform and Citizens for the Republic Education Fund. Both nonprofits were described as nonpartisan social welfare organizations. The "nonpartisan" designation allowed the groups to meet an IRS standard and run issue ads—as long as they were not funded by or coordinated with a political candidate. Yet every dime of the $3 million that the two nonpartisan Triad organizations spent in the 1996 election cycle was spent on twenty-nine Republican congressional candidates. Neither the public nor the candidates attacked by the ads bought with Triad money knew what individuals paid for them. Because Triad was a corporation and not a political action committee, it was exempt from disclosure laws. It was a drop box where contributors who "maxed out" their federal giving could send additional money to help their candidates. And perfect cover for donors who didn't want their names in the public record.

Triad was also one of those shadowy political organizations that will make you believe Hillary Clinton's claim about "a vast right-wing conspiracy." Carolyn Malenick, Triad's sole proprietor, was a graduate of Jerry Falwell's Liberty University and a close friend of the Falwell family. Her entire professional life had been devoted to raising money for extreme right-wing causes and candidates. She began her career with direct-mail pioneer Richard Viguerie. Then she raised money for Ollie North's Freedom Alliance and for North's failed campaign for the U.S. Senate. Her main funder at Triad was Pennsylvania multi-millionaire Robert Cone, a zealous anti-abortion-rights crusader—until his family toy company lost several personal injury lawsuits and he put his heart and political contributions into the tort reform movement. Cone even appeared in Triad's marketing video (though the corporation sold nothing and served only as a political operation).

For Triad, Pete Cloeren was a perfect mark: a guy with deep pockets and a track record (albeit a short one) of contributing to conservative Republicans. Even if it was just one candidate, he did have deep pockets.

DeLay and Babin were not Triad insiders; DeLay, in fact, was beginning to build his own huge fundraising operation. But he knew that Triad along with the Thurmond and Gill campaigns were conduits through which he could maximize Cloeren's giving. So he hooked Cloeren up with Malenick, who did for him what her corporation did for other big donors: took his money and moved it on to the candidate of his choice. A Senate committee looking at Triad found that "on occasions multiple PACs received checks from the same individual within a matter of days. All of the PACs receiving the contributions then made contributions to one candidate within days of one another." Precisely as the $5,000 Cloeren sent to Citizens United found its way back to the Babin campaign.

As the general election campaign began, Babin's opponent, Jim Turner, was blindsided by ads linking him to gay rights and early release of prisoners. ("God, guns, and gays" campaigns are formulaic fare in Texas; you remind voters that you favor God and guns and that your opponent is aligned with gays.) The ads attacking Turner were paid for by Citizens for Reform. Turner had no idea which "individual citizens" wrote the checks to pay for the attack ads.

To anyone reading Federal Election Commission filings, it would seem that workers at Cloeren Inc. had joined together in a rare show of support—in the form of $1,000 contributions for the congressional campaign of a dentist from a small town sixty miles away. A *Beaumont Enterprise* reporter looked at the list and didn't buy it. Maybe it was the *Enterprise* news story that caught the attention of the FBI. Whatever did it, Pete Cloeren was suddenly the target of a criminal investigation. Cloeren cooperated, phoning Babin to discuss the campaign contributions while FBI agents recorded their conversations.

The investigation wasn't exactly deep cover. When Cloeren called to get Babin's comments on tape, the dentist began to grouse about the Feds coming at them, probably, he said, because one of Cloeren's disgruntled employees tipped them off. According to Cloeren's affidavit, Babin reassured him that at least he had picked up the checks, so they couldn't be investigated for mail fraud. Ben Ginsberg, a lawyer who once worked for the Republican National Committee, had warned Babin about mail fraud.

Cloeren also taped conversations with Walter Whetsell, the Babin campaign consultant who steered Cloeren toward Triad. Whetsell must not have shared Babin's concern about the FBI investigation. According to Cloeren's sworn account, Whetsell talked freely about the conversation Cloeren had with DeLay and Babin at the country club in Orange. Whetsell also had been in touch with Ginsberg regarding possible exposure to criminal prosecution. Yet he seemed unaware the Feds were watching (and listening).

Cloeren cut himself a deal, though federal prosecutors didn't cut him much slack. He wouldn't do any jail time but would plead guilty to misdemeanor violations of federal campaign finance law. He paid a $200,000 fine, and his company paid another

$200,000 fine. His relationship with DeLay, Babin, and Triad cost him a half million dollars if you take into account attorneys' fees, fines, and his actual contributions. His candidate didn't even win the election. "I presently have no business or personal relationship with Representative DeLay, Mr. Babin, Mr. Whetsell, or Mr. Mills," Cloeren wrote at the end of the affidavit he submitted to the House Committee on Government Reform.

"It seems like they really took advantage of him," said a local businessman who knows Cloeren casually. There's a certain journalistic economy of scale in the Triad story. Its small size makes it easier to follow the money. From Cloeren to his employees and finally to Babin. Or from Cloeren to Triad in Washington, to one of the Triad entities, then back to the Babin campaign. Or from Cloeren to the Thurmond and Gill campaigns then back to Babin. Soft money (corporate funds illegal to spend) sent to an entity not required to report it, or to a congressional campaign that could turn it around and send it back as hard money (individual, PAC, or organizational money legal to spend). This is precisely what the fundraising operation that has come to be called DeLay Inc. does on a much larger scale, and with the extra incentive a leader of Congress brings to the process of asking for money.

The Triad affair also illustrates the impunity with which campaign fundraisers operate. How is it that no one other than Peter Cloeren got popped for the Triad fundraising scheme? A Democratic member of Congress who asked that his name not be used said Clinton Attorney General Janet Reno's lack of enthusiasm for prosecuting illegal fundraising didn't help. Reno had put herself in a box. Once she refused to appoint a special prosecutor to look into allegations about improper fundraising in the Clinton White House, any Department of Justice enforcement action against Republicans would appear to be partisan.

Congressional oversight was equally politicized. Committees in both houses were controlled by Republicans and largely focused on Clinton's fundraising. Democrats were pointing to

Triad, arguing that there was more to investigate than the phone calls President Clinton and Vice President Al Gore made to funders, and the names of donors who had slept in the Lincoln Bedroom. Considering the magnitude of the White House fundraising operation and the serious questions raised about it, it's not surprising that Republicans in Congress had little interest in a small-time shell game in Texas. Yet Government Reform Chair Dan Burton's conduct was so egregious that it gave partisan excess a bad name. Burton had his sights set on ClintonGore '96 and wouldn't look at what Triad had done in the same year.

Not only did Burton refuse to look at Triad. He blocked committee Democrats from conducting their investigation. Burton held his ground until California Democrat Henry Waxman put him on the spot in public. Waxman made such a compelling argument at a mid-May '98 committee hearing that Burton agreed to allow minority members of the committee to subpoena summaries of FBI interrogations of Triad subjects. Burton quickly reneged, however, implying that Waxman was coordinating his investigation of DeLay with other congressional Democrats who had filed a racketeering suit against DeLay and his fundraising operations.

Though he wasn't able to hold hearings or subpoena witnesses, Waxman persisted, and Peter Cloeren was able to tell his story to Congress. Waxman sent a minority staff member to Texas to look into Babin, DeLay, Triad, et al. But the scope of his investigation was limited. There is no doubt that the Triad/Babin affair was dwarfed by Clinton-Gore's fundraising. But Triad was never adequately examined by the House and Senate committees looking into fundraising irregularities. Lacking the authority to issue subpoenas and schedule hearings, committee Democrats were checkmated. (Much of the material here cited is in the public record because it was in the minority reports of House and Senate committees.)

When no one was prosecuted after Peter Cloeren cooperated with the Feds and paid a $400,000 fine, he filed a complaint with the Federal Election Commission. After conducting an investigation, the FEC legal staff recommended $4,544,000 in fines: $1,149,000 against Triad; $1,818,000 against Citizens for the Republic Education Fund; and $1,577,000 against Citizens for Reform. The commissioners, always responsive to political pressure, ignored the recommendations of their own staff, dropped the fines against the two nonprofits, and reduced Triad's fine to $200,000.

Tom DeLay got a walk on the deal he had done on Peter Cloeren, which DeLay claimed involved no more than speaking to Cloeren for three minutes at lunch. ("I don't know this man from Adam," said DeLay.) Whether it was DeLay's three minutes or the ninety minutes Cloeren swore to in his affidavit, DeLay's visit to Orange, Texas, occurred as he was moving into major league fundraising. By the time he opened a Texas branch in 2001, DeLay Inc. was raising money in volumes never seen in the United States Congress. Nothing compares. No member of Congress—except members raising money for their own presidential campaigns—had ever raised the amount of political money raised by Tom DeLay. The Texan elected majority leader in 2003 is in a class of his own.

Fred Wertheimer has dedicated his entire career to campaign-finance reform. Previously with the public-interest group Common Cause and more recently with Democracy 21, which focuses exclusively on campaign finance, Wertheimer has filed complaints, worked on legislation, directed investigations, and testified before congressional committees. When it comes to DeLay, Wertheimer gropes for metaphors adequate to fit the subject.

"All politicians raise money," Wertheimer said in an interview in his Washington office. "But this is different. He is different. It's what he's about. It is as if political money is in his DNA."

Wertheimer also predicted, months before a criminal investigation looking into DeLay's fundraising in Texas, that the majority leader was taking extraordinary risks. "He's always close to the edge. It's like skating near the edge of a cliff. Sooner or later you're going to get too close. Ultimately," Wertheimer said, "all these guys overreach."

DeLay's huge fundraising machine traces its beginning to 1994, when he won election to the third highest position in the House only to have Gingrich slash his budget and thereby take some of his power. He didn't get mad; he began the process by which he would get even. DeLay understood that PAC spending is an investment in power. While some members of Congress use their PAC money to support big staffs and pay for lavish living, DeLay realized that to increase his political power, he would have to increase his giving to other Republican candidates. As soon as he was elected to a leadership position, he beefed up his PAC. He hired Karl Gallant, a right-wing fundraiser who had worked for the anti-union National Right to Work Committee and the Ramhurst Corporation, a stealth group created by the tobacco industry to lobby and organize "grassroots" pro-smoking campaigns.

Gallant was a perfect match: a tobacco lobbyist who was also a professional anti-union activist. The industry signaled its support by contributing $27,000–$17,000 from R. J. Reynolds and $10,000 from Philip Morris. But DeLay needed more than tobacco money to fund his "revolution." In 1995, one Texas corporation was synonymous with bold, deregulated, corporate success and flush with the cash DeLay needed. Cultivating Enron as a patron was as logical as hooking up with Big Tobacco. After all, DeLay had been fighting Enron's fight when it was a regional gas pipeline company trying to grow its way out of the Southwest. He might as well be paid for it. DeLay and Lay were a perfect political marriage. "Tom DeReg" ascribed to the same canon of unfettered capitalism that Enron CEO Ken Lay was using to turn Enron into a company that could sell bandwidth in

Texas, remarketed electricity in California, and nuclear power in the Marianas.

And Lay played in the big leagues. He was a major donor to the elder George Bush, dined and overnighted with George and Barbara at the White House, co-chaired Bush's 1992 campaign, chaired and helped underwrite the 1992 Republican national convention in Houston, and provided the Republican Party with $1.5 million in soft money. He also had invested heavily in the 1994 gubernatorial campaign of George W. Bush. The list of people who could provide DeLay with such instant access to big political donors was a short one and Ken Lay was at the top.

As DeLay called on Enron to help him raise the money that would allow him to compete with Gingrich's leadership PAC, he was careful not to offend Gingrich. He devised a plan that wouldn't offend the image-conscious Speaker. He would honor Gingrich at an ARMPAC (Americans for a Republican Majority PAC) fundraiser in Houston. It would be sponsored by Enron. Donors writing checks for $5,000 or more could buy a photograph taken with DeLay and his boss, Speaker of the House Newt Gingrich.

The year before the Houston fundraiser, Gingrich's GOPAC had outspent DeLay's ARMPAC two-to-one: $1.5 million to $780,000. The Houston event was the beginning of a campaign to close the fundraising gap. Enron and its executives brought in $280,000, betting against the odds on an ambitious politician whose Sugar Land home was thirty miles out the Southwest Freeway from Enron's sleek downtown office tower.

The Houston event was the beginning of a friendship that would endure until Enron's vertical collapse six years later. Before Ken Lay's company went down, it had contributed half a million to ARMPAC—almost as much as the $750,000 it had donated to George W. Bush. The fundraising event was also the beginning of a cozy relationship between Enron and DeLay's staff. Joining Karl Gallant on the ARMPAC makeover team was Jim Ellis, another R. J. Reynolds political operative, who would

later run DeLay's controversial 2002 fundraising campaign in
Texas. In 1998, at a meeting with Enron lobbyists in his Sugar
Land home, DeLay helped secure a $750,000 Enron consulting
contract for Gallant and Ed Buckham—who was still DeLay's
chief of staff and had not quite resigned to set up his lobbying
firm, the Alexander Strategy Group. Also joining Gallant at
ARMPAC was Robert Mills, the same Robert Mills who ran
DeLay's 1996 campaign and helped DeLay get between Pete
Cloeren and his money. (DeLay's wife, Christine, a retired
teacher, would also get in on the lobbying deal, earning $40,000
a year as an Alexander Strategy groupie.)

You couldn't tell it by sitting in the Rayburn Building hearing
room in spring 1998, watching Henry Waxman and Dan Burton
feud over FBI records, but Robert Mills and his relationship
with Tom DeLay were part of the subtext of that feud. House
Government Reform chair Dan Burton had shut down the Triad
investigation in 1998 when he got wind of a Democratic Congressional Committee RICO suit filed against DeLay and his
funding operation. Mills was one of the defendants. "RICO"
refers to suits filed under the Racketeer Influenced Corrupt Organizations Act. If a judge certifies a RICO suit and allows it to
proceed, the plaintiff has broad discovery power. In other words,
with the court's authority, the party that filed the suit can demand all the defendant's relevant paper, computer, bank, and
phone records. There is also the right to conduct depositions of
anyone with information relevant to the case. Other than a criminal investigation, the discovery process provided by the RICO
statute is about as bad as it gets for a political fundraiser.

When federal Judge Thomas Penfield Jackson, who presided
over the Microsoft anti-trust case, certified the Democrats'
RICO suit against DeLay, congressional Republicans went
apeshit. Burton, one of the dominant primates in the House,
was out in front. He reneged on the agreement on subpoena of
FBI material that he had made at a committee hearing in early
May. That was enough to send Henry Waxman brachiating

across the Rayburn Building. "I've never had this happen in my adult life," said Waxman. "How can you operate in this institution if a chairman gave his word in front of all those members then goes back on it?" The angry attack from the short, bald, pugnacious California Democrat didn't convince Burton. The Government Reform Committee he chaired would not subpoena FBI summaries of Triad interviews. The content of interviews regarding Triad, Babin, DeLay, and Mills would not be introduced into the public record.

If Bob Mills wasn't the sketchiest character named in the RICO suit the Democrats filed, he certainly was fronting for the sketchiest operation. To certify a RICO suit, plaintiffs must convince a judge there is reason to believe the defendant is involved in a criminal enterprise and that there is a pattern of racketeering activity. Democrats filing suit alleged that three "associated organizations" related to DeLay were involved in racketeering activity. One of them was the U.S. Family Network, which had been run by Mills. The others were the Republican Majority Issues Committee, directed by Karl Gallant, and Jim Ellis's Americans for Economic Growth.

Mills's U.S. Family Network would have been hard to explain to a jury, if the Democrats hadn't folded and settled the suit first. The nonprofit operation shared office space with ARM-PAC and the Alexander Strategy Group, the Ed Buckham operation that provided full employment for DeLay staff alumni. Mills was U.S. Family's director until the suit was filed, when he quietly departed. Reports that he had stolen $35,000 from the Council for Government Reform, where he served as director until signing on with DeLay's campaign in 1995, made him too hot to keep on staff. Mills didn't have a bar card. But he could have given Brian Babin some hard-earned advice about postal fraud. Of the $35,000 Mills stole from the conservative advocacy group he directed, $5,400 was a postal refund check.

Mills had one of the hottest vitas in Washington. Before his brief tenure at the Council for Government Reform, he had been the subject of an FEC investigation into another organization: United Conservatives of America.

The FEC was looking into United Conservatives' huge debts, which investigators believed were somehow used to hide illegal corporate donations. When the investigation began, Mills disappeared, ignoring calls from FEC lawyers and leaving investigators' certified letters piling up in a P.O. box.

Maybe Mills found Jesus when he went to work for Tom DeLay's U.S. Family Network, which Mills said would focus on Christian right voter turnout. But his mission statement didn't square with expenditures. Initially, the meager $15,000 it had in the bank in 1996 limited outreach to Christians. But a year later it had raised $476,000 and quickly acquired a Capitol Hill townhouse for $325,000, a $149,000 skybox at the MCI Center, home of Washington's NBA and NHL franchise, and a $27,000 GMC truck that the Capitol Hill newspaper *Roll Call* traced to Ed Buckham's Maryland residence. U.S. Family also paid a $59,000 yearly salary to Buckham's wife. Odd expenditures, it seems, for a group registered with the IRS as a 501(c)(4) "social welfare" organization and focused on Christian conservatives.

By 1999, Mills was out. But the Reverend Buckham—an ordained Christian minister and a secular fundraiser—and the Family Network made the news again. The $500,000 donation it received from the National Republican Congressional Committee was the largest single donation the NRCC made that year. The huge cash transfer was never approved by the NRCC executive committee. Tom Davis, the Virginia congressman DeLay had made NRCC chair, cut the check because he knew Ed Buckham would use the money to support Republican House candidates. Almost as odd as the carte blanche half million from the NRCC was a $1 million contribution from an unnamed benefactor.

U.S. Family was designed "to conceal or disguise the nature, location, source, ownership, or control of the proceeds," alleged the Democrats who sued DeLay and his fundraisers. "There is no accountability," Wertheimer said in an interview. "No one knows who is providing these large sums of money." The editorial board at *Roll Call* was equally critical. "[T]he NRCC has dumped this money into a black hole, where the sun doesn't shine—or disinfect."

Roll Call also engaged in some informed speculation about what U.S. Family was probably really about. "Our natural suspicion is that the U.S. Family Network will do and say things for GOP candidates and against their opponents that the NRCC would be embarrassed to be identified with. The close connections between the Network, Buckham, and DeLay also invite suspicions that coordination of one sort or another will take place—supposedly a no-no under campaign finance law." The Democrats, according to *Roll Call,* had been screaming to the FEC, and got no responses. So they sued.

It was a coordinated, big-money effort that the Democrats who filed the RICO suit hoped to stop. Or at least slow down. Wertheimer suspects that the DCCC didn't really want to take DeLay and his funding operation to court. The blowback from a jury ruling would have imposed the same fundraising restrictions on fundraisers from both parties. And the discovery process in a civil suit is a two-way street. Republicans would have demanded records from the Democrats who had sued them. "I think they wanted to freeze the linebackers," Wertheimer said. Bob Bauer and Mark Elias (the Perkins & Coie lawyers who filed the suit and who refused to be interviewed) are not campaign finance reformers. They are lawyers who advise Democrats on campaign finance law and track Republican campaign spending. Their interest was not necessarily the public interest.

Despite its odd behavior and dodgy funding sources, the U.S. Family Network wasn't the main target of the lawsuit. The Republican Majority Issues Committee (RMIC) was the fundraising operation that Democrats considered the Death Star. It, too, was a DeLay-Buckham enterprise. But it made no pretense about courting Christian voters. In the spring of 1998, the two men sat in the oversized dining room chairs of a Pennsylvania Avenue restaurant overlooking the cascading fountain at the navy memorial. "A power dining hot spot," 701 is renowned for its vodka, caviar, and flights of fine wines. ("Dry" for years, De-Lay now drinks red wine.) 701 was a long way from the Barbecue Barn back in Sugar Land, but DeLay had come to appreciate fine dining. In fairness to him, he was on the PAC's tab, and his social life is given over to fundraising dinners. In the past, De-Lay had introduced Buckham as his minister. On this occasion the two men were seated in an opulent restaurant, praying to the one god universally worshipped in Washington: Mammon.

Buckham believed that RMIC could easily raise $25 million for Republican candidates in the 2000 campaign. And because it was not connected to the party, none of the donors would ever be identified. RMIC intended to spend millions on twenty-five congressional races. "It was a novel idea because of its potential to raise huge amounts of money virtually in secrecy," wrote *Washington Post* reporter Juliet Eilperin. "It was audacious in its willingness to push the boundaries of campaign finance law. And it reflected the fundamental belief of DeLay that Republicans and their allies can always tap new sources of wealth to help their party." Americans for Economic Growth, the third "associated organization" sued by the Democrats, was run by Jim Ellis, a longtime DeLay associate and former member of his staff, who also worked for Buckham at the Alexander Strategy Group. According to the lawsuit, DeLay, Gallant, Ellis, Mills, et al. were "extorting" contributions from individuals with interests before Congress.

The RICO suit threatened to expose the intricate and corrupt relationships between big contributors and members of Congress who served their interests. A highly regarded federal judge sitting in a District of Columbia courtroom had given the plaintiffs a green light. Reporters were poring over the allegations made in the complaint.

Then the Democrats and DeLay settled.

Just as he had in the Triad case, Tom DeLay had dodged the bullet. "The suit was dismissed," DeLay was still reminding reporters at a March 2004 press conference. In case anyone in the press corps had forgotten, he reminded us: "It was a partisan lawsuit."

Both statements are true. In part. Judge Jackson, no doubt delighted to have *Democratic Congressional Campaign Committee, Inc. v. Tom DeLay et al.* off his docket, dismissed the suit because both parties withdrew. There were no litigants. And while it was partisan, as are most suits filed against politicians, the judge's certification of the lawsuit spoke to its merit.

"We shut it down," Bob Bauer said of the suit. "There is no DeLay shadow network. We didn't have to worry about it in 2000, and we don't have to worry about it in 2002." DeLay saw it differently: "They have waved the white flag of surrender in the courts," he said.

At best the lawyers hired by the Democrats did what Wertheimer said they intended. They "froze the linebackers." They didn't shut down the franchise. The RIMC was, at least for the coming election, out of business.

"He's not said he's going to stop raising money for anybody," said DeLay chief of staff Susan Hirschmann. If the sentence is tough to parse, the meaning is clear. Tom DeLay was not leaving the money chase. By 2003, DeLay's various fundraising enterprises were bringing in $12,785 a day, a total of $14 million from January 2000 to December 2002, according to Wertheimer's Democracy 21. It was a conservative estimate, looking only at groups with which DeLay was immediately involved.

If DeLay had started out scrambling for money, building his own PAC, and hiring political consultant Mildred Webber to handicap the House races where he could get the best return on $780,000, ten years later lobbyists are coming to him. Not at the huge cattle calls where a donor is only expected to drop off a $1,000 check before moving on to the next event. But rather at smaller gatherings in exclusive restaurants, where donors get face time as they very publicly hand $20,000 checks to fundraising operatives hovering over the candidate. At one ROMP (Retain Our Republican Majority PAC) affair at the Capitol Hill Club, DeLay introduced the lineup of Republican House candidates as lobbyists and trade association presidents handed over their checks. He even provided Vanna White lookalikes: two attractive blond women holding up a giant check, adjusting the amount as the money came in. The total on this particular evening was $1.3 million.

Susan Hirschmann had it right: "He's not said he's going to stop raising money for anybody." And he's not. Two-thirds of the way through the 2004 election cycle that began in 2003, the majority leader had raised $2.28 million and distributed $528,000 to candidates. (Speaker of the House Denny Hastert had raised only $1.68 million.) The $2.28 million was moved through DeLay's personal political action committee. Totals on his extended operation were not yet compiled.

But the extended fundraising operation was raising so much money that it was turning it over to other campaigns to give away. And Jim Ellis, who had been with Tom DeLay since the big fundraising campaigns began, said they were so flush they might be moving into more state elections, where they could help Republicans take control of state legislatures.

Integrated into the K Street Project, the coordinated shakedown of the corporate lobby, the huge fundraising machine Tom DeLay ran seems capable of extracting money and servicing its clients like nothing ever seen in Washington. Tom DeLay is at the top of his game. And so far, bulletproof.

EIGHT

Revolt Within the Revolution

By 1997 DeLay's suite of offices in the Capitol was the Republicans' command central. Sixty-five House members were on his team of deputy and assistant whips. On every piece of legislation important to the House Republican Conference, he handed them slips marked "No, Leaning No, Undecided, Leaning Yes, Yes." Printed on the back was a Conference summary of the bill. They were charged with keeping those slips of DeLay's intelligence current at all times, allowing him to keep an accurate running count and know when GOP colleagues needed to be coaxed or pressured to follow the party line. (He rarely bothered to try to persuade Democrats.) The décor of DeLay's office ran to blue walls, silk-covered furniture, coiled bullwhips positioned like wall art and sculptures, and tables with replicas of his favorite golf holes. "I play wherever anyone will take me," DeLay joshed, and people took him golfing and fact-finding a great number of places these days. In 1997 the Asia-Pacific Exchange Foundation picked up an $18,000 tab for a two-week fact-finding tour of Asian countries by DeLay and his wife. The same year he and a staffer spent $30,000 on Concorde supersonic flights between Paris and Washington—forging a relationship between the majority whip's office and Russian officials. DeLay was flying high and savoring his ascent to power, but there were irritants in his life. Chief among them was the one represented in his golf display by a ball, a photograph, and the inscription: "Slick Willie: Good Lie Guaranteed."

Bill Clinton had looked so vulnerable in 1996, but the GOP

primaries delivered Bob Dole, whose campaign was so detached and half-hearted that he demanded schedulers get him back to Washington home and hearth by each nightfall. The subject of Clinton made DeLay twitch with agitation. "This is very important to me," he said before anyone had heard of Monica Lewinsky. "I think Bill Clinton is the representative of the demoralization of America during my generation."

On top of that annoyance, the Republican revolution proclaimed by the Contract with America had ended up resembling one of a vastly different persuasion involving men named Lenin, Trotsky, and Stalin. Not that Tom DeLay would ever have a rival stalked with an axe, but he dwelled on intrigue and betrayal. Any ill that befell him was always somebody else's fault, and he nursed deep and bitter grudges against enemies and allies alike. DeLay's relationship with Newt Gingrich had always been prickly. When Gingrich had run for whip in 1989, DeLay had backed his opponent, Ed Madigan. Then DeLay had defeated Gingrich's guy, Pennsylvania Congressman Bob Walker, in the 1995 whip race. But there was more to DeLay's mistrust than past jockeying in GOP leadership races. When Gingrich was asked to list his intellectual influences, he answered with transparent pleasure and inference that it was a large intellect to fill: Lincoln, Jefferson, Franklin Roosevelt, Isaac Asimov, Alexis de Tocqueville, Tom Clancy, Arnold Toynbee, *Zen and the Art of Archery,* the 1913 Girl Scout Handbook, and the Sydney Pollack/Robert Redford movie *Jeremiah Johnson.* Gingrich was a gadfly and a social theorist. DeLay was put off by Gingrich's hauteur and penchant for offering things like "Five Pillars of American Civilization," "Nine Vision-Level Principles of Personal Strength," "Seven Welfare State Cripplers of Progress." Gingrich said he had fifty boxes full of quotes and clips of writing that he processed into his philosophy and vision, but he never emphasized the Bible, the Word of God. DeLay probably thought Gingrich was as full of shit as a Christmas turkey. He questioned the depth of Gingrich's commitment as a conservative. DeLay's idea of the revolution was a tough all-out fight for America's soul and direction. Gingrich, to his mind, was a think-tank pontificator and a flake.

And from the first weeks after they took power in 1995, De-Lay had brooded over his treatment by Gingrich and Dick Armey. DeLay and Armey had been lumped together since their arrival on Capitol Hill amid the Texas Six-Pack. Sure, DeLay said some outrageous things, but Armey hogged the attention of the press, stomping around in his cowboy boots and spouting lines of country music. A great number of conservatives loved Armey, for his economic positions and for his sass. "Your president is not that important to us," he barked at House Democrats, referring to Clinton. "Your charm is overrated," he informed Hillary, when she was First Lady.

But one advantage DeLay always had over Gingrich and Armey was that the evangelical Christians believed he was one of them. The Speaker and majority leader condescended to the Christian right, and the evangelicals knew it. Neither Gingrich nor Armey were true congregants in the evangelical movement that provides the base for the modern Republican Party.

Apart from the overcrowded egos, DeLay felt ganged-up on and wronged by Gingrich and Armey when they appropriated a million dollars from the whip's budget in 1995. DeLay reacted as if they had stolen from him personally. Across the hall from De-Lay's office was a suite occupied by Gingrich and the fourth key revolutionary and author of the Contract, upstate New Yorker Bill Paxon. Paxon had taken over the chairmanship of a bloated, debt-ridden National Republican Congressional Committee and made it into a top fundraiser and recruiter of candidates for the party. He was widely perceived in Washington as a loyal lieutenant of Gingrich, who had created a special leadership position for him—but then DeLay and Armey were supposed to be, as they say in Texas, asshole buddies, too.

Paxon was a star in tortoise-shell glasses. Yearbook hand-some, he was single when elected, then proposed to Staten Island Republican Representative Susan Molinari on the floor of the House. The couple instantly became Hill celebrities. Trim, erect, described by one writer as "well scrubbed," he was everything DeLay was not. Molinari, who occupied the seat once held by her father, Guy, was attractive and charming. DeLay and Paxon admired each other's convictions and political skills, and they enjoyed other topics of conversation as well, though De-Lay had—and resented having—a reputation as an unpolished hayseed. Though he had cut back his problem drinking, he still had a passion for wine, and for knowing about varieties of grapes, wineries, vintages, and regions. Paxon was also a oenophile. And he belonged to Chowder & Marching, a clubby Republican leadership fraternity. Paxon knew the prestige of membership mattered to DeLay, and perhaps even more, that social exclusion nettled him, so he spoke up for the whip and helped get him into the club. "Paxon is a remarkable manipulator," said one congressman. "He knew what he could do to make Tom think he was his new best friend." In the privacy of their richly furnished offices DeLay and Paxon kept their own notes on the state and health of the revolution. Gingrich and Armey went on their separate and loquacious ways, performing on *Meet the Press* and other high-toned forums, oblivious to muttering in the ranks. High-profile House Republicans like South Carolina's Lindsey Graham and Oklahoma's Steve Largent and J. C. Watts (the latter two enlarged by their fame as star football players) wanted a concerted plan of attack to cut taxes and stymie Clinton's presidency. Though Gingrich and Armey demanded allegiance, neither possessed enough instincts as team players to be real leaders. Conservative firebrands saw that Gingrich was consumed with being a celebrity. Armey had always prided himself on being a lone wolf. He first got in leadership races, he said, because of his interest in forcing issues, not hanging out. He came to look on the newcomers as a bunch of malcontents. Meanwhile DeLay continued to feed his colleagues and fill their glasses in the blue-walled suite after long days on the floor. He kept up with their golf handicaps, gave them rides to the airport, got jobs for their kids and wives.

By the end of their first Congress in the majority, DeLay was the Hammer—he had finally lived up to the name that Tony Blankley says was first given to him by a reporter. "We're going to only fund those programs we want to fund," he said imperiously in 1995. "We're in charge. We don't have to negotiate with the Senate. We don't have to negotiate with the Democrats." The House Republicans had swept into the majority believing that Clinton was beaten, and they played brinksmanship with him, thinking they could bully him into yielding to their 1995 budget demands—if Clinton didn't concede, they would let the federal government run out of money and just shut the behemoth down. But the ultimate poker game DeLay boasted about went badly for House Republicans. Clinton called their bluff, and the Republicans overplayed their hand. Gingrich soon understood that forcing a shutdown of the federal government in the dead of winter had backfired. But in DeLay's view they got scorched and the Contract with America fizzled only because the other side had a better set of flack communicators. He remained fervent in his belief that they had lost that fight because they failed to stand their ground.

At the end of that Congress Clinton humiliated the GOP by drubbing Dole in the presidential election with patronizing ease. Conservatives saw Gingrich wobbling in his charge of leadership, growing more distant and distracted as personal troubles mounted. Gingrich, who had essentially forced Texas Democrat Jim Wright out of the speakership for hiking up his royalties on a vanity book, accepted a $4.5 million advance from a New York publisher owned by Rupert Murdoch for his book *To Renew America,* and the adverse publicity made him give up the deal. In response to the conservatives' emphasis on family values, reporters dug up unflattering stories about the lead conservative's spotty performance as a husband. They portrayed Gingrich as a man who could, while consulting notes on a legal pad, inform his first wife, who lay ill with cancer, that he no longer loved her and was leaving her for another woman. Now his second marriage was in trouble, too. Gingrich's PAC got careless in its fundraising and was fined $300,000 by the Federal Election Commission. His approval ratings plunged as fast as they had risen.

Paxon and DeLay began a series of meetings over the course of two weeks in July of 1997, egging on House malcontents and fanning the flames of insurrection. Some members quietly began to make the argument that Gingrich had to go.

The role of Armey in the coup was hotly debated. Some observers believed he had encouraged the plotters from the start. Others thought that typically he just didn't think and react quickly enough to clear and explain himself. Others said that Paxon and DeLay had deftly blindsided him. However it happened, the participants in a culminating tense meeting, who included DeLay, Paxon, and Armey, and Ohio Republican John Boehner, came close to launching their coup to overthrow Gingrich.

DeLay told the House revolutionaries that he was prepared to vote to remove Gingrich when they met with the full House Republican Conference. Coming from the whip, who exercised perhaps as much power as any one member of Congress, DeLay's endorsement of the ouster was the most important moment in the two weeks of meetings. Several of those participants believed they owed their election to the PAC money he had provided them in their first race for Congress.

DeLay was almost certainly "running the show," said a former congressional staff member who was close to leadership at the time. But DeLay never put his name forward for Speaker. It was either Armey or Paxon who would take the place of Gingrich. DeLay's friend Paxon was clearly the more adept plotter and had the inside track. Some believed that in their many nights of talking about wine and politics, they had struck a deal—Paxon would be the Speaker and DeLay would force out Armey as majority leader. "Armey was given to walking around talking," said the staffer who observed the intrigue. "He was never as politic. He spent far too much time in the open, in the halls, mumbling about what was going on. He wasn't as cautious as the others."

The plotters set a date in July, then reportedly at Armey's urging gave it a night's sleep. In the light of day they backed away from going public with a revolt that had filled their private offices with so much drama, and the storm seemed to blow over. But a reporter for *The Hill,* Sandy Hume, got wind of it and the story was all over town. The leaders of the plot were scrambling, trying to cover their asses, as what looked like a Shakespearean drama began to unfold around them. By multiple accounts a furious scene erupted in a hallway. Armey refused to lend his name to a cover story proposed by DeLay and Paxon. A florid DeLay bellowed curses and grabbed Armey by his necktie. If the Texans had ever been friends, they were no more.

"Gingrich, by that time, was wounded," said his former press aide Tony Blankley. "He had fought fight after fight and when you are in such a position you begin to die a death of a thousand cuts."

Gingrich convened a full meeting of the Republican Conference, which lasted a grueling three hours. DeLay, by all accounts, delivered a brilliant speech, accepting just enough responsibility for the near-coup to be considered a participant but not quite enough to be considered the ringleader. "It was a bravura performance," a Republican staffer said. "The baring of the breast, or just enough of it, saved him." It also helped that DeLay had never positioned himself as a candidate to replace Gingrich when he was toppled.

DeLay's press person at the time, John Feehery, who went to work for Dennis Hastert when he became Speaker, framed DeLay's version to reporters: though he had not initially been one of the plotters, he had met with them and openly said he would vote to overthrow Newt. It was a failure of judgment. At the time, the press aide said, his boss was "physically and mentally exhausted. . . . He made the statement, but he immediately re-gretted saying it. He didn't mean it."

A House member who was inside the Conference saw it quite differently. He shook his head, remembering DeLay's perfor-mance. "He told the caucus, 'I just had too much wine that night, and I wasn't thinking clearly.' People who had been in those meetings knew he'd been in on it all along. But they said nothing. They let him get away with it."

A wounded Gingrich was forgiving, at least in public. "It was fabulous," he said oddly as he emerged from his meeting with the caucus. "It's over." There was one line of authority in the House, he had told his colleagues, and he was at the top of it.

But Gingrich never recovered.

Tom DeLay was pitch perfect in his speech to the Confer-ence. And he was covered. Before going into the emergency Conference meeting with Gingrich, the House dissidents warned that if Gingrich and his backers moved against DeLay, they were prepared to move against Gingrich and Armey.

"You don't know what happened unless you were in the meet-ing room where they did their plotting," said a member of the Clinton team who was watching the House. "So you have to look at who is standing at the end of one of these fights. Who comes out on top." One member of the Republican Conference had no doubt, saying that DeLay was the plotter out to over-throw Newt. "I will tell you unequivocally that the seventeen members that were in that room with Tom DeLay had that im-pression," said Arizona representative Matt Salmon.

Was DeLay Brutus? we asked a Gingrich aide.

"Brutus?" he said. "No. Not Brutus. Remember your history. Remember Shakespeare. Brutus's betrayal was so important be-cause he was so close and so loyal to Caesar. And because he had himself given so much to Rome.

"DeLay was Cassius."

Not the noble, ambivalent Brutus, but Cassius, the dangerous man of resentment, the plotter with the lean and hungry look.

Whipping the President

"They're going to fuck us!"

Majority Whip Tom DeLay was livid. And determined that the staff members he summoned to his office in September 1998 would seize control of the impeachment machinery. "They're going to fuck us!" he hissed at his staff. "They're going to screw us. They're going to leave us and they're going to screw Newt and Dick in the back."

At this point in DeLay's career, Newt Gingrich was an obstacle in the Republican Party's (and DeLay's) path to power. If De-Lay hadn't thought Gingrich could be had, he wouldn't have plotted to overthrow him a year earlier. But Gingrich was still Speaker of the House. And Dick Armey was still majority leader. Two failed professors, DeLay thought, too often too slow to react.

Now minority leader Richard Gephardt and the Democrats were playing Gingrich and Armey for fools. DeLay wasn't about to let Gephardt save Bill Clinton while DeLay had the power to destroy him—or at least so badly weaken him that the final two years of his presidency would be a failure. "This is going to be the most important thing I do in my political career," DeLay had said of the impeachment of Bill Clinton. And now Gingrich and Armey were about to let Clinton escape. All because Richard Gephardt alone was smarter than the two of them together.

But not as smart—or ruthless—as Tom DeLay. The Republican whip was inserting himself between the two Republican leaders and the Republican House Conference. Gingrich was history and Armey was ineffectual. DeLay alone would direct House Republicans toward a historic vote to impeach Bill Clinton.

The national drama that consumed the American public between 1998 and 1999 is impossible to forget. It was the season of the witch hunt, the United States House of Representatives was the crucible, and New York Congressman Gary Ackerman's motion to convene the Judiciary Committee in Salem, Massachusetts seemed as sensible as it was sarcastic.

The House was in a state of chaos. Newt Gingrich had attacked Bill Clinton for six years of his presidency and come out of the strife a badly mauled second-best. In the run-up to the midterm elections in November 1998, Gingrich had boasted that the Republicans would pick up more than twenty seats. Instead they lost five. The news of Gingrich's extramarital affair was about to break, and with his leadership already battered by the coup fiasco and an ethics investigation, he announced after the election that he would be stepping down as Speaker. Now Clinton's licentious recklessness had brought him to the brink of political ruin. With Tom DeLay's help, Louisiana's Bob Livingston had won enough pledges from GOP colleagues to succeed Gingrich, but he would be leading a chamber that was on the verge of impeaching Bill Clinton for lying about sex. Beyond Clinton there was the presidency, at risk as it had not been since Richard Nixon started plotting his Watergate cover-up thirty years earlier. That sobering fact occurred to Livingston as he prepared to ascend to the office of the Speaker the week before Christmas in 1998. "We've got to stop this," he told an aide. "This is crazy. We're about to impeach the President of the United States."

It had been 130 years since the House of Representatives had undertaken its solemn duty to begin the constitutional process of removing a president from office for "high crimes and misdemeanors." It was not self-doubt or nagging concerns about hypocrisy that tore at Livingston. His years of lying about his own infidelity were a separate issue. He had grave doubts about whether impeachment was an appropriate response to Bill Clinton's foolish relationship with a White House intern—and the subsequent lying to cover it up. If Livingston had ignored his wedding vows, he was devoutly faithful to the oath of office he took when he was elected to the House of Representatives. Appropriations Committee Chairman Bob Livingston was an institutionalist, and the institution of the presidency was about to be put at risk.

Everything could have been stopped the night Speaker-designate Livingston grappled with his convictions before sitting down to write the speech that would begin the impeachment. Or earlier. There was a way out: a public vote to censure the president. It was the clear preference of a bipartisan majority in the House. Had Livingston demanded—or allowed—censure rather than impeachment, the country would have been spared the madness that would culminate with the Chief Justice of the United States presiding over a Senate impeachment trial. Some of the collateral damage could have been stopped, too, such as *Hustler* publisher Larry Flynt's going public with his documented account of Livingston's infidelity just three days before he was to formally become the Speaker, Monica Lewinsky's degrading videotaped testimony at the Mayflower Hotel, and the hostile partisan division of the House of Representatives.

It did not stop. It could not be stopped. Because Tom DeLay would not allow it to be stopped. Far more than Gingrich had been, DeLay was obsessed with taking down Bill Clinton. As the national tragedy unfolded, DeLay would keep the pressure on Livingston, whom he personally moved into the Speaker's office when Gingrich collapsed. He would browbeat and intimidate the moderates in the House, threatening to end the careers of anyone who didn't vote to impeach. And he would inflame the Southern conservatives, who were the political muscle to make impeachment happen. Again and again, at critical moments,

DeLay inserted himself into the process, as he did when Richard Gephardt came up with the proposal to censure the president and withhold several years of his presidential pension benefits ("censure-plus"). Gephardt might be smart enough "to screw Newt and Dick in the back" and provide an escape for the president. But he wasn't going to fool Tom DeLay.

Tom DeLay hated Bill Clinton. Clinton was the cad who always seemed to get away with everything. The kind of guy DeLay hated when he was a hard-hitting, bantamweight defensive lineman at Calallan High School in South Texas. Clinton was the A student with a little too much Elvis in him. The good-looking guy who played the saxophone in the band and always seemed to get the girl—sometimes your girl. DeLay hated Clinton's White House dinner parties with Barbra Streisand. He hated Bill Clinton's $75 haircuts. He hated the way good suits always seemed to fit him. He hated his erect bearing, his height, his Southern-boy charm, and his calculated avoidance of military service during the Vietnam war—even if DeLay himself had also managed to avoid serving.

But more than anything, Tom DeLay woke up every day hating the fact that William Jefferson Clinton was president of the United States. The "Democrat" Party was "socialist" and Clinton was its leader. DeLay's terminology was in part rhetorical fuel to fire up the Republican base. But it was also part of the core conviction of a conviction politician. The hatred was only exacerbated by Clinton's ability to outmaneuver congressional Republicans who had finally won a majority in both houses—after nearly half a century in the minority.

Clinton had to be impeached because he could not be defeated. "They believed he was Godzilla," recalled a House staffer who worked on the impeachment. "No matter what they would throw at him, they couldn't stop him. He kept coming at them." When Republicans won the House in 1994, after Democrats passed an unpopular gun control bill and allowed the Republicans and health insurance lobby to hang Hillary's failed health care reform around the Democrats' necks, Clinton should have been dead. Yet he absorbed the fury of the House Republicans' Contract with America, most of which never was enacted, and in doing so made them look foolish. When the anti-tax ideologues in the House refused to pass his 1995 budget or a continuing resolution to keep government offices open, they thought they finally had Bill Clinton in a box. Yet the president somehow convinced the American public that the House Republicans were responsible for the closed national parks and furloughed federal employees. Undaunted by the public, DeLay whipped House members into intractable opposition to Clinton's budget. And they were holding. Until Clinton and Leon Panetta seduced Bob Dole, the Kansas senator who was so traditional he still believed in bipartisan government. No matter what the Republican leaders of the Gingrich-DeLay revolution did to weaken him, Bill Clinton tenaciously clung to and judiciously used the power of the presidency. His involvement with Monica Lewinsky presented House Republicans the opportunity to seize that power or at least weaken it. It was an opportunity the majority whip from Texas was not about to pass up. "They knew they couldn't beat him," said the former house staffer. "So they had to destroy him. If they didn't impeach him they wouldn't have been able to win back the presidency. They wouldn't be able to achieve the absolute dominance they were planning."

According to Clinton's White House counsel Lanny Davis, a team of White House advisers prepared for the possibility of impeachment by dividing House Republicans into two categories: one group that had genuine intellectual concerns about impeachable offenses, and a faction that personalized the issues and was driven by a personal dislike of President Clinton. The first group held a sincere intellectual position that the president had lied in a civil deposition and that it was an impeachable offense to have done so. Davis points to Lindsey Graham, now a senator from South Carolina, and former California Representative Jim Rogan. They held what Davis, five years after the fact, still describes as an "honorable position." They were also open to discussion and negotiation. Davis described a second group of House Republicans as "a cadre of ideologues, beholden to the Christian right [who] made impeachment a highly partisan and personal issue and acted out of hatred for Bill Clinton." Their position on impeachment had hardened and they were unapproachable; no discussion and no negotiation could move them.

Tom DeLay was the most inflexible member of the no-discussion and no-negotiation faction. Even Bob Barr, the Georgia Republican who defined the extreme right wing of the Republican Conference and who wrote a pro-impeachment book before any impeachable offense was identified, would consider censure in lieu of impeachment. Tom DeLay refused to entertain any talk of compromise. "He believed Bill Clinton was evil," Davis said. His position on impeachment mattered far more than Bob Barr's. As majority whip, DeLay ran a tightly organized team of sixty-seven deputies with whom he met regularly. Clinton's advisers knew that devising a strategy to work with DeLay would be difficult, Davis said in an interview. Devising a strategy to deal with DeLay was not difficult. It was impossible. Even as they prepared for the worst, Clinton's scandal team did not anticipate the extremes to which the majority whip from Texas would go to take down the president.

Bucked up by his two closest aides, Mike Scanlon and Tony Rudy, DeLay organized a political operation with a clearly articulated goal: the end of Bill Clinton's presidency. They called it "The Campaign." DeLay and his staff set up a war room. There would be a daily message for the press. Regular communication with members of the Republican Conference. Dear Colleague letters, from the majority whip to Republican House members, when issues needed "clarification." Regular strategy sessions. A discreet vote-counting organization that circumvented the formal whip operation DeLay ran. "Blast-faxing" daily talking points to as many as two hundred radio and TV stations. Soliciting conservative talk show producers, who were booking DeLay for as many as ten interviews a day. DeLay's staff, according to a House staff member who was mired in the impeachment fight, even compiled a list of finance chairs of Republican House members facing tight elections. "They started all this," a committee staffer said in an interview, "long before there was enough evidence for members of their conference to make an informed decision. They even put out the word that they would 'primary' anyone who voted wrong on impeachment."

Though damaged, in 1998 Gingrich was still the Speaker, and as the scandal expanded—from an investigation of Clinton's role in a real estate deal while he was governor of Arkansas into Independent Counsel Ken Starr's investigation of Clinton's illicit relationship with Lewinsky—Gingrich seized the moment. He believed that impeachment was good politics, the big national issue that would allow House Republicans to expand their narrow majority by more than twenty seats. The electoral laws of gravity ensured that the party holding the presidency always lost House seats in off-year elections. Clinton and Lewinsky had enhanced those laws. Not only would the Republicans win seats in the House, Gingrich argued. They would win big.

But Gingrich was continually outmaneuvered by his Democratic counterpart, Dick Gephardt. The Speaker could always be counted on to overreach, which was precisely what Gephardt encouraged him to do. In *The Breach*, a remarkable account of the impeachment fight, *Washington Post* reporter Peter Baker describes Gephardt's plan to encourage Gingrich to overplay his hand. "We win by losing," Gephardt told House Democrats, again and again. The Democrats would win by losing in committee and floor votes to release all the evidence to the public, including the videotape of the president testifying before the grand jury. When that happened, the public would see the prosecution as a persecution, and Speaker Gingrich would begin to look like Inspector Javert.

Gephardt was right. Voters didn't share Gingrich's obsession with impeaching the president. Newt's predictions of twenty-plus House seats gained by the GOP in the fall of '98 came out minus-five. When that happened Newt Gingrich lost the support of his caucus. He had overplayed his party's impeachment hand. His tenure as Speaker, which began with such a bang in 1995, would end with a whimper in 1998.

Right after the midterm election, Davis said, there was an opportunity to persuade the House to censure rather than impeach the president. "We won that amazing victory. Not a victory per se, but we didn't lose. We gained seats." If someone as extreme as Bob Barr was willing to at least discuss censure in lieu of impeachment, then it was, Davis believes, the ideal solution. "We had a very very small window of opportunity that occurred right after that election . . . that was the moment that we could have done the deal and beaten DeLay. We could have gone to Lindsey Graham, we could have gone to the group of intellectual dissidents, let's call them, or intellectual critics, as opposed to those driven by emotion and hatred. And we could have said, 'you write the resolution. You describe the [President's] behavior any way you want to, as long as it's within reason.'"

As the ground under him began to shift, Tom DeLay became the kingmaker. He called upon Bob Livingston to take Gingrich's place and he used the whip's organization to help secure the votes to make Livingston Speaker. Or Speaker-designate. Before it could become official, reports of Livingston's infidelity were released by Larry Flynt. Helen Thorpe was following DeLay at the moment and captured that political earthquake in a telling profile in *Texas Monthly*:

> In the office of the majority whip, oblivious to the tableau of
> disorder around them, DeLay's staff moved with a remarkable

singularity of purpose. A contained fury gripped the office. ("There's this Vulcan mind-meld that exists between us," Mike Scanlon, DeLay's press secretary, said later.) At the epicenter of the tumult, behind a polished wooden desk, sat DeLay. He was feeling utterly confident of Clinton's downfall. "Looks like the coffin's nailed shut," he said. Just then his chief of staff stuck her head into the office. "The Speaker needs to speak to you," she said. "Which Speaker?" asked DeLay. . . . "Elect," she said, indicating that it was Livingston. . . . That evening, the Speaker-unelect issued a statement to the press. DeLay was one of the last figures to emerge from a Republican conference after the news broke. I tagged along as he quick-stepped up a flight of stairs surrounded by reporters. DeLay's face wore a mask of dismayed wrath. "How do you feel about this?" I asked him, "Sick," he answered. Scanlon intervened then, heading off any further discussion. "No questions! No questions!" he started yelling. "A little personal time!"

As Livingston collapsed, DeLay again tightened his hold on power. Even as he stood on the floor of the House with his eyes welling up with tears, describing Bob Livingston as "this good man," his deputy whips were locking up the votes to elect Denny Hastert Speaker. More quickly than DeLay had made Bob Livingston Speaker-elect, he cut him loose once he was damaged goods.

Livingston's demise might have provided Democrats a second chance to avoid an impeachment vote. But by that time DeLay was in charge. He was the most powerful member of the body that would decide the fate of the president.

Lanny Davis had left his White House position and was out making the president's case on TV talk shows. He often found himself in studio greenrooms with Lindsey Graham, Orrin Hatch, John McCain, Jim Rogan, Henry Hyde, and other Republicans from Congress who were stating their party's position. "I got great intelligence as to what they would go for,"

Davis said. Reasonable members of the House were telling him they were willing to compromise.

But Davis also sensed a hardening of the position inside the White House, as Clinton began to listen to advisers who believed they could beat the whole rap—censure and impeachment. While the White House was deliberating, DeLay seized the moment. "That's when Tom DeLay intervened and put a stop to all conversations," Davis said. "I was told he will not let them even bring up [censure in lieu of impeachment] in the caucus. So he's the most important piece in all of this."

Once DeLay stepped in, he never relinquished control of the campaign or the war room, relentlessly pursuing Clinton until the historic vote was cast on the House floor.

Scanlon, the twenty-seven-year-old DeLay staffer who within six years would become a multi-millionaire lobbyist by trading on his boss's name, set the tone early on. His e-mail response to a message from his colleague Tony Rudy suggests a war room mentality that was as pathologically hostile as it was sophomoric.

"God Bless you Tony Rudy—are we the only ones with political instincts—This whole thing about not kicking someone when they are down is BS—Not only do you kick him—you kick him until he passes out—then beat him over the head with the baseball bat—then roll him up in an old rug—and throw him off the cliff into the pounding surf."

Even if Scanlon was talking in jest, he was referring to the constitutional responsibility to impeach the president of the United States. It's hard to see how this suggested a fair hearing for Clinton. And Rudy and Scanlon would remain—along with DeLay chief of staff Susan Hirschmann—DeLay's closest advisers throughout the impeachment fight.

Before he could get Clinton off the cliff and into the pounding surf, DeLay had to first kill the growing movement to censure the president—or to combine censure with a penalty of some sort, such as forfeiture of a certain number of years of presidential retirement benefits or forfeiture of his law license.

In late September, almost a month before the 1998 election, De-Lay had written a letter to Republican House members warning them that censure was not within their constitutional powers. He followed with a second "Dear Colleagues" letter a week later. This time he was more forceful: "Any talk of censure or censure plus should be stopped." He buttressed his argument in op-ed articles in the *Wall Street Journal* and the *Washington Times*, where three weeks before the scheduled vote, he called censure "an idea born out of desperate imagination by those too timid to uphold their own sworn oath to 'support and defend' the Constitution."

The fight to block censure became the central focus of De-Lay's House operation. Democrats emboldened by the election results continued their efforts to offer a compromise that would attract moderate Republicans and conservative Democrats inclined to support impeachment. Republican Henry Hyde, as some Democrats on Clinton's team admit to this day, initially recognized the magnitude of what the Congress was undertaking. As chair of the House Judiciary Committee, Hyde was determined to be judicious. At one point, he even permitted the Judiciary Committee to vote on a Democratic motion to censure.

He was no match for the former bug man from Sugar Land, however. DeLay doubted Hyde's partisan commitment and was furious with Hyde for allowing the censure vote. That vote also intensified DeLay's hostility to the House tradition of independent committee chairmen, a hostility that he shared with Gingrich and that they both worked to undermine. Though De-Lay helped position Bob Livingston as Gingrich's successor, he worried about Livingston's independence. The Louisiana congressman had served on the Appropriations Committee, becoming chairman when Republicans took control of the House. Livingston was notorious for his angry outbursts, which some saw as the calculated use of anger to intimidate opponents. He was guilty of collaborating with Democrats on the committee.

Almost as bad, Livingston worked with James Dyer, a pragmatic
Republican staff member who earned bipartisan respect as
Appropriations majority staff director. ("Approps," where the
best fiscal wonks in the House are reverently referred to as "ap-
propriators," is one of the most demanding committee assignments in the Congress. The committee would remain one of the
last bastions of bipartisan cooperation until the second year of
the Bush presidency, when the leadership's plan to consolidate
power at the top was almost complete.) Livingston had made a
lot of promises to win enough pledges to ensure his election as
Speaker, but he could not have pulled it off without DeLay's
whip organization. But Livingston might still exercise his independence and, working with Hyde, allow a Democratic censure
motion to come to the floor. To ensure that the President would
be impeached, DeLay had to kill and bury the censure compromise.

Livingston's rise and fall was so fast—a matter of weeks—that
the voting public outside Washington was aware of him only
when the media reported his ignominious demise. He may have
been a distinguished congressman, but in the frantic telenovela
of sex, lies, and impeachment, he was a blip on the screen. In
that short period between DeLay's campaign to make Livingston Speaker-designate and Livingston's collapse, however,
DeLay quickly and effectively moved to eliminate any possibility of a censure vote.

What DeLay did to bury any prospect of censure is told in
detail in Peter Baker's book. Working in DeLay's office was an
aide who had recently left Newt Gingrich's sinking ship. DeLay
directed her to draft three letters. One to Gingrich, soon to be
the ex-Speaker, and to his designated successor, Bob Livingston,
was to be signed by Henry Hyde. It outlined Hyde's opposition
to any vote on censure. The second letter was from Hyde to Livingston alone, briefly restating what was written in the first letter. The third letter was (perhaps) intended for Gingrich's
signature, stating that he would summon members of the

House to Washington on Thursday the following week to vote on impeachment—and would allow no censure vote.

DeLay wanted the letters signed quickly and dispatched his aide to procure the signatures. Hyde agreed to sign when the majority whip's aide told him it represented the will of the leadership—even if it only represented the will of the majority whip. In Livingston's office, DeLay's aide persuaded Livingston's aide to sign the letter in Livingston's absence, after the congressman agreed in a phone conversation. When the aide still balked and said he would prefer to wait for his boss's signature, he was told he had known Livingston for a long time and therefore had to know that Bob Livingston rarely changed his mind. He also got a warning from DeLay: "It's really important that we get it out now." When Gingrich couldn't be reached to sign his letter, his former aide, the same woman who was now working for Tom DeLay, signed it herself, copying (or forging) Newt's signature from sample stationery she had held onto. The letters were released to the news media immediately after Hyde adjourned the Judiciary Committee for the day, so it appeared to the public (and to Democrats holding out for censure) that the Republican House leadership had met and decided against a censure vote. In fact, it was Tom DeLay and one aide closing the door on censure while the Judiciary Committee was tied up in session and Gingrich and Livingston were not in the Capitol.

After sandbagging Judiciary Committee Chair Hyde, DeLay highjacked his committee. Susan Hirschmann, at the time DeLay's chief of staff, had talked DeLay out of formally "whipping" the impeachment vote. That is, using his position as majority whip, openly count and line up votes for impeachment. So DeLay turned the Judiciary Committee into a whip organization, providing staff members with whip cards and instructions on vote counts and the intricacies of whipping House members.

With censure eliminated by DeLay's swift, bold (and some might say dishonest) maneuver, he could focus on muscling wavering Republicans into voting to impeach Clinton. In his book

The Clinton Wars, Clinton senior adviser Sidney Blumenthal tells of one Republican who crossed DeLay early in the impeachment fight and found himself "primaried"—facing an opponent in the 2000 primary at the time almost two years away! Another moderate Republican, New York Congressman Peter King, was openly talking to Democrats and had stated his misgivings about impeachment. A DeLay aide pulled King aside and warned that his boss would "make the next two years the toughest of your life."

"Coming out of the [1998] election, everyone thought impeachment was dead," King told Blumenthal. "I didn't hear anyone discuss impeachment. Then DeLay assumed control. . . . In most districts in the country a majority was against impeachment. But a majority who voted in Republican primaries was for impeachment. When you put your individual members under the gun, a lot of them could get killed in a primary. That was the way he did it. I heard Christian radio stations going after Republicans. Right-wing groups were stirring it up in parts of the country outside of the Northeast. Most of the pressure went through the Christian right network. It happened over a ten-day period. The whole world changed."

For Republicans who needed additional encouragement, DeLay had one trump card to play. It was what Blumenthal described in an interview as "the document dump." Much of the material Whitewater Independent Counsel Kenneth Starr had gathered in his investigation but had elected not to include in his report was moved into a room in the Ford Building—a nondescript congressional office building a few blocks northwest of the Capitol. DeLay began to talk about incriminating material in the "evidence room," insisting that House members look at the evidence before making up their minds. But the room was closed to everyone except members of the Judiciary Committee. The room quickly became known as the "sex vault." That, at least, is what Democrats were led to believe, based on an agreement reached with Judiciary Committee Chair Henry Hyde.

Somehow, the rules changed; without informing House Democrats, Hyde opened up the room. (A source close to the Judiciary Committee confirmed Blumenthal's account, as did
another House staffer.)

The "evidence" included notes from investigators' interviews, affidavits, depositions, and claims by "Jane Doe 5":
Juanita Broaddrick, who had told investigators that Clinton
forced himself on her twenty-five years earlier. There was material in the room that no lawyer would consider evidence, yet, as
a former Judiciary Committee staffer explained in an interview,
DeLay insisted that members of the Republican Conference
look at it before making up their minds.

So Republican House members quietly began to shuttle over
to the Ford annex to read through files. "Henry [Hyde] wanted
to do this properly, but he was like a spinning top when DeLay
got started," the House source said. According to the same
source, DeLay let Republican members know the evidence in
the "sex vault" could be made public in their districts during primary races.

The warning was sufficient. Republicans who had reservations about impeachment understood their leadership would
use an anti-impeachment vote against them. In other words:
vote wrong and the leadership would recruit a primary opponent who would make the vote and the lurid contents of the evidence room a campaign issue. The position of moderate
Republicans was made more difficult because DeLay had eliminated the alternative to impeachment: a vote to censure the
president.

DeLay didn't stop until the House cast its vote to impeach.
Most of what happened happened behind closed doors. "He
broke that last twenty arms," said a bitter member of Clinton's
White House staff, who described DeLay's aggressive tactics as
unethical and unprincipled.

Until all the memoirs are written, the public will not know the
extent of DeLay's orthopedic work. King, a New York moderate,

spoke out early and took a beating. Peter Baker tells how DeLay got to lame-duck Republican John Fox, who had lost his seat in the 1998 election. Fox opposed impeachment, and because he had already lost his election, DeLay was left with little leverage. Yet he found a way. When he heard that Fox was traveling to the Middle East with the president, he called one of his go-to rabbis. Seattle-based Rabbi Daniel Lapin, founder of a right-wing ecumenical Jewish-Christian group called Toward Tradition, phoned Fox and told them the country would be better off if it were rid of a president who would take a phone call from a congressman while getting oral sex from an intern. "Lapin" is "rabbit" in the French, so Rabbi Rabbit, a bewildered Jew torn between Jesus and the Messiah to come, led the less-than-resolute Fox down the path toward impeachment.

For other Jewish House members, DeLay used a more secular approach. He told Ben Gillman, a Long Island Republican concluding a three-decade career in the House, that he would be stripped of the chairmanship of the House Foreign Relations Committee if he didn't vote to impeach. Gillman, at the pinnacle (and end) of his career, was close to tears as DeLay explained to him the consequences of a vote against impeachment, according to two House sources. In the end he capitulated. "DeLay treated a distinguished senior member of Congress like a dime store clerk," said a lobbyist who asked to remain anonymous. Gillman's constituents were bewildered by his last-minute change of heart. As were angry editorial page writers in his moderate district.

Even some conservative Republicans were shocked by the extremes to which DeLay was willing to go. In one stunning moment on the eve of the House vote on impeachment, Clinton announced an attack on Iraq, where intelligence indicated that Saddam Hussein was in violation of the United Nations ban on chemical, biological, and nuclear weapons. Livingston agreed to put off the vote, at least for a day. DeLay was enraged. At a rare closed briefing of House and Senate leaders, where CIA Director George Tenet joined Secretary of Defense William Cohen and Hugh Shelton of the Joint Chiefs of Staff, DeLay was over the top. "Is there any reason why we couldn't go on?" he demanded. He was referring to the impeachment vote. Cohen tried to avoid advising Congress on its constitutional duty, but DeLay kept pressing. He demanded that Cohen tell him if there was "any national security reason why we shouldn't go ahead." Cohen, a former senator from Maine and the lone Republican in a Democratic cabinet, seemed stunned by the question. "It's been the tradition throughout history that when we have people out there with the risk of dying it's good to have bipartisan support."

"It was the strangest day in ten years' working here," said a woman who worked for a Democratic representative at the time. She referred to the day Bob Livingston announced he was leaving the Congress, shortly before the vote on impeachment began. "Livingston came out and it was obvious there was something wrong. He always had that bearing, straight up. But when he came out he was looking down, his shoulders were bent. I said, 'something is wrong with him.' I'd never seen him like that."

Livingston felt as bad as he looked. Several informants had taken up the offer *Hustler* publisher Larry Flynt's made in a full-page ad in the *New York Times*. Flynt offered to pay for proof that specific members of Congress were involved in extramarital affairs. (How he missed Newt Gingrich, few in Washington seem to understand.) Livingston told DeLay he'd been "Larry Flynted."

DeLay had the votes and the power. Why did he hesitate to fulfill his dream and make himself Speaker then? DeLay later said it was because he was too hot, that the all-out fight against Clinton had made him "nuclear." Some observers speculated that DeLay feared he was about to be Flynted himself. A rumor about DeLay's family values had dogged him since his days in the Texas legislature. In the days when he wore sideburns and a mustache, he was alleged to have fathered a daughter in an affair with a woman who worked in Austin. Many years later, the story picked up steam when a Capitol Hill newspaper published a photo of DeLay standing beside a young woman. The matter-of-fact caption identified her as his daughter. Whoever she was, she was not Danielle DeLay. Democrats who ran against DeLay in the twenty-second district periodically pushed the rumor. In the early nineties a man who identified himself as a private investigator approached several political reporters and editors in Texas with documents, a name, and a photograph of a girl in an Austin high school annual. One of the authors of this book was among the reporters who sent the dirt merchant on his way. What difference did it make if it were true? But the allegation took on more resonance when DeLay embarked on a relentless moralistic tear about another man's marital behavior.

DeLay and his defenders claimed he was a victim of his virtue, that the smear had begun right then, in 1994. This was his version of the truth behind the photograph: Christine De-Lay's passionate cause was neglect and abuse of children, and she had become a court-appointed volunteer and had agonized over a sixteen-year-old girl who had been a victim of abuse and was a chronic runaway. No foster parents could be persuaded to take her in. Tom and Christine DeLay filled the breach. Political advisers urged him not to do it. The girl was a volatile teenager—the situation could blow up in his face. DeLay had a great number of things going on in his life. But with a company being sold, a lawsuit being settled and avenged, and a campaign for reelection that was part of the Contract with America crusade to win a Republican House and neuter the presidency of Bill Clinton, the congressman from Sugar Land and his wife found time to complete a mandatory course on parenting. They took the sixteen-year-old in, and, as James Dobson phrased it in the book that changed DeLay's life, they dared to discipline her. Within a few months she hit the road again. The DeLays would be foster parents to two other children in years to come, with happier results. During the impeachment vendetta against Clinton, the story about the alleged daughter in Austin naturally surfaced in Washington. DeLay raged that his enemies were making out that unfortunate runaway as his natural child. The age of the foster child would be about right. According to *Rolling Stone,* DeLay called together his top staff and railed that his enemies were "out to destroy" his family by circulating this slur. An ex-member of DeLay's staff described him saying, "I don't have to do this. I could quit my job and make millions of dollars."

"Why don't you?" someone said.

"Because I still have things I want to do."

Larry Flynt later said he looked at the DeLay story but it didn't meet the standard of proof that justified his going public. (The professional pornographer set a very high standard when he set out to illustrate the hypocrisy of the president's accusers.) In truth, DeLay was probably not terribly concerned about the story.

When the vote was cast, after one of the most tumultuous days in the history of the American Congress, the House voted to impeach Bill Clinton. Tom DeLay had prevailed. But his treatment of the impeachment of the president as if it were a floor fight over a special-interest bill marked the end of the bi-partisan cooperation by which the House had conducted the people's business for more than two hundred years.

"He deprived the country and the Congress of a satisfactory solution," said Lanny Davis. Censure, Davis said, would have been a partial victory for House Democrats who wanted to avoid impeachment and for House and Senate Republicans who wanted the president held accountable for his transgressions. Instead, in a protracted national spectacle, Clinton was impeached by the House vote and vindicated by the Senate.

If the Democrats could win by losing, so could DeLay. His relentless pursuit of Bill Clinton strengthened his House leadership position. "That's right," said Joe Allen, a Vinson & Elkins lawyer who was the single most important political kingmaker in Houston until his close association with Enron made his blessing a curse. Allen was agreeing with Houston's nominally Democratic mayor, Bob Lanier, who held that DeLay couldn't lose in his fight to impeach Clinton. "That's right," a laughing Allen said. "Looks good on a résumé, doesn't it?"

If the backing of his hometown pols and rainmakers, along with what some refer to as the House's "banshee Republicans," and the support of the Christian right, wasn't enough to justify his crusade, DeLay could point to a higher authority. As the House prepared to begin debate on impeachment, DeLay gathered his staff in his conference room adjacent to the floor and had all of them join hands and pray. "It's not about winning or losing. It's not about politics. This is a very serious moment. We need to pray for strength," he said, as tears streamed down his face. "Please know," he said in that very Protestant style of prayer that is a talk with the Lord, "that we're not happy about doing this. We see this as our responsibility."

"Political systems always find an equilibrium," said a former Judiciary Committee staff member. "That's what was happening in the House, when a bipartisan majority wanted to vote to censure the President and put the affair behind them. Tom DeLay wouldn't let that equilibrium happen."

TEN

K Street Kingpin

In October 1998 Dave McCurdy was sitting in an airport in the nation's capital sweating out his future. The past had been no sweat. McCurdy was a political natural. Like Bill Clinton he was both a co-founder and one-term national chair of the centrist Democratic Leadership Council. He had served fourteen years in Congress. He had earned the respect of his colleagues, the chairmanship of the House Intelligence Committee and a House Armed Services subcommittee. Tall, handsome, and moderate, McCurdy was also quick to master the technical and political arcana that could overwhelm members of the Intelligence Committee. His CV was a political consultant's dream: economics graduate study abroad, a law practice, a judge advocate general's commission in the Air Force Reserve, a seat in Congress, a wife with a career as a pediatric psychiatrist, and three kids. He was Bill Clinton without the Gennifer Flowers baggage. Democrats pushed him toward the 1992 presidential primaries. *Newsday* described him as one of "a group of younger, fresher politicians . . . who will shake up the system." He even had a campaign theme—"the New American Order"—whatever that was supposed to mean. There were a few formulaic "testing the water" stories. Then McCurdy backed away from the crowded pack that gave the country Bill Clinton.

Two years later, McCurdy ran for the Oklahoma Senate seat that opened up when David Boren retired. But 1994 wasn't a good year for Democrats in the South, where Republicans run god-guns-and-gays campaigns at even the most moderate Democrats, and the Contract with America caught on. James Inhofe defined McCurdy as a "Clinton liberal," and ran his campaign for the Senate seat against Bill Clinton. It worked. For the first time in fourteen years Dave McCurdy was a civilian. Four years later, he was back on Capitol Hill, where he faced a bigger challenge than Inhofe. Standing squarely in McCurdy's career path was House Majority Whip Tom DeLay. DeLay was even insisting that a Republican get the job McCurdy had just landed. That Republican was Bill Paxon, who had taken a bullet for DeLay when their 1997 attempt to topple Newt Gingrich failed. Paxon had conspired with DeLay against Gingrich, and his betrayal cost him the special leadership position Newt had created for him; so he left the Congress. DeLay wanted the job McCurdy had landed to reward Paxon.

McCurdy started working the phones, calling friends, advisers, and former colleagues in Congress, like Democrat-turned-Republican Billy Tauzin of Louisiana. But the lukewarm endorsement of Tauzin and other Southern Republicans wouldn't win him the vote of confidence he needed in the Republican House. Not when the most feared and ruthless member of the leadership openly opposed him. Dave McCurdy was flying to Phoenix.

After a five-month search by an executive recruiting firm, McCurdy had won the lobby lottery: the top spot at the Electronic Industries Alliance. He would direct a trade organization with an annual budget of more than $50 million and a staff of 260. If it wasn't a seat on the Senate Foreign Relations Committee, the EIA president job would pay four times more than he would have earned in the Senate. No fundraising, no campaigns, no juggling schedules to make three morning committee meetings. So when he was offered the office vacated by retiring EIA president Peter McCloskey, Dave McCurdy said yes.

Tom DeLay said no.

The Republican's focus on the lobby wasn't new. Since the party took control of the House in 1994, DeLay had been leaning on trade associations and lobbying firms to hire Republicans. His muscular tactics could be defended, up to a point. Democrats had dominated Congress for almost half a century. Lobbying firms and trade associations hire Congressional alumni and staffers who have easy access to the party in power, so Democrats also dominated the lobby. Once the Republicans took control of the House and Senate, it was predictable that the Democrats' dominance of K Street—the downtown D.C. strip that is to political influence what Wall Street is to finance—would end. It was also predictable that the Republicans would do all they could to hurry the process along. Newt Gingrich was barely settled into the Speaker's office when he began to warn K Street firms about insufficient Republican representation in the lobby. Congressional Democrats, Gingrich warned lobbyists in his signature-mark, overblown style, "are the enemy of the American people."

Unlike Newt, who was always so rhetorically over the top, DeLay was quiet and cunning. Where you got bluster from Gingrich, with DeLay, as a colleague said, it was "a smile and a swift knee to the groin." Rather than pound the table and demand more Republican hires, DeLay rewrote the informal rules by personally vetoing the hiring of Dave McCurdy. "When I heard it, I thought, 'This is really nutty,'" said a trade association president who helped enlist someone to go in and "explain to DeLay how unreasonable his actions were." At least they seemed unreasonable at the time. First, DeLay put out the word that McCurdy would not be welcome in Republican leadership offices. By denying him access to the leadership, DeLay was rendering McCurdy impotent as a lobbyist. When the EIA stood by its hire, DeLay made a tactical move that surprised his more conventional Republican colleagues. He pulled from the House calendar a bill the EIA and a large business coalition had been working on for two years.

The Digital Millennium Copyright Act provided safeguards for intellectual property on the Internet. It was required to

implement guidelines in a treaty written by the World Intellectual Property Organization. Without it, cyber theft of American software, music, and videos would become even bigger
business in China, Mexico, and a dozen other countries. With
it, most of the world would accept the basic protections of U.S.
copyright law. The treaty had been signed by 128 nations. The
House bill implementing it had broad bipartisan support, had
been backed by the Clinton administration, approved by the
House Judiciary and Commerce committees, voted out of the
House, and unanimously approved by the Senate. All that was
needed for the president to sign it into law was a final House
vote on the conference committee report. "DeLay acted like he
didn't give a shit about any of the process that went into this,"
said an industry lobbyist who had worked on the bill. "We had
never seen a member threaten legislation over an issue like
this."

Not only had it been through the process, the WIPO bill was
business—all business. Its lonely opposition had consisted of
consumer advocates and computer wonks—people DeLay goes
out of his way to ignore. It was the sort of economic development proposal universally embraced by Republicans. Utah Senator Orrin Hatch pushed it through the Senate, calling it the
most important bill the Congress would pass in 1998. The Motion Picture Association, the Recording Industry Association of
America, software companies all sent their heavy hitters to
committees where the bill was heard. When DeLay used his position as majority whip to block its final passage in the House,
he sent K Street a loud, crude message. He also probably broke
the law. He wasn't blocking a pork-barrel provision some House
member had hidden in a piece of legislation. This was the meat
and potatoes of Big American Business. The message was not
only crude, it was clear: any big hires by lobbying firms would
require the approval of the Republican leadership. And when
representatives of lobbying firms and trade associations came to

ask DeLay to sign off on a hire, they had better be prepared to answer three questions.

- Is the candidate a Republican?
- How much has the candidate contributed to the Republican Party, candidates, and PACs?
- Has the candidate contributed to the Democratic Party, candidates, and PACs?

DeLay knew the answer to each of the questions. But going through the process helped domesticate the K Street supplicants who showed up to ask the majority whip for his blessing. In the words of a defense industry lobbyist: "They show you real quick who was in charge."

DeLay had been close to the edge in the past. Yet he had never fired a lobbyist. But by 1998 his Americans for a Republican Majority PAC (ARMPAC) had put so much money into Republican House campaigns that he was above reproach. So he was rewriting the rules. He was also giving new meaning to the name of the oil patch product that paid his father Charlie DeLay's mortgage while he worked for Storm Drilling: Texas Crude.

While he was putting the muscle on the lobby, he and his staff were giving the finger to any colleague who dared question him. When GOP conference chair John Boehner complained that holding up legislation was too heavy handed, DeLay roughed him up at a Speaker's office leadership meeting: "Who died and made you god of coalitions?" DeLay angrily asked. When New York Democrat Jerrold Nadler protested and called for an Ethics Committee investigation, DeLay spokesman Mike Scanlon was dismissive. "The last time I checked," Scanlon said, "there was nothing wrong with voicing displeasure about a situation like this one. . . . We don't appreciate Nadler's heavy-handed tactics." Calling Nadler's protestations heavy handed—after DeLay had pulled a bill from the floor over a hire that offended him—was truly inspired.

Nadler couldn't believe DeLay was holding up legislation to coerce a trade association into hiring a lobbyist: "It was outrageous," Nadler said, still fuming four years after the fact. "They pulled a bill off the floor of the House. They took an official action. For what, to coerce a trade association? That meets the legal definition of extortion as I understand it."

The airport slots in nearby Las Vegas would have provided Dave McCurdy better odds than he expected in Phoenix, where his fate was to be decided by the EIA board. DeLay had already called retiring president Peter McCloskey to warn him about hiring McCurdy. Billy Tauzin had put the word out that his recent Washington meeting with McCurdy was not an endorsement. Lobbyists from EIA affiliates were openly working against him. A Republican insider named John Palafoutas, who lobbied for AMP Inc., a corporation that belonged to the EIA, told board members that McCurdy was damaged goods. Palafoutas had arrived in Phoenix to convey a message from Gingrich's chief of staff: "Tell the EIA they ought to be careful about Dave McCurdy." He also warned them that "the leadership is angry." There were others. A Phillips Electronics lobbyist said he was hearing "a lot of negative things on the Hill" and feared McCurdy was a liability. But the beleaguered EIA president-elect made his case before the board. Outgoing president McCloskey spoke on his behalf. "I knew our organization. There was no way we were going to change or minds," said McCloskey. "We had made our decision. We had put a lot of work into selecting Dave McCurdy. I knew that." McCloskey said he had spoken to DeLay and told him the hiring decision would stand. McCloskey and McCurdy prevailed. Or thought they

had. Until DeLay and Gingrich instructed their staffs to allow
no communication with anyone from the Electronics Industry
Association.

The EIA found a way to tactfully back down. It hired Adrien
MacGillvray, a former aide to John Kasich, who at the time
chaired the House Budget Committee. And retained the services of former Republican Congressman Robert Walker, the
president of a Washington lobbying firm. The same Bob Walker
DeLay had knocked out of the whip's race three years earlier.
McCurdy could keep his job. But two Republicans tight with
the House leadership would be working with him. "The message was clear and Mr. DeLay did a very good job in sending that
message," said EIA vice president Mark Rosenker.

A year later MacGillvray was doing EIA's deals on the Hill,
using established relationships to connect with aides to every
member of the Republican leadership team. She even got facetime with DeLay chief of staff Susan Hirschmann. Hirschmann—who like many other key staffers would remain a DeLay
operative after moving on to a K Street firm in 2003—was furious when McCurdy was hired, only calming down after the
trade association capitulated. McCurdy was never going to be
embraced by the Republican leadership. But MacGillvray was.
"Susan wants me to be successful," MacGillvray said. "She rec-
ognizes that this is an important and powerful industry."
MacGillvray might have been flogging her stock with her comments to the press. But she was also making wise investments.
Shortly after EIA hired her she attended a fundraiser for ARM-
PAC. McCurdy had become the big-picture guy—stepping in
when he was needed. "For example, he recently made several
telephone calls to Democrats when the Senate was considering
the Y2K bill," according to the *National Journal*.

The legislative trade press—*Roll Call* and the *National Journal*—followed the story. And the *Washington Post*, which does
Washington inside baseball better than any other big national

daily, gave its Capitol bureau the hit away sign. Predictably, their reporting was thorough and revealing. But the story had no legs. American news consumers have little appetite for stories about the business lobby. (Not even HBO could sex it up enough to sell it in its brief *K Street* dramatic series in 2003.) Congress was adjourning for an election recess. And there was Clinton-Lewinsky. Even if the story was fading as the public turned away from Kenneth Starr and back toward Bill Clinton, it still had more shelf-life than a pissing match between the Republican leadership and a Washington trade association. So Newt Gingrich, who would soon be irrelevant, and DeLay, who was in the process of quietly expropriating Newt's power, walked away unscathed.

That's unfortunate.

Because Tom DeLay's public mugging of Dave McCurdy was a rare opportunity for the public to understand the House leadership's hostile takeover of the lobby. Regarding the way the country's business is done in Washington, this was a huge story. "It finally came to light," said Hilary Rosen, at the time the president of the Recording Industry Association of America (RIAA). "It came out in the press. DeLay sort of denied it and there was a little bit of public contrition. But that was all."

For a brief moment in 1998 the "K Street Project" emerged from the shadows to redefine the relationship between the Congress and the business lobby. Then it moved back underground, where it continues to work, through regular meetings of House and Senate leaders taking their cues from Grover Norquist, leader of Americans for Tax Reform. DeLay is the enforcer. Norquist does a lot of the headwork and the organizational heavy lifting. But Grover Norquist never has been "in" government. In fact the Reagan ideologue, who came out of the national College Republicans ten years after Karl Rove, is averse to government. He says he wants to starve the federal government "until it's small enough to drown in a bathtub," even if starving it requires using the machinery of government. It was

Norquist's idea to use public records to compile lists of party affiliations and political contributions of lobbyists working on the
Hill. Early on, he turned the lists over to DeLay, who used them
to threaten lobbyists. Later, spreadsheets published on his
Americans for Tax Reform website would include names; firms
or trade associations; previous work histories; party affiliations
gleaned from voting records; and amounts contributed to Republican and Democratic candidates and PACs. "I can't talk to
you about DeLay," said a high-dollar Texas lobbyist both authors
of this book have known for decades. "He has people looking at
my party affiliation and all my contributions."

DeLay was the first leader in Congress to openly use the
Norquist list to select lobbyists. In 1995, soon after the new Republican House majority elected Gingrich Speaker and him
whip, DeLay invited lobbyists over for a get-acquainted session.
Then he sat each of them down before a list of the 400 top political donors in the profession. To make it easier to understand,
he had his staff prepare a "friendly" and "unfriendly" list. Lobbyists whose misfortune it was to make the unfriendly list—that
is, those giving money to Democrats and not enough to Republicans —understood what they had to do. To make sure they got
it, DeLay told them: "If you're going to play in our revolution,
you've got to live by our rules." Most fell in line and started writing checks. In 1998 DeLay changed the rules. No longer was the
old Sicilian practice of "paying *tributo*" sufficient. Lobbyists
would need résumés and references that established their party
bona fides. All others would be shut out. By attacking McCurdy,
DeLay openly defined the new relationship between the Republican Congress and the Lobby. No one, it seemed, could stop
him.

On its best days, the House Ethics Committee, officially known
as the House Committee on Standards of Official Conduct, is a

chickenshit operation.* The only committee evenly divided between Republicans and Democrats, and charged with oversight
of ethical transgressions of members, it is one of the smallest
committees in the modern Congress. Not that it needs to be
bigger. If you can count on anything in Washington, you can
count on the Ethics Committee doing nothing. Not because the
ethical conduct of House members is not in need of attention.
The committee is irrelevant because of what is known as "The
Truce." The bipartisan agreement is fairly straightforward. You
don't file ethics complaints against us and we won't file ethics
complaints against you. So nobody files ethics complaints. And
the Ethics Committee reprimands nobody.

Yet a year after the McCurdy incident, the Ethics Committee
awoke from its slumber and did something that was nothing less
than stunning. Without a complaint filed by any member of
Congress, the committee launched its own investigation of the
DeLay-McCurdy affair and ruled that what the majority whip
had done was improper. In a private letter, which DeLay's office
refuses to release, it rebuked DeLay and told him he could not
consider a political affiliation when taking an official action in
Congress. It wasn't a fine or censure, but it was something. The
committee also sent a memo to every member of the House, in-

---

*The "truce" was finally broken in June 2004, by Houston Congressman Chris
Bell, a white Democrat defeated by an African American in the Democratic
primary. Bell's district was turned into one of the Gerrymandered "Bantus-
tans" drawn to concentrate the state's blacks and Hispanics into a few minority districts, thus making most other congressional districts safer for
Republicans. Bell's complaint included the $25,000 Westar contribution to
DeLay's PAC, and the alleged violations of Texas law by spending corporate
money on state House races. It was the first time in seven years that a House
member filed a complaint before the Ethics Committee, and, predictably, it
was opposed by the all-too-predictable House Democratic leadership. The
complaint was drafted by Citizens for Responsibility and Ethics in Washington, a newcomer to the public interest advocacy community currently doing
the work of the moribund Ethics Committee.

forming them that as government officials they are "prohibited from taking or withholding any official action on the basis of partisan affiliation or the campaign contributions or support of the involved individuals."

DeLay chief of staff Tony Rudy, who would later move on to the lobby, said his boss was "happy the committee has disposed of this matter." DeLay was contrite. "Sometimes I get a little overpassionate in my desire to get things done," he told Tim Russert of *Meet the Press*. "Sometimes I say things I shouldn't say and the ethics committee reminded me."

DeLay and other members of Congress were barred from using *official* acts in Congress to intimidate people. In other words, don't pull a bill from the House floor to coerce a hire in the lobby. That was it.

Dave McCurdy kept his head down and his mouth shut. "I don't think we were ever frozen out," said the EIA's Mark Rosenker. "No one ever called this organization and made a threat to us." So an act of extortion by a public official acting under the color of the United States Constitution was quietly "disposed of." DeLay would later tell McCurdy that the fight over his job was "nothing personal," according to one House source close to the incident.

There were no more overt threats to block legislation. The K Street Project that started as a fight for partisan equity in campaign contributions evolved into something less visible but more elaborate and powerful: a political machine that shut off lobby contributions to the Democratic Party, increased lobby contributions to the Republican Party, and closed the corporate lobby to Democratic job applicants. Grover Norquist's list became the Blue Book on the market value of lobbyists. "It was like this new rule everyone knew they had to live with," said Rosen, who would leave her job with the RIAA in 2003.

Before she left, the K Street Project sent word to Rosen. After the Republicans took control of the House she had hired Mitch Glazier, a Republican Senate staffer with a background in intellectual property rights. It was a good hire, easily justified by Glazier's understanding of intellectual property right law. That he was a Republican gave him added value. And because he had been on the "right" side of the impeachment fight, he was okay by DeLay. Glazier would provide the RIAA access to office suites where Rosen was no longer welcome—like Norquist's "Wednesday Group" tactics-and-strategy sessions for Republican lobbyists, staffers, and legislators.

"Mitch came into my office one day," Rosen said. "He had just come back from the [Norquist] Wednesday Group, right before the Senate went Republican [2002]. He said, 'You know, I got handed a list today of all your political contributions. And all the RIAA political contributions. Obviously you are leaning Democrat because everyone recognized you as a top Democratic giver among business lobbyists. You've got to give more money [to Republicans]; that's number one. We have to even out our contributions.'" Rosen asked Glazier how he responded. He said he had laughed. He didn't think what they were demanding was practical. Nor did Rosen. "But then he said, 'You know, I think they're serious.'" Glazier had one other warning to convey to his boss: It was number two. "We were all warned that if the Republicans take the Senate, no more money is to go to Democrats."

"It was that overt," Rosen said.

Ten years after it began, the K Street Project is part of DeLay's larger leadership combine. In the Senate it's run by Pennsylvania Senator Rick Santorum, who regularly meets with lobbyists to approve of their hires. Across the rotunda Mildred Webber, the political consultant DeLay used when he was a neophyte charting his ascent to power, organizes K Street strategy meetings for her new boss, House majority whip Roy Blunt. Webber consults with former DeLay chief of staff Susan Hirschmann, who followed the money to a K Street lobby shop.

The list of former DeLay staffers who have moved downtown include Hirschmann, at Williams & Jensen; Karl Gallant (when he's not running one of DeLay's PACs) is at the Alexander Strategy Group, along with former DeLay staff counsel Tony Rudy. Glenn LeMunyon is at Tate-LeMunyon. Tom Pyle lobbies for Koch Industries. William Jarrell is at Washington Strategies. Drew Maloney works for the Federalist Group. Jim Dowell works for the American Association of Health Plans. Until recently (more on this to come) DeLay's adviser and unofficial American Consul to the Marianas, Jack Abramoff worked for Greenberg Traurig. Abramoff's protégé there and in subsequent lobbyist ventures has been Mike Scanlon, the former DeLay press aide and attack dog during Clinton's impeachment.

What Rosen described in 1998 as a new rule for lobbyists was routine by 2003. Lobbyists were vetted by Santorum or Blunt, and occasionally someone would be told they had to go. Julie Domenick was the top lobbyist at the Investment Company Institute (ICI) when House Financial Services Committee Chair Michael Oxley decided she had to go. But Oxley got sloppy and Domenick's job was probably saved by loose talk at a Christmas party in a downtown Washington hotel. There, Oxley's chief of staff and a lobbyist who had previously worked in Roy Blunt's office told the group that Domenick was on her way out. If ICI moved her along quietly, the *Washington Post* reported, Oxley's ongoing probe of the mutual fund industry would be less painful.

Press reports described Oxley as offended because Domenick hadn't promptly made a courtesy call when he was named chairman. A whispering campaign circulated about Domenick being "too close" to certain Democratic senators, which she was. Oxley was reportedly angry about her seeking direction from Massachusetts Congressman Barney Frank, the ranking Democrat on Financial Services. All of which amounted to a rather weak justification to demand someone's job. *Washington Monthly*'s Nick Confessore got closer to the heart of the story:

> What explains Oxley's decision is the same thing that explains why the Bush administration would risk angering voters by

attempting to privatize Medicare: the GOP needs K Street's
muscle for long-term ideological projects to remake the national government. For years, conservatives have been pushing
to divert part of Social Security into private investment accounts. Such a move, GOP operatives argued, would provide
millions of new customers and potentially trillions of dollars to
the mutual fund industry that would manage the private accounts. The profits earned would, of course, be shared with the
GOP in the form of campaign contributions. In other words, by
sluicing the funds collected by the federal government's largest
social insurance program through businesses loyal to the GOP,
the party would instantly convert the crown jewels of Democratic governance into a pillar of the new Republican machine.
But to make the plan a reality, the GOP needed groups like the
ICI to get behind the idea—by funding pro-privatization think
tanks, running issue ads attacking anti-privatization Democrats, and so on. The ICI, however, had always been lukewarm
to privatization, for which conservatives blamed Domenick.
Hence, the GOP machine decided she had to go. In the end, to
quell the Oxley scandal, Domenick was allowed to keep her job.
But ICI hired a former general counsel to Newt Gingrich to
work alongside her, and the GOP's campaign to get K Street behind Social Security privatization continues.

Confessore was getting at the important third phase of the K
Street Project: congressional Republicans using the lobby to implement their own partisan agenda. It's one of Washington's
best-kept secrets. Washington reporter Robert Dreyfuss managed to get inside the story for the *Texas Observer*. Dreyfuss
found that DeLay was expanding his kitchen cabinet for occasional lobbying campaigns, bringing lobbyists in and requiring
them to pressure Congressman to support a bill backed by the
leadership. In the summer of 2000, for example, lobbyists
friendly to DeLay were called in for a meeting in the Capitol
basement and given marching orders regarding passing Presi-

dent Bush's $700 billion tax cut. "We'd occasionally get a hundred people into a room to talk about what the tax cut was going to look like," Blunt said. The tax cut group was chaired by Mike Baroody of the National Association of Manufacturers.

Lobbyists called into a meeting of the tax cut task force were told they were expected to get out and sell the bill to "their members"—that is, members of their trade associations and clients. The bill was not yet written and lobbyists were not allowed to ask about provisions their clients would want in the bill. They were told their clients should contact members of the House and tell them the president's tax cuts had to be passed. The small details—what their clients wanted in the bill—would be taken care of later. A House source was surprised by the direct approach. "You're all here because you're the best lobbyists in town and because you're loyal Republicans," they were told. "The job of this coalition, frankly, is to pass the President's tax cut bill the first day it comes to the floor for a vote, whatever the details look like."

"I always thought my job is to look out for my client's interest," one lobbyist told a reporter. "Suddenly I'm working for the Republican Party." Hill publications have also reported that Republican lobbyists are calling on congressmen, "whipping legislation" unrelated to their clients—acting on orders from the Republican House leadership. Rosen said she was told that it was her job to deliver the votes of Democratic members because all the lobbyists in movies and recording are tight with Democrats. She was also told that the RIAA would have to do mailings and other advocacy in support of the Bush tax cut bills. All of this represents a perversion of the relationship between lobbyists and elected officials. Prior to the K Street Project, lobbyists told members of Congress what bills they wanted passed. Now the tail is wagging (and whipping) the dog.

The K Street Project that DeLay, Santorum, and Norquist run has public policy and political consequences that will last for at least a quarter of a century. By disciplining the lobby, and making it an extension of the Republican House Conference, DeLay has expanded his influence far beyond the House. Lobbyists are being ordered to do the party's bidding. Lobbyists are told to lean on House members to whom they have contributed money and tell them how the party wants them to vote. Lobbyists are required to contribute money to the majority party—if they are to have access to the Speaker and committee chairs to advance their clients' interests. With the political contributions from the lobby come the contributions from the corporate clients they represent.

As Democratic money dries up and Democratic patronage disappears, Tom DeLay is thinking ahead to a full generation in control of Congress. And why not? Seizing control of the lobby was the final brilliant, if cynical, move in a struggle for absolute power. And they did it with very little attention from the press, the public, and the courts.

"Who cares if DeLay bullies lobbyists?" asked *Slate*'s Timothy Noah. Noah argued that if lobbyists are treated "like the help," the lobby won't be so appealing for members of Congress—such as Billy Tauzin, who shamelessly offered to go to work for the big pharmacy lobby after writing their prescription drug bill. Can a captive lobby be good for politics and policy? Not hardly—to borrow a phrase from the majority leader. While liberals tend to demonize lobbyists, they have become an essential part of the permanent government and an essential part of the process. And they are now part of a Republican machine that has accumulated power that is without precedent in the modern Congress.

They are also utterly lacking the critical self-awareness that could have discouraged their most egregious behavior, according to Hilary Rosen:

> As a business lobbyist you're always sort of cognizant of the
> red-face test. Yes, it's your job to seek things from public policy

that are to the advantage of your client and that are to the advantage of your company. And that put more money in the pockets of your executives and your shareholders. And make greater profits. But there was always this sort of—call it the red-face test, call it the front page of the *Washington Post* test. Whatever you do, it has to stand some sunshine. If it couldn't stand the scrutiny of some sunshine, it was inappropriate. I think the change . . . through this sort of club that has been created, is that there is no red-face test. There is no front page of the *Washington Post* test anymore. That standard has become if it's criminal or not.

Massachusetts Democrat Barney Frank says members of the House and lobbyists have come to accept the new rules DeLay put into place when he set out to bust Dave McCurdy. In ten years the K Street Project has been internalized. "They don't even have to use threats anymore. Everyone is conditioned to behave a certain way." A Republican lobbyist almost echoes Frank. "Now, everybody factors DeLay into their thinking," said Mark Iskowitz.

To explain the K Street Project, New York Congressman Jerrold Nadler, who speaks in staccato paragraphs, finds a point of reference that's close to home. Maybe it's because his district lies across the Hudson from the gritty Jersey waterfront industries controlled by HBO's Soprano family, but Jerrold Nadler isn't as genteel as Barney Frank. "Barney is right," Nadler said. "They have institutionalized it. They're like the mob. When the mob bosses start out, they tell you if you don't pay them what they ask for, they are going to bomb your store. After a while, they don't need to threaten you anymore. You just hand the money over when they show up to collect it."

Nadler sympathizes with the lobbyist who worries that he's working for the Republican Party rather than his client. "Under this system," Nadler said, "when he is working for the Republican Leadership, he is working in the interest of his client. Because if he doesn't do what they tell him, the Republican Party is going to screw his client."

The new system is going to be with us for a while. "It's a nice start," DeLay said of the changes House Republicans have made on K Street. "You don't change a culture that's been built up over forty or fifty years in six years. We've made good progress."

Grover Norquist agrees.

"We're not finished yet."

ELEVEN

Saipan

At first look the island of Saipan is a tropical paradise: white sand beaches, palm trees billowing in the breeze, glimmering turquoise sea, dramatic rock cliffs rising from the mist and foam of crashing waves, reefs teeming with wildly hued fish, snorkelers, and scuba divers. Saipan is also the name of a small city beside the sea that is the capital of the Commonwealth of the Northern Mariana Islands. In the late 1990s this remote outpost of America, 9,000 miles across the Pacific from California, offered a vision of what the nation might look like if Tom DeLay had his deregulatory way. DeLay's adventure in Saipan illustrates how his agenda had changed: from trying to disable the EPA to imposing his ideology and will on whole territories and economies. And the implementation of his ideas would increase the riches of the loyalists who in turn keep the maw of his political leviathan stuffed with money. Here was a land newly born to American dominion, a place and people that had never been corrupted by federal regulation. Saipan was his grand experiment—a construction of the world as he wished it to be. "It is a perfect Petri dish of capitalism," DeLay enthused about Saipan in 1997. "It's like my Galapagos Island."

The free-market laboratory experiment and the opportunities of vast profit that Saipan spawned could be carried out in virtual secrecy. Few Americans born after World War II are aware that

Saipan exists. If you surf the Internet for references, you are most often rewarded with obituaries of old Marines. In mid-1944 Saipan, which rises from the Pacific near Guam, became a crucial objective in America's tortuous strategy of island-hopping toward fortress Japan. When Saipan fell, the United States would be positioned to build an airfield on nearby Tinian from which the decisive bombing missions of the war were flown. But the strategic victory did not come easily; Marines speak of Saipan with the same reverence and horror they attach to Iwo Jima and Guadalcanal. The U.S. military committed 70,000 troops to overwhelm a forty-seven-square-mile island. The GIs suffered nearly 17,000 casualties during the twenty-five-day battle, including 3,225 killed in action. The slaughter of the Japanese on Saipan was almost unimaginable. The recorded total of their soldiers killed was 23,811 — five hundred per square mile of the atoll they lost. And, though estimates vary, up to 18,000 civilians jumped to their deaths from the towering cliffs, rather than give up to the advancing Marines. The mass suicide convinced the U.S. military that the Japanese would never surrender to invaders of their homeland: Saipan moved Harry Truman toward his decision to drop the atomic bomb.

After the war, the Marianas became a trust territory of the United Nations, the United States its administering authority. The navy governed the islands until 1962, when their rule was transferred to the Department of the Interior. In 1975, during the administration of Gerald Ford, the islanders voted overwhelmingly in a self-rule plebiscite to continue embracing the sovereignty of the United States as a commonwealth. Eleven years passed before Ronald Reagan formally made that covenant into law. Though the Marianas' indigenous peoples had won their prized U.S. citizenship, the entire population then amounted to one small town. In an effort to jump-start an economy, federal negotiators granted control of immigration, wage, and workplace standards to the commonwealth government. That's when the islands grabbed the attention of rich people in Hong Kong, Taiwan, and South Korea.

The most affluent and powerful man in the Marianas was a naturalized U.S. citizen named Willie Tan. Tan Holdings Corporation, founded by the tycoon's father in Hong Kong, included Saipan's largest garment factories, several hotels, a bank, travel agencies, ice cream parlors; the largest newspaper in the islands, the *Saipan Tribune,* was the company's mouthpiece. Tan and other venture capitalists had realized they could create a garment industry that was fully protected by U.S. trade laws and virtually immune to the obstructions of federal regulation. Imports from the U.S. came into the Marianas duty-free and without quotas, and exports from the islands moved past U.S Customs without stirring so much as a breeze. For the venture capitalists on Saipan, the commonwealth status enabled them to circumvent quotas on Chinese textile exports to the United States. The investment capital behind the factories was largely Chinese. The plants were run like factories in China. Even the fabric was Chinese.

All the capitalists needed was a labor force. The indigenous islanders had no future as executives in this industry, nor did they fit the desired mold of factory workers. The Marianas capitalists instead contracted with recruitment squads that roved the provinces of China, the Philippines, Thailand, Bangladesh, Sri Lanka, and other Asian countries. The arm's-length arrangement meant the recruiters' methods could not be directly connected to corporations chartered in the United States. Typically, the recruits were obligated to pay $5,000 to $7,000 for the privilege of signing one-year labor contracts that enabled them to work and receive housing and health care benefits in the U.S. In the places they came from, $5,000 to $7,000 was a fortune. Large families and communities of peasants raised the money for some of these young workers, whose riches earned in America were supposed to help feed and clothe them. But many recruits could never raise that kind of money. Some were steered to loan sharks in the Asian countries who had working arrangements with the recruitment agencies; more signed agreements in which they would see none of their wages until the "recruitment fees" were paid back. They were indentured workers, at best.

Many of these people had not seen any of the world beyond their villages. Several Bangladeshi men, hired to work in security, were told and believed they could ride the train from Saipan to Los Angeles. Chinese workers who became pregnant were forced to return to China to have an abortion or else have it performed at a clinic on Saipan. Most of the immigrant workers were women, many of them mothers of small children. One could spot their arrivals in Saipan. They came off the plane and were hustled through immigration and aboard buses, their faces staring out in bewilderment and apprehension as the drivers sped through the winding back streets of the capital city. White beaches, emerald water, and resort hotels frequented by Korean and Japanese tourists were not the Saipan they saw. Their new homes were security-fenced compounds set far back in the jungle. With maybe a sheet thrown over a cord for privacy, the women slept on cots, as many as ten jammed in one small room. They had a dripping showerhead with no privacy or hot water, and a single toilet they lined up to share. Rats and cockroaches roamed freely. On the one day each week they were allowed to leave the compound, they were let out through a gate in a security fence by an armed guard. They had an early curfew, and knew better than to miss it.

There were about thirty factories. The young women worked upwards of seventy hours a week with no overtime pay, sometimes around the clock for two or three days to meet impossible quotas. They were paid $3.05 an hour to keep the sewing machines humming (the federal minimum wage was then $5.15 an hour). Three-plus bucks an hour must have sounded like an extravagant wage to poor girls in the backwaters of Asia, but they quickly found out they had no chance of coming out ahead; the employers billed them for their lodging and food, on top of withholding for the thousands of dollars many still owed on their contracts. Squares of raw fabric were piled up around their machines as high as they could reach; a glaring electronic production counter nagged them to work harder, longer, faster. The air was filled with dust and lint. Workers were not afforded the low-cost filter masks commonly worn by people with respiratory difficulties; for relief they wore rags over their noses and mouths like the bandanas of Old West desperadoes. If they fell asleep and ran a needle through a finger, there was no first aid station; all they got was a rebuke from a shouting supervisor who called them stupid. And those were the lucky ones.

On arrival in Saipan some workers found that their contracts were worthless. They were told their employer had gone bankrupt. They were stuck on Saipan, and as for their loss of money—too bad. Day laborers who had thought they were going to be security guards piled on top of each other at night in one-room hovels and explored ideas like selling their kidneys to raise enough money to go home. Saipan became a fixture of the booming global sex trade. Young Chinese women recruited for restaurant jobs were ordered to work in karaoke and topless bars where managers told them they had to drink and have sex with customers. They received no pay for this coerced prostitution. The so-called bar fines for their services went to their employers.

Even officials in the laissez-faire administrations of Ronald Reagan and George Bush the Elder were alarmed by the instant garment industry in the Marianas. In 1986 the Interior Department of the Reagan administration voiced concerns that the economy, culture, and legal system of the native islanders were buckling under the strain of the mass influx of foreign workers, and proposed an immigration cap to keep the once-pristine island from turning into an industrial slum. In 1992 Bush administration officials testified to Congress that the garment industry on Saipan had been built on a foundation of cheap alien labor, favorable tariff treatment for goods shipped to U.S. markets from the Marianas, and tax breaks, rebates, and other assistance underwritten by the federal government. "Outsourcing" was not then the omnipresent and ugly word it has become today. Brand-name clothiers favored by American shoppers were having their cake and eating it, too. They could take advantage of third-world wages and labor practices and undercut the domestic textile industry, but (unlike sweatshop industries in neighboring Asian countries) their competitive advantage was not offset by import tariffs—because of the Marianas' commonwealth status they could ship garments bearing the proud label "Made in the U.S.A." Companies taking advantage of the free rein extended to manufacturers in Saipan included Gap, Sears, Wal-Mart, J. C. Penney, J. Crew, Tommy Hilfiger, Ralph Lauren, Anne Taylor, Liz Claiborne, Brooks Brothers, and Abercrombie & Fitch.

Meanwhile the population of the islands increased by 36 percent over five years in the nineties, to 58,000. Now a minority in their country, the indigenous Micronesians struggled to maintain their culture and make a living off scarce government jobs and in the limited service and tourism industries—their unemployment rate shot to fourteen percent, twice the average of other U.S. citizens.

Stories about the Marianas reached George Miller, a congressman who represents the East Bay area near San Francisco. Miller is the ranking Democrat of the House Committee on Resources, which has jurisdiction over U.S. territories and commonwealths. In 1992, when the Democrats still controlled the House, he chaired the committee and convened a hearing on the garment industry in the Marianas (known in U.S. federalspeak as CNMI for Commonwealth of the Northern Mariana Islands). Miller said at the hearing, "I am concerned by the attitude that it is acceptable to underpay and mistreat alien workers who are willing to accept substandard conditions in the CNMI that are better than their homeland. It is unacceptable when U.S. farmers abuse Mexican field workers, and it is unacceptable when CNMI garment manufacturers abuse Chinese workers. It cannot be tolerated anywhere."

But rhetoric from a California congressman was not the chief concern of Saipan's capitalists and politicians. In 1992 the U.S. Labor Department sued five garment factories owned by Willie Tan. The Tan companies were fined $9 million as restitution for 1,200 employees who had been locked in worksites and barracks and obliged to work 84 hours a week with no overtime pay. It was the largest fine ever imposed by the Labor Department. Then in 1995, accounts of abuse on Saipan prompted the Philippines to impose a startling moratorium on granting its citizens work visas in the Marianas. Negotiations between the commonwealth and the Philippines ensued at once; ardent promises were made and heard. Soon the Philippines lifted the moratorium and busied itself writing new work visas — 3,000 Filipinos arrived at Saipan during the last quarter of 1996 alone.

But in mid-1997 Bill Clinton wrote Marianas governor Froilan Tenorio saying that "certain labor practices in the islands . . . are inconsistent with our country's values," and proposed federalizing the Marianas' labor and immigration laws — in other words, workers on Saipan would have the same legal rights as U.S. workers. The ruling clique on Saipan decided some heavy-duty lobbying and image tending was in order. That was when the Marianas Islands became the fervent ideological cause and favorite beach of right-wing Republicans on Capitol Hill. The Marianas' GOP boosters included Dick Armey and John Boehner. But Tom DeLay aggressively took the lead.

In 1997 Governor Tenorio had traveled to Washington and called on DeLay, who lionized the commonwealth and its leader in a speech to House colleagues. "Governor Tenorio did not come to Washington looking for taxpayer benefits, welfare, or handouts," DeLay bragged on the man. "He came to promote his market reforms. . . . During his administration, Governor Tenorio has actively pursued and courted business around the globe to open shop in the CNMI. Like President Reagan in the 1980s, Tenorio has kept taxes low. Low tax rates have actually increased productivity, which in turn increased revenue for the government of the CNMI. Additionally, the Governor has recognized the importance of trade and has demonstrated how trade with Asian markets can bring prosperity. The economic changes that have taken place in the CNMI have been nothing short of miraculous."

The Marianas Miracle funded a sweet, high-profit, low-maintenance account of the most arch-conservative top-dollar lobbyist in Washington. Unlike other luminaries of the K Street Project, Jack Abramoff had never worked on DeLay's staff in Congress. He had been a star politico of the GOP when DeLay was still in the Texas Legislature. A high school weightlifting champion and a teetotaler of Orthodox Jewish faith, Abramoff strutted with the far right at Brandeis, a Massachusetts campus usually dominated by left-wingers. In 1981 he moved to Washington, where he got a law degree at Georgetown and chaired the College Republican National Committee. Democrats have nothing that resembles that collegiate proving ground of the GOP. Karl Rove, Lee Atwater, Ralph Reed, Grover Norquist, and Jack Abramoff all got their starts as College Republicans, and they zoomed to the top strata of American politics. Abramoff hired Reed as his top deputy in the collegiate group, and—his strong Jewish faith no apparent hindrance—later helped Reed found the Christian Coalition. Abramoff is also very close to Norquist. The young star politicos of the GOP convinced themselves they possessed the power to change the world, and their conviction has never wavered. Abramoff was the executive director of Reagan's grass-roots lobbying organization, Citizens for America. Later he produced a video on Ollie North that included the ex-Marine filibuster's soon-to-be famous slide show about heroic Nicaraguan Contras. Some senior Republicans grumbled that Abramoff's indiscretion blew the cover of Iran-Contra. A Reagan administration official eased him out of its lineup with a remark that an overeager young man had gone "off the reservation." (The term would come to have an almost literal meaning when Abramoff was entangled in an Indian gaming lobbying scam years later.)

During the eighties Abramoff lobbied in Washington for the dictatorship of Zaire and founded the International Freedom Foundation, which worked to build support for the apartheid regime in South Africa. He took a turn as a Hollywood movie producer in South Africa. *Red Scorpion* was a thriller pitting Soviet agents and assassins against U.S.-supported guerrillas in Angola and Namibia. The movie opened in 1989 on 1,268 screens, a healthy showing, but it was picketed in Washington and rebuked by the United Nations over the moviemakers' use of military equipment loaned by the South Africans—an alleged violation of cultural sanctions against the regime. Abramoff produced a few more movies, making no apology for their exuberant violence. "In my movies, the bad guys get killed," he boasted. Not for a moment did he doubt who the bad guys were.

Abramoff became a charter member of Tom DeLay's "kitchen cabinet" of like-minded lobbyists and former aides when DeLay became whip in 1995. Abramoff worked in the D.C. lobbying office of Seattle's oldest law firm, Preston Gates, and then jumped to a K Street competitor, Greenberg Traurig. In both books the Marianas were a gold mine account. His public relations campaign, financed by the office of Governor Tenorio, turned the Marianas into a Republican playground. In 1997 the Marianas taxpayers picked up the tab for 88 week-long junkets at a reported $5,500 per traveler. Seven members of the House, five wives, one child, and 75 aides crossed nine time zones to find facts while golfing, snorkeling, and deepening their tans. Because the Marianas were U.S. territory, and its government was paying for the vacations, these paragons of government ethics did not have to disclose the junkets on their official travel reports.

Tom DeLay, his wife Christine, his daughter Dani, and three staff members arrived to celebrate the New Year's holiday in 1998. They stayed in a posh Hyatt Regency and found time for a couple of rounds of golf under the caring watch of the staffs of the governor and Willie Tan. At a dinner in honor of Tan, DeLay recalled enlightening conversations he had enjoyed with various powers in the Marianas and oozed with deference to "the Mogul."

> When [the Mogul] came to my office in the Capitol, he told me about the conservative policies that the CNMI has implemented. When I met the Governor, he told me about his proposals to pass a flat tax and school choice for children. When I played golf with [two Marianas officials] in Houston, they told me about the attempts of the Clinton Administration to kill prosperity on the islands. And when one of my closest and dearest friends, Jack Abramoff, your most able representative in Washington, D.C., invited me to the islands, I wanted to see firsthand the free market success in the CNMI and the progress and reform you have made. Even though I have only been here for twenty-four hours, I have witnessed the economic success of the CNMI and I have witnessed the friendship and good will of its people.

DeLay went on to rail about an administrator in the Office of Insular Affairs—a sub-agency of the Interior Department—whom his hosts found troublesome. "Pardon me, but does this man have a vote in the United States Congress? I don't think so. . . . You are up against the forces of big labor and the radical left. Dick Armey and I made a promise to defend the islands' present system. Stand firm. Resist evil. Remember that all truth and blessings emanate from our Creator. God bless you and the people of the Northern Marianas."

DeLay said that in front of news cameras from ABC. But he was not easily embarrassed, nor inclined to back down. When he returned from the trip and a reporter pressed him about sweatshops in the Marianas, he said, "I saw some of those factories. They were air-conditioned. I didn't see anyone sweating." Then he laughed. Inspired by the labor model he saw on Saipan, he threw out a daring and philosophical idea: the United States should establish an identical "guest worker" program "where particular companies can bring Mexican workers in." The Mexicans would be paid "at whatever wage the market will bear."

Unfortunately, a few weeks before DeLay's trip, the Marianas had held a gubernatorial election, and the incumbent had been turned out by his Uncle Pedro. The new Governor Tenorio dropped broad hints he was not entirely on board with DeLay's vision for the commonwealth. That same January in 1998, as the U.S. Senate prepared to conduct hearings on the Marianas, someone leaked to the press an e-mail written by Jack Abramoff. In it the lobbyist called for a congressional and public relations counter-offensive that would characterize Clinton administration policy as a federal takeover of the islands. Abramoff's e-mailed memorandum to his clients and the commonwealth's GOP champions said the junkets to the island had proved most fruitful. The e-mail called for continuing "impeachment" of the Interior Department bureaucrat and "working with the garment industry to get friendly workers (one Chinese, one Filipino, one Bangladeshi) to D.C. for the hearings." (That spectacle of American condescension never materialized.) The e-mail strongly implied that Willie Tan would bankroll much of the proposed campaign on Capitol Hill. "We don't have a relationship with Tan and we never will," Abramoff told one reporter with a straight face. It was a curiously brazen lie—Tan had been one of the three recipients of Abramoff's e-mail.

Meanwhile, Representative George Miller and his chief of staff accepted the new governor's invitation to come to Saipan for his inauguration. This, too, was a fact-finding mission, but they were looking for a different kind of fact. The Californians were taken on tours of a garment factory in which women labored placidly and appeared to relax over dinner in a cafeteria. "At the hotel nobody would come near us," said Miller, a tall and sharp-voiced man with erect bearing and silver-gray hair and mustache.

> They were terrified. But when we got back people were literally slipping notes under our doors. One of the cleaning ladies handed us a message from a relative who worked in this place where we'd been. It said that as soon as we were gone, they had to drop their food and get back to work—they had been off the clock while we were there. The relative said, "Tell the congressmen they've been had."
>
> So we sent word that at eight o'clock we'd be at this church way back in the island. At midnight people were still crowding in the church to tell us what their lives were like. It was incredible. The economy and immigration were so skewed that Marianas islanders had houses full of servants and were living on food stamps. Workers were being abused in so many ways. They had no rights, young women were being forced into prostitution, yet here's Mr. Conservative Morality, Tom DeLay, telling the world that this is a good system.

Back in Washington Miller was turned aside by the committee chairman, Don Young, an Alaska Republican. "We were told in no uncertain terms that there were not going to be any hearings on Saipan," said Miller. "I told the chairman, 'Why not? They're having hearings in the Senate.' He said, 'Well, we're not going to have them in the House. This is above my pay grade. The Whip has said he's not going to let that happen.'" The Whip of course was Tom DeLay.

The Senate hearings produced detailed testimony elaborating on what Miller had heard. The resulting legislation focused on the "Made in the U.S.A." label, proposing that any garment bearing that endorsement should actually be made by American workers. More than 200 members of the House co-sponsored the bill. But on the islands, political leaders and factory owners protested that enactment of the legislation would cost the local economy $85 million a year. The Marianas' lobbyist, Jack Abramoff, likened the industrialists to innocent people who were victimized at Nuremburg in the punishment of the Nazis. "These are immoral laws designed to destroy the economic laws of a people. [Conservatives] see in this battle a microcosm of an overall battle. . . . What these guys in the CNMI are trying to do is build a life without being wards of the state."

Tom DeLay made a similar pitch for the Marianas: "You've got a part of the world that was totally dependent on the federal government that now wants to get rid of the federal government. They now want to be self-sustaining and self-sufficient, and anywhere in the world where you have people that want to do that, we ought to be supportive."

Everyone on DeLay's team was certainly supportive. When Abramoff was organizing that airlift of congressmen, staffs, and families to the private beach of Republicans, Bill Jarrell, a lobbyist who had been DeLay's deputy chief of staff, was working on logistics and legalities to keep them out of trouble. Accompanying DeLay on the New Year's getaway were Ed Buckham, a former chief of staff turned political director of DeLay's ARMPAC, and Mike Scanlon, the young communications director who would articulate the impeachment jihad against Bill Clinton and with Abramoff later bill four Indian tribes an astounding $45 million for lobbying and PR. Another longtime top aide of DeLay, Tony Rudy, left the congressional staff to join the Abramoff and Scanlon lobbying team. The *Saipan Tribune* hailed Rudy as "the most helpful staffer for the CNMI in its history" and "a super hero."

But none of the lobbyists helping Saipan's clique were quite as venerated as Abramoff. The *Tribune* called him "our Michael Jordan." According to the public auditor, Abramoff alone carried off $7,940,000 from the islands between 1995 and 2001. Association with DeLay was a valuable entree for those lobbyists. To clients who feared the terrain of federal regulation, they invoked DeLay's name as if it were a magic wand—the man could get things fixed. By all accounts, the lobbying campaign conceived by Abramoff and the legislative barricade erected by DeLay carried many days for Saipan's ruling clique when trouble arose in Washington. The Marianas campaigns instructed the lobbyists in ways to arrange even more extravagant paydays in the future. In idealizing the far-flung archipelago as his Petri dish of capitalism, DeLay demonstrated how deregulation was an absolute in his approach to government—and how far the reach of his power extended beyond a congressional district in Texas. In an emotional column praising the work of Abramoff in November 1998, the publisher of the *Saipan Tribune* all but tremored in his reverence toward DeLay: "Let's not lose grace with the Kingmaker of the U.S. House of Representatives."

They might have all ended their days still enraptured by the wonders they had wrought in their Pacific paradise if not for a dispute that erupted between the Mogul and DeLay—amplified by one of the worst corporate scandals in American history. The garment industry in the Marianas was putting a strain on the islands' power capacity. There were frequent power outages, and resort hotels relied on generators. Willie Tan lorded over everything on Saipan from sweatshops to ice cream parlors; when proposals for a new $120 million 80-megawatt power plant emerged in the late nineties, the Tan Holdings Corporation naturally assumed that it was entitled to the largest business deal ever seen on the islands. But Tom DeLay kept book on the favors that he granted, and for this payback he signaled that the Marianas contract would be reserved for his old friends at Enron. Hired by the commonwealth's utilities corporation to analyze the bids, a Kansas City engineering firm concluded that the best proposal came from neither the Tan group nor Enron. But the squall out of both camps was so ferocious that the public auditor hastily called for a new round of bidding.

Enron CEO Ken Lay had participated in early organizational meetings of Tom DeLay's ARMPAC. Enron had loved Project Relief and channeled hundreds of thousands of dollars into DeLay's politics and future. In turn, DeLay had been an indefatigable champion of deregulation of the utility industry in Congress in 1996 and 1997. But Enron no longer wanted just to break up monopolies and use existing grids to move the electricity it sold. It had grandiose plans to construct power plants all over the world—from Bolivia to India to the Marianas Islands. Ed Buckham, DeLay's former congressional chief of staff who became a political director of ARMPAC, accompanied DeLay and his family on the trek to bring in the New Year, then set up the Alexander Strategies Group, the lobbying firm composed entirely of former DeLay staffers. Enron then contracted Buckham to lobby on "energy deregulation issues in the Marianas Islands." One can see how Enron officials believed that the fix was in.

When Buckham told DeLay in 1999 that a Japanese-U.S. consortium appeared to be winning the competition, DeLay wrote the Commonwealth Utilities Corporation demanding that the bidding be reopened. The so-called Congressman from Enron was laying claim to being de facto Congressman from Saipan. Equally untroubled by matters of jurisdiction, one of DeLay's far-right House allies, Helen Chenoweth-Hage of Idaho, wrote a letter threatening a federal investigation of the utilities company if it rejected the Enron bid. Officials on Saipan panicked; the legislature passed a bill that forced the utility to hand the business to Enron. Over the furious protests of Willie Tan's group, in May 2000 the utility's board voted 3-2 to award the contract to Enron. It gave the business of finalizing the contract language to Fulbright & Jaworski, a Houston mega-firm. The Mogul had come up against a power that was greater than his own. "There were all kinds of political pushes from the top and the side and every way," said a manager of the commonwealth's utilities company. "There were all kinds of political interference. [The government officials] didn't want to understand it." They said, "Just do it! Give Enron the contract."

One thing Enron executives never lacked was brass. In March 2001, the utilities company and Enron announced they had closed a deal for a scaled-down 60-megawatt plant. Just a month later Enron flabbergasted the islanders by breaking off the talks and announcing it had lost all interest in the Marianas project. Enron had kept its adventure in the Pacific afloat, knowing that it was sailing into those waters aboard the *Titanic*. In December of that year, Enron filed for the biggest corporate bankruptcy in American history. DeLay, who had frantically been trying to push through a bill that would have given Enron a $250 million tax rebate and some breathing room, told a TV reporter in Houston that he was "heartbroken." But, unlike Senator Kay Bailey Hutchison and other Texas Republicans, DeLay did not return one nickel of Enron contributions as a gesture to shareholders and employees. As long as he contained the political damage, it was no real skin off his back—nor those of his lobbyist pals Jack Abramoff, Mike Scanlon, and Ed Buckham. The Marianas are, of course, just a footnote in the Enron implosion saga. On Saipan today the lights still flicker. None of the bidders that had been shoved aside in the power play could be persuaded to come back to the table. Construction of the plant has been shelved indefinitely. On Saipan the episode is known as the Enron Fiasco.

In 1998, just four months after DeLay told the Mogul and other factory owners that that their shining example of unfettered capitalism was under attack by big labor and the radical left, the U.S. Department of Labor announced that three garment companies on Saipan had been charged with violating U.S. law. In all, the Department of Labor recovered $2.1 million in unpaid wages for 1,315 workers on Saipan that year. In 1999 the federal government obliged one of the companies to pay $987,000 in unpaid wages to 427 workers who had been compelled to work up to twelve weeks without pay. In 2000 that company and another pled guilty to criminal contempt and, though nobody went to jail, they were ordered to pay fines of $100,000. "The United States is serious about ending worker exploitation in the CNMI," said the Clinton administration's secretary of labor, Alexis M. Herman. "We will not hesitate to pursue criminal action in cases where companies disregard court orders."

In response to lawsuits seeking up to a billion dollars worth of damages for workers in the sweatshops, a spokesman for Tommy Hilfiger said: "The Company is proud of its monitoring program and has taken all reasonable efforts to ensure a proper work environment. . . . Currently, approximately two percent of Tommy Hilfiger production is allocated to Saipan. . . . If it should develop that any remedial action is required, then Tommy Hilfiger will play a leadership role in effecting any such actions." Wal-Mart issued a haughty claim that the company "does not conduct business with factories in Saipan. . . . We are continually working to educate our associates and vendors about our policies and our zero-tolerance position with regard to illegal or unethical working conditions." At the time of that claim, according to a well-respected investigatory report in the *Westchester County Weekly,* Wal-Mart had reportedly contracted with a garment factory called, appropriately, Mirage to act as its agent on Saipan. Top

clothing retailers continue to sell the blouses and tank tops sewn
by young Asian women in the Marianas and stamped for competitive advantage: "Made in the U.S.A." The wage in Saipan's garment factories is still $3.05 an hour.

One day in the spring of 2004 George Miller, the California
congressman, was reflecting on the Marianas. He said that im-
proved conditions in the factories have resulted from the election and policies of Governor Pedro Tenorio, not a change of
heart in Washington. "The other folks in the Marianas are doing
everything they can to get rid of him and regain the hold they
had. There's not going to be permanent change unless there's a
legislative fix, and . . . DeLay's not going to let that happen."

Like many House Democrats, Miller had an air of grudging
admiration when he spoke of the majority leader. "Last week in
California he made a speech to some bankers. He told them,
'We've got the House, we've got the Senate, and if we get another term in the White House, it's 'Katy, bar the door.'" Miller
shook his head and chuckled at the implications of that
metaphor. "It was hard to miss the echoes of him a few weeks
ago when President Bush proposed his guest worker program
from Mexico. Now, these workers are going to be committed to
a single employer, they have no rights, they can be fired at any
time. Where have we heard that before? Why, the Marianas Islands." Miller reflected on what he had seen on Saipan six years
earlier. "Those people were working as hard as they could possibly work. They could be fired at any moment, deported at any
moment. Because contracts were bogus some of them had been
made into outlaws, living in hiding. They came over there looking for better opportunity, and what they walked into was a
cesspool of human misery."

Another laugh without humor. "We're engaged in this race to
globalization, and we go the last mile, and at the finish line we
find Tom DeLay, making a virtue of slavery."

TWELVE

Remaking Texas . . .
and American Democracy

After the protracted 2000 presidential election was over, a member of George W. Bush's campaign remarked to the *New York Times* about the titanic struggle in Florida: "If you ever were or wanted to be a Republican, you were down there." DeLay responded to the emergency of the Bush-Gore deadlock in characteristic fashion. He sent around Capitol Hill an urgent call for staffers who could take vacation or temporary leave and, with all expenses paid by the Bush campaign, take to the streets in Miami-Dade County. Described in a few accounts as a mob, on November 26 protesters pushed aside security and shrieked, banged on doors, and whanged signs against interior windows at the Miami-Dade County election department, prompting officials to abort their recount. Gore workers alleged their candidate lost votes in that disorder and called the protesters "brown shirts." Identified as leaders of that demonstration and a subsequent one in Fort Lauderdale were a DeLay fundraising worker named Michael Murphey and Thomas Pyle, a policy analyst on DeLay's congressional staff.

Just a few months after the Supreme Court put the Florida recount out of its misery and handed the presidency to George W. Bush, Tom DeLay was driving around Austin with ARMPAC's political director, Jim Ellis. It was early 2001, and the two men were brainstorming. The president's hand had to be strengthened. What could they do to make the Texas congressional delegation as overwhelmingly Republican as they perceived the state to be?

In their Austin drive-around, according to Juliet Eilperin of the *Washington Post,* DeLay and Ellis came up with a daring plan: target a few linchpin races where Republican victories would enable the party to break the Democrats' lock on the Texas House of Representatives, help recruit the strongest possible candidates of far-right bent, and then pour in money and assistance just as ARMPAC had done in so many congressional races. Then the Legislature could push through a redistricting plan that would allow gerrymandering arithmetic to accomplish what the Republicans couldn't achieve in elections. Soon the Texas congressional delegation would include an appropriate majority of lockstep conservative Republicans (who would, among other virtues, show their gratitude in the event DeLay offered himself for Speaker).

DeLay's power had reached such heights that he would soon have the governor of Texas, the lieutenant governor, and both houses of the Legislature—the entire leadership of state government—performing for him like dancing bears. The pandemonium that he set off in Texas was the flip side of the old adage that all politics is local. By drawing the Texas map so that five to seven more seats would be handed to the GOP, in one brash swipe he meant to perpetuate a conservative GOP majority and agenda in the U.S. House until the roosters quit crowing and the sun stayed down. The return of pulling this off amounted to a right-wing wish list—placing more and more restrictions on abortion, drilling in the Arctic National Wildlife Refuge, eliminating the capital gains tax, all but putting the hated Environmental Protection Agency and Occupational Health and Safety Administration out of business. Katy, bar the door!

The biggest obstacle to this plan, DeLay and Ellis figured, was Pete Laney, the Speaker of the Texas House. Laney was a quiet and well-liked Democrat from a wind-raked farm town in the Panhandle. With a tuberous nose, piercing blue eyes, and a shrewd sense of humor, Laney had gotten along well with Bush when he was governor and in quantum ways had made Bush's life and work easier, and had stood beside Bush in the Texas Capitol and vouched for Bush's bipartisanship when the Supreme Court handed Bush his fiercely disputed presidency. After a national census such as the one in 2000, by law congressional districts have to be reapportioned. Under Laney's leadership, the Texas House had offered a plan in 2001 but couldn't agree to terms with the Senate. Despite DeLay's aversion to the federal judiciary, he thought Republicans stood a better chance of getting what the national party needed from a three-judge federal appeals panel than from trying to legislate a compromise with Democrats. The House redistricting committee passed a plan that had Laney's stamp of approval, but the State Senate, where Republicans had a majority, stalled and it never came up for a vote. The GOP maneuver backfired. Reportedly alarmed that a completely redrawn map might be challenged and make the state unable to hold the 2002 elections on schedule, the judges chose not to revise much of the Laney-backed plan. And it was a longstanding custom that the plans remain in place for a decade, until the next census. Except when compelled by suits involving the Voting Rights Act, state legislatures had initiated congressional redistricting in non-census years just once since the nineteenth century.

One of the few Texas legislators who was close to DeLay and had served with him during his three terms in the statehouse was a man from the hometown of Bush's youth, Midland. Tom Craddick was a salesman of the mud that is used to seal and lubricate the drilling of oil wells. Craddick had been shuttling between Midland and the Legislature since the sixties; he had once been known as a rebel and reformer who ganged up with liberal Democrats to oust a corrupt leadership team of conservative Democrats. For a long time he was a friend of Pete Laney. But since the late eighties, he had chaired the House Republican Conference.

Craddick longed to be Speaker, and as the years and sessions passed and each attempt to beat Laney failed, his ideological rhetoric sharpened, his narrow face and mouth grew more pinched, and not so many stories were told about his sense of humor. Craddick had other rivals, moderate Republicans, who also aspired to the Speakership. But DeLay believed that Craddick was the one Speaker candidate who could enforce discipline and push through the redistricting plan he wanted. Republicans on the right *had* to take control of the House, make Craddick Speaker, and put redistricting back on the legislative agenda—to hell with custom and the census.

Karl Rove was laying similar groundwork for his strategy in the midterm congressional elections of 2002. He was plotting legislative blitzkriegs designed to revive congressional redistricting and create additional GOP seats in Ohio and Colorado. A moderate Republican governor in Ohio and a state supreme court in Colorado foiled those maneuvers. That made success of DeLay's Texas intrigue more essential. Like many politicians, Bush believed loyalty was a primary measure of a person's strength of character; the president had plenty of reasons to be loyal to Pete Laney. But the cloak Bush had worn as governor of Texas camouflaged his own very conservative agenda and vision of the future. He had a hunger to win all fights, and he listened to and trusted Rove. Bush maintained a distance and looked the other way while Rove indulged his pleasure at tinkering with redistricting in Texas, and urged DeLay to help take Laney down.

It was a formidable alliance that went to the top of American conservatism and government. Still, Rove and Tom DeLay made strange bedfellows. One was a snob who lusted for the intellectual glamour of having a PhD but never completed the necessary work—the other a social climber who reckoned himself a champion of the common man. One condescended to and used the evangelical Christian right; the other claimed to personify it. One tried to frighten Republicans into staying on message, exactly as the messenger delivered it, on grounds that it was the gospel brought straight down from the president; the other was nobody's puppet and especially enjoyed aggravating Bush. But Rove and DeLay shared the mission of making the United States into a Republican nation. Theirs was a marriage of convenience, not love.

In September 2001 DeLay founded a new offshoot organization, Texans for a Republican Majority (TRMPAC—the acronym soon made its way into the political lexicon as *trimpack*). DeLay positioned himself as chairman of an "honorary" board, appointed Jim Ellis its director, and ordered Ellis to make sure their daring plan was carried through. To get things rolling, ARMPAC gave the new baby its first $50,000. Everything was to be modeled on the way ARMPAC raised money and jammed it into carefully selected congressional races, and TRMPAC's fundraisers went back to the same proven feed troughs. Forty-three percent of the contributions came from interests outside Texas that had no business pending with its State Legislature. Certain transactions seemed just bizarre. Why would the Barona Mission Indians and the Mississippi Choctaws give $6,000 to TRMPAC? Because longtime DeLay ally Jack Abramoff was the Choctaws' lobbyist, and he took credit for convincing DeLay, a few years earlier, that their casino revenue was not taxable. The largest contribution, $100,000, came from the Boston-based Alliance for Quality Nursing Home Care. Some claims were later made that a couple of Texas companies were part of the organization, but the middleman in that transaction was one Haley Barbour, the drawling old party warhorse who was then lobbying for the consortium of nursing home companies trying to block Medicare cuts (and, lending more evidence that in American politics all ambitions and reputations are redeemable short of the grave, was mounting a successful campaign for governor of Mississippi). Barbour had been quite thick with DeLay and ARMPAC. In Kansas City, Westar

Energy sent $25,000 to TRMPAC in hopes of securing "a place at the table," as one executive put it, at a House-Senate conference committee in Washington, not in Austin.

And so it went for TRMPAC through 2002. Bacardi USA, $20,000. Philip Morris Management Group, $25,000. Old Country Store, Inc., $25,000. Burlington Northern Santa Fe Railway, $25,000. Sears, Roebuck & Company, $25,000. Constellation Energy Group, $27,500. Diversified Collection Service, Inc.—a California company that helps the IRS collect taxes—$50,000. In a memo in September, a fundraiser named Susan Lilly recorded the breathless day she and Representative Beverly Woolley had spent drumming up support and bucks in Houston. Seven fifteen A.M. "Wheels down" at a Houston airport. Nine A.M. Moran Resources, 10 A.M. Vinson & Elkins (a mega-law firm)—in all, five appointments squeezed between traffic and a one-hour lunch break before the 4:15 "Wheels up" of the flight back to Austin. Handwritten notes around the itinerary reported "35K day + 25 Reliant"—that being a big energy firm. Sixty thousand dollars in one day's work was quite an impressive haul. Lilly's compressed notes expressed in varying specificity what the money-givers expected in return.

Hired to be TRMPAC's executive director was a Texas consultant and former employee of Karl Rove, John Colyandro. "He didn't raise a nickel personally," Colyandro said of DeLay. "But he gave us instant credibility." The director's subsequent claim that DeLay maintained an arm's-length relationship with TRMPAC would choke a shark. The claim that his board membership was only honorary might leave it to a jury to decide if DeLay had a legal obligation to know how the money was being spent, but he sat in on financial planning sessions. His daughter Dani Ferro was paid a reported $27,600 to organize fundraising events.

Ellis, Colyandro, and others identified twenty-one House districts and two Senate seats in Texas that they believed were in play. TRMPAC raised $1.55 million during the 2002 campaign cycle and spent almost all of it in those races. But help from TRMPAC was only part of the Republican largesse. Six donors, including TRMPAC and ARMPAC, reported contributions of $2.88 million, and on top of that, an organization called the Texas Association of Business (TAB), which made no bones about being a devoted patron of the Republican Party, poured $1.9 million into "issue ads" designed to help the chosen few. An average bump of $200,000 per candidate is a huge advantage in any race for the Texas Legislature. In fact that would more than cover the entire budgets of most races. These are elected officials who make $7,200 a year. By design they are part-time politicians.

Apart from the unprecedented money put into their coffers, the Republicans had some attractive candidates. They tended toward young spruced-up white guys with an ability to quote Scripture. They knew why they were being helped—they would deliver the House to their party, and then they would do what the party's honchos told them to do. Tom DeLay was one such honcho; Karl Rove was another. In mid-October Colyandro e-mailed TRMPAC's accountant that he should expect a check for $152,000 from a donor in San Antonio. Fourteen Republican candidates were to share that amount, and the accountant was told to send the checks to Tom Craddick at his office in Midland. The man who had the honchos' blessing as the next Speaker had the honor and responsibility of delivering those checks.

The Republicans had Bush in the White House and strength from the top to the bottom of the statewide ballot. Texans reelected Governor Rick Perry and sent a new Republican U.S. senator, John Cornyn, to Washington to succeed the retired Phil Gramm. Republicans held all twenty-seven statewide offices and dominated the State Senate. And by a margin of 88-62, at long last the Republicans controlled the Texas House of Representatives. In the postscripts and analysis of election night, it became a verity and commonplace that Texas no longer *had* a Democratic Party.

Eighteen of the twenty-one candidates backed by TRMPAC and five other big donors won in the legislative races. The triumph set off a frenzy of backslapping and claiming credit for the Republicans' grand day. The Texas Association of Business issued a boastful press release: "There was a unique opportunity to change the face of the legislature. . . . That is why at the close of the session in 2001, TAB devoted all its efforts to raising money to promote pro-business candidates in key House and Senate races." The head of the organization, a former GOP legislator, boasted that their efforts "blew the doors off" the 2002 election. Two days after votes were cast, Tom Craddick called a press conference. Everything was in place for him to oust Pete Laney. The invitation to the press conference and tacit kickoff of Tom Craddick's race for Speaker contained a line of small print at the bottom: "Paid for by Texans for a Republican Majority."

When Craddick walked into the lovefest, the winners broke into wild cheering and applause. Everything between Craddick's bifocals and nose and chin folded into the joy of his grin. Now that the prize was in his grasp, he moved quickly. The Speaker's race in the Texas Legislature is run and won behind closed doors, as it is in Congress. Craddick brushed aside the challenges of two moderate Republicans while offering choice committee assignments and chairmanships to black and Hispanic Democrats—who came to be called "the cross-dressers." Some saw the way it was going and believed, or at least rationalized, that they could help their constituencies by jumping off the sinking ship of Pete Laney. The old-style Democrat who had stood up for a beleaguered GOP president and fellow Texan made calls until he saw it was useless. Laney released his pledges; Craddick's ascendance was assured. The new Legislature convened in January 2003. On the first day Craddick was sworn in as Speaker of the House. Seated in the front row was the old friend who finally made Craddick's dream come true. That man now owned Tom Craddick, and his name was Tom DeLay.

For much of the session, talk of redistricting was downplayed. Governor Rick Perry dismissed it with a football metaphor: "It's like, 'Do you want to go run your wind sprints again?'" The new lieutenant governor, David Dewhurst, was working hard to transform his image from that of a street fighter who bought his elections with his personal wealth into a consensus builder with some bright ideas in his well-groomed head. Dewhurst grumbled that redistricting was a distraction from more pressing business of the Senate, likening it to "the flu." The new Republican attorney general, Greg Abbott, issued an opinion that spring that the congressional districts drawn by the three-judge panel in 2001 were valid. Even Craddick sounded pessimistic that they had enough time to get a redistricting bill through the chamber. But Tom DeLay was an alumnus of the Texas House, and there he had plenty of arms that he could twist.

Craddick set up his new domain to run like the House in Washington under DeLay and his allies. Old hands in the Capitol were startled by the open coordination of Craddick's team and the business lobby. Texas ranked forty-ninth among the states in social services, but the Republicans gutted the programs anyway. A quarter million kids lost health insurance that the federal government would have largely financed. During a committee hearing, a Houston representative named Debbie Riddle addressed the big picture. "Where did this idea come from that everybody deserves free education? Free medical care? Free whatever? It comes from Moscow. It comes from Russia. It comes straight from the pit of hell." This was the new brain trust of the Texas Legislature.

Except for the few Democrats who had decided to back Craddick for Speaker, the minority opposition was shut out of the legislative process. Pete Laney was banished by the leadership, bereft even of committee assignments. Democrats were not consulted on important bills—they weren't even informed. As the session wore on, the Democrats were increasingly dispirited and embittered.

Meanwhile, Jim Ellis shuttled in and out of Austin. Ellis kept DeLay meticulously informed of the progress being made by TRMPAC. Driven by DeLay like mules whipped by an old-time teamster, Republicans in the Legislature were pressured to eliminate white Democrats from the state's congressional delegation by giving them no place to run. Despite the blowout in the 2002 elections, Democrats had won 17 of 32 congressional elections in Texas. DeLay's gerrymandering strategy was risky, for it would alienate, energize, and bring fully out of the margins skillful young Hispanic and African-American legislators in the Democratic ranks. But Republicans were confident that if they drew the map right, there was little chance that John Ashcroft's Justice Department would rule that the plan violated the Voting Rights Act by diminishing minority voting strength, or that legal challenges would persuade a federal judiciary dominated by conservative Republicans. High on the Republican hit list were Austin's Lloyd Doggett, Dallas's Martin Frost, and Waco's Chet Edwards. Among conservative Republicans, Doggett was the most-hated Democrat on Capitol Hill. Sure of his Austin constituency, he was liberal and caustic and relentless in his lambasting of George W. Bush. Frost, an ex-television weathercaster, had been a ruthless player at gerrymandering when the Democrats had the upper hand. Edwards was troublesome because, even though his district grew more Republican without any help from redistricting, he kept winning. The Republicans also wanted to get rid of an East Texan named Max Sandlin and even Charlie Stenholm, a conservative west Texan who had been one of the most prominent Boll Weevils—Democrats who rallied to the economic policies and leadership of Ronald Reagan. Of course, if loyalty for past bipartisan service wasn't going to protect Pete Laney, it wasn't likely to reach far enough back to help Charlie Stenholm.

Confident that his lieutenants were pulling off the coup in Texas, DeLay continued to make his estimate of himself known in Washington. One night in early May, according to the *Washington Post,* DeLay was participating in a fundraiser at a Ruth's Chris Steak House. The majority leader was smoking a cigar. The restaurant manager came over and said the gentleman would have to put it out. The building was owned by the federal government; even in the private restaurant the federal no-smoking policy applied. DeLay was reported to have roared, "I *am* the federal government!" Sent along afterward to cover for the boss, a DeLay spokesman said the manager and the newspaper were mistaken—the congressman had just said that he was *with* the federal government.

On a more positive note for DeLay, a few days later the redistricting committee in Austin suddenly kicked out a bill and proposed map. To Democrats, this gerrymandering was over the top—an outrage and insult. Elliott Naishtat had migrated to Austin as a VISTA volunteer from Queens and had ridden Ann Richards's coattails into a liberal central Austin House seat in 1990. Naishtat was agog at what the Republicans were trying to do now. The state capital would be divided in three districts so that the GOP could get rid of Lloyd Doggett. Austin's ethnically diverse and environmentally sensitive south side would be handed to Lamar Smith, a Republican of nativist views who lives in San Antonio, 85 miles away. Austin was always being punished in the Legislature for its snooty airs and liberalism. But what to make of Lockhart? Southeast of Austin, the little town would also be cut in three congressional districts. "They want to split the high school off from its football stadium!" Naishtat cried.

Waco, a city that had remained entirely within a single congressional district for a century would be divided at the Brazos River. The purpose was to separate Chet Edwards from the black community's vote. Edwards was also to be cut off from the sprawling army base to the west of Waco. Fort Hood was the largest employer in the area, and Edwards was a member of the House Armed Services Committee. Willing to let that position of influence go to somebody in another state, the Republicans wanted to put Edwards in a stacked-deck race against a woman in the Texas House whose obsession was disparaging people who applied for the government's health and social service programs.

The redistricting plan voted out of the committee was hurtling toward passage like a runaway train. The Republicans weren't even going to hold public hearings. The only way to stop this, Democrats realized, was to run out the clock on the legislative session. If fifty-one of them left the state and stuck together, they could break the quorum and bring the House to a standstill—they could kill the redistricting bill. Someone observed that they had better pick a state with a Democratic governor who wouldn't heed pleas to have them arrested. Democratic Caucus chairman Jim Dunnam, a lawyer from Waco, had in-laws who often vacationed in Ardmore, Oklahoma. In this way a reasonably attractive small town that evoked the word *aardvark* became the destination of Democrats who gathered at an Embassy Suites Hotel in Austin the night of May 11.

"Eventually," wrote Naishtat (for a speech to Massachusetts Democrats that would be a bigger hit than an address delivered the same night by John Kerry), "we gathered in the hotel parking lot, loading baggage onto two chartered buses, visiting well-wishers, volunteers, and advisors, all sworn to secrecy, all there to help us make a clean escape. We wondered if DPS [Department of Public Safety] troopers would converge on us, try to detain or illegally arrest us, shoot out a tire or two. We'd done nothing wrong yet. The House was scheduled to convene at nine the next morning. We counted forty-seven and headed north. Three members would join us in the morning; a handful would hide out on their own. We ate fried chicken, fretted about whether the others would make it, and settled in to watch the movie *Catch Me If You Can*." (Several "cross-dressing" Democrats had not been told about the plan.)

However brief and futile, the revolt of the "Killer D's" was a national sensation. The House had adjourned for Mother's Day, and most Republicans had left Austin for the holiday. Craddick and his team were caught flat-footed the next morning. Seeing that the House had too few members to attain a quorum, he ordered a lockdown of the chamber. Nobody could leave. Capitol staff started hauling in cots where the captured House members could sleep. It was quickly noted, though, that most of the hostages were Republicans. Capitol staff quietly returned and hauled away the cots. Craddick banged his gavel and ordered the House to stand at ease. At a press conference reporters hooted and asked him where the Democrats had gone. What had become of the vaunted GOP intelligence? The best Craddick could do was sneer that the runaways were "Chicken D's."

Governor Perry went on TV with a lecture to these Democrats who were laying down on the job. "Come home," he said with a bit of a smile. In a less amiable moment he ordered troopers to find the fugitives, arrest them, and haul them back. The troopers barged in to the Capitol offices of the runaways and tried to browbeat staffers, warning them they could be prosecuted as felons for assisting fugitives. On reported orders of Perry, troopers harangued nurses in a neo-natal hospital ward in Galveston where a House member's wife had given birth to premature twins. The wife of a representative in El Paso learned by cell phone that troopers were inside her home, without a warrant, interrogating her seventeen-year-old daughter.

In the Ardmore Holiday Inn, the fugitives were hardly living it up. Following a short night's sleep they gathered in a small conference room with laptops and copies of bills that were still pending before the House. They knew it wouldn't be long before they were discovered, and to counter the GOP public relations onslaught they wanted to be able to prove they were working. One member from El Paso showed up in his wheelchair, raising their spirits greatly. Another from the Rio Grande Valley, who had a death in his family, sent word that he'd be sitting it out in

Matamoros, Mexico. The Democrats learned that their leader and hero, the banished Speaker Pete Laney, was on his way by air from the Panhandle. "We knew the DPS was going to be looking for us," Naishtat later said. "But we never dreamed that they'd put *federal* officers on our trail."

Tom DeLay was livid. A lawyer on his staff called the Justice Department to inquire if the FBI had the authority to arrest the Democrats. From Austin, DeLay got a report that a bunch of Democrats were aboard Pete Laney's plane. Laney's craft was a Piper turbo-prop; how many fugitives could there have been? But they didn't need to bring in all the runaways. A few Democrats—notably a flamboyant black entertainment lawyer from Houston named Ron Wilson—were on the Craddick team and had reported for the vote. One more Democrat on the floor would give Craddick his quorum. A caller from DeLay's office helpfully provided the Federal Aviation Administration with the tail number of Laney's plane, and a DPS investigator implied to the Department of Homeland Security that an "overdue" plane carrying state officials could have crashed or might even be victim of terrorists. A search was put out for the plane, which landed uneventfully in Ardmore and delivered Laney, who was traveling alone, to his admirers.

The Democrats knew the jig was up when they saw reporters in the hotel lobby the night after they arrived. They were approached by a nervous Texas state trooper who acknowledged he had no authority to arrest them—he asked if he could give any of them a ride back to Austin. Ever sure of himself, DeLay told the *Houston Chronicle* that calling in federal marshals or FBI agents to arrest the fugitives was justified because redistricting involved congressional seats, which made it a federal matter. Ardmore swarmed with national press. CNN's Judy Woodruff asked one legislator if he didn't feel "a little silly doing this." But the Killer D's stuck it out in Ardmore for four days. They forced Craddick to gavel the House session to a close without a vote on redistricting.

The episode was farcical, no doubt about it. But another CNN commentator, Bill Schneider, reported that "Texas authorities had followed up on DeLay's suggestion and asked the feds to help round up lawmakers on the lam." Even before the Democrats got back on their buses and came back across the Red River, state troopers in Austin were anxious about what they had done. One DPS official ordered all field notes, photos, and computer records of the manhunt destroyed. Investigations were also underway at the Federal Aviation Administration, Department of Homeland Security, and Department of Justice. In an internal Justice Department report, an official wrote that that DeLay's requests to call in the FBI had gone unheeded because they were, in a word, "wacko."

The flight of the Killer D's had been a small victory and, it appeared, a pyrrhic one. Governor Rick Perry at once called another thirty-day special session to get a redistricting bill passed. Democrats were catching all sorts of hell, especially on talk radio, for running off to Ardmore, but Republicans were besieged by newspaper editorials calling DeLay's crusade a mistake and travesty and waste of tax revenue. "The editorials are wrong," he replied from Capitol Hill.

Under intense pressure from the press and local political leaders, the Republicans this time consented to a brief schedule of public hearings around the state. In Houston Ron Wilson, the entertainment lawyer who had joined the Craddick team, impugned the motives of an erstwhile friend and fellow legislator, Garnet Coleman, by saying he made his money hacking for Democratic consultants. "I'm not the one who drove here in a Lamberghini!" Coleman shouted.

The June 29 hearing in the border city of Brownsville was the most rambunctious. Richard Raymond, a handsome and pugnacious Democrat from Laredo, had been ordered to the west

Texas town of Lubbock, far from his Hispanic constituency on the border. He went to the hearing in the Rio Grande Valley anyway. A group of Hispanic veterans affiliated with the civil rights organization the GI Forum (which is generally Democratic) came down from the coast from Corpus Christi to have their say. One of the GOP legislators did not show up; Raymond and the other Democrats quickly staged a press conference, saying once more the Republicans had failed to produce a quorum.

The chairman, a Methodist minister named Joe Crabb, decided to convene it anyway. The other Republican, Mike Krusee, represented the conservative suburbs that had grown around Austin's north side. According to a Corpus Christi writer named Susan Reeves, who showed up with the veterans, the GOP legislators were promptly shouted down. They scuttled behind a curtain at the rear of the hall on the University of Texas–Brownsville campus. Krusee was shouting in a cell phone, "Get me the Governor! I need to speak to the Governor immediately!"

They tried again with Krusee growing angry and agitated. A veteran of some years came to the microphone and started addressing the crowd. Krusee told him to be quiet or sit down. A uniformed campus cop, who apparently feared the situation might get out of hand, approached the old vet warily. A woman with the Corpus Christi group started shouting, "Are you going to arrest a veteran, Representative Crabb?"

It got wilder. Krusee rebuked a campus cop for not maintaining order. The veterans started singing "God Bless America," and the portly preacher sang along. The crowd was chanting "*Sí, se puede*" — (yes, we can, roughly translated). Another vet approached the mike. Ordered to state his name, address, and Social Security number, the man refused. Susan Reeves was hardly a detached reporter, but she had a vivid prose style. She wrote that Krusee "glared at the person in the sound booth in the back of the auditorium, and drew his hand across his neck in a slashing motion, telling the sound man to turn off the microphone." Krusee called it a day, but Crabb and the old vets stayed on, singing more "God Bless America."

Bedlam reigned in a committee room of the Capitol in Austin five nights later. Everywhere one looked, redistricting protesters wore lapel pins inspired by an international traffic symbol: against a white background, enclosed in a circle with a diagonal red slash of negation, was the name *DeLay*. In Congress and within the administration in Washington, Republicans believed that DeLay was engaged in an act of courage and heroism. But to Texas Democrats, he was the unseen ogre, the man they loved to hate. If DeLay had walked in the room that night he would have needed bodyguards.

The Austin hearing on a new map drawn by Weatherford Representative Phil King—in whose office TRMPAC's Jim Ellis had set up his advisory shop that spring—was supposed to have begun that afternoon. A few minutes after two, Crabb had gaveled the hearing to order and brusquely announced that King needed "several more hours" to finish drawing his map. "The committee will stand adjourned until seven P.M.," announced Crabb. "We will take testimony then."

A member of the committee, Ruth McLendon, a black Democrat from San Antonio, stared at Crabb then gestured toward the crowd. "Mr. Chairman, these people are going to have to wait *five hours* before they can testify?"

At that point the yelling had begun.

"I had to take off work for this!" someone cried.

"The democratic process is being overruled!" shouted another.

Richard Raymond was a son of the same brush country that had given the world Tom DeLay. Raymond's great-grandfather was well-remembered as a *patrón* of politics in Webb County and Laredo. As a youth Raymond had worked for several Texas Democratic politicians, among them U.S. Senator Lloyd Bentsen, and on the Washington staff of his hero, Illinois Senator Paul Simon. Raymond was first elected as a state rep from Pharr County, lost a statewide race for land commissioner to the

enormously funded David Dewhurst, then moved with his family to Laredo and got elected to the Legislature again. In the interest of making a living, he was laboring through his first year
of law school at the University of Texas, but his seat on the redistricting committee had thrust him in the spotlight—he
would sure find the time. In Webb County the Democrats still
carried elections by eighty and ninety percent. The chaparral
that DeLay roamed as a boy outside Mirando City was the only
terrain left in the state where the Democrats could stage a real
comeback. Raymond might not be the future of the Texas Democratic Party, but someone like him was.

Raymond's nemesis on the committee was Krusee, who was
known to think of himself as a logical choice to succeed Tom
Craddick as Speaker. Krusee had to be feeling somewhat
bruised by redistricting. He had offered to carry the bill, only to
be vilified at the hearing in Brownsville, and now he was looking
at another surly crowd and the prospect of staying up all night.
Because they all had orders from DeLay? What was he getting
out of it?

Joe Crabb yielded to the sheer press of bodies and announced
that the hearing would move into a room that had the seating
and dimensions of a movie theater. More jeers and grumbles,
now mixed with cheers. Finally, the crowd speckled with slash-
DeLay lapel pins got its Austin hearing. Phil King, a mustachioed
GOP representative from Weatherford, near Fort Worth, had a
calm and soothing demeanor, and he was called on first by
Crabb. King explained the intricacies of the plan and concessions to public concerns; the scheme would, he claimed, increase
representation by blacks and Hispanics in the Texas delegation.
But when San Antonio's Mike Villareal (projected by some Democrats as another star of the future) asked King to spell out the
political purpose of the map, King left a brief pause and sighed.
"The purpose was simply to seek a few more Republican congressional seats in Washington and to better hold on to a Republican majority and help President Bush in his endeavors."

Boos resounded throughout the hall. King smiled and gave them a nod. "We have a few Democrats in the audience."

Raymond rolled his shoulders and leaned into his mike. "Mr. King, I appreciate your honesty. My concern is that you are trying to do this at the expense of people who've worked real, real hard to have voting rights, too." The crowd roared its approval. In the ensuing exchange King raised his voice once: "It's just my map! You can draw one, too!" Everyone on the committee was in for a long night—which went on until five the next morning.

Krusee, who looked grim and testy, was seated between Raymond and King. Raymond kept going back to the contretemps with the GI Forum and the veteran who had been asked for his Social Security number. Krusee, who had begun to turn red, raised his hand at Crabb and glared past Raymond. "My recollection of Brownsville," he complimented the chairman, "was that you were doing everything you could to solicit and invite input from the public, and that the intimidation I saw was from Democrats and the Democratic Party."

"Let me respond to that, Mr. Chairman," said Raymond. "I was there, too. Those who were opposed were World War II and Korean veterans. None of them threatened anybody in any way. But I guess Mr. Krusee was a little uncomfortable listening to Hispanic veterans standing up for their rights and protesting a process that was flawed and illegal. But I can assure you, Mr. Krusee, that there was nothing to be *scared of*. They were just standing up for their voting rights, that's all. If I or some World War II veterans frightened you, I apologize."

Several people in the audience laughed aloud at the taunt. Smoke was all but blowing out of Krusee's ears. As Raymond and Krusee continued to rag each other, Crabb watched them with the dismay he would have shown if a schoolboy fist fight had broken out on his congregation's lawn. "Gentlemen, gentlemen!" he begged them to behave.

Civility in Texas politics had completely broken down. Governor Perry called a third special session, and finally a bill cleared the House. The Senate, which has thirty members, had a reputation of being convivial and clubby. The Democrats had been beaten down to eleven Senate seats, but if they stuck together—and a procedural rule that had never been suspended was observed—they could stop redistricting. The rule held that for any bill to be referred to the floor for a vote, it had to have support of a two-thirds majority. (Once that happened, in most cases a simple majority ensured the bill's passage.) But the two-thirds agreement was a rule, not a law. And it was enforced at the discretion of the Republican lieutenant governor, David Dewhurst. In his rookie session, Dewhurst was the surprise star of the Legislature. Tall and handsome, well dressed and manicured, he liked to show off his skill roping calves from a sprinting quarter horse. Dewhurst was hugely ambitious and rich. Members of his staff spoke dreamily of a future Dewhurst presidency. But it was a delicate moment for him now. He knew he risked squandering his fast start if he threw out the two-thirds rule.

A much-respected GOP senator from east Texas named Bill Ratliff had strong opinions about the responsibilities of the lieutenant governor. Ratliff, in fact, had served as interim lieutenant governor when the position was vacated by the elected lieutenant governor who took the place of departing governor George W. Bush. Ratliff held that Dewhurst would damage government in Texas for more than just a legislative session if he changed that gentlemen's rule to get a redistricting bill. Dewhurst was none too pleased that the old man preached at him in public. One day Karl Rove called Ratliff from the White House to chat. Rove carefully avoided trying to pin him down on a vote, but mentioned that passage "could be important to the President." In the end Ratliff didn't toe the GOP line—but he also didn't stand with the Democrats, who were eager to cast him as their principled ally and rescuer. Ratliff announced by the end of the year that he was burned out and it was time for him to retire.

The pressure applied by influential right-wing ideologue Grover Norquist was not as subtle as Rove's. "The whole world is watching," he said of Dewhurst in the *New York Times,* one week after the raucous hearings in Texas. "He can't possibly screw up." The *Denver Post* quoted Norquist as calling bipartisanship "another name for date rape," and in that story Norquist laid out the big picture: in the new American order moderate Democrats would simply disappear. "They will go so that no Texan need grow up thinking that being a Democrat is acceptable behavior." What radical Republicans seemed to envision was a political system for the nation, not just Texas, that resembled one sustained in Mexico for seventy years under the PRI, the Partido Revolucionario Institucional. There could be opposition parties, but the party claiming the ideological mantle of the revolution would be an oligarchy that nominated champions who won every major election. Norquist would later elaborate in the *New Yorker.* The goal of Republicans was to put to lasting rout the twentieth century's accumulation of trial lawyers, labor unions, and educators hung up on the idea that only public schools could receive government support. "When that happens," Norquist said, "the Democratic Party will have ceased to be the economic statist party. They can be the weird-sex party, they can be the tree-hugger party, they can be the secularists-against-the-religious-zealots party. There are a lot of different things they can be." Norquist fancied himself a witty fellow.

If that weren't enough pressure, Bush's longtime speechwriter and confidante Karen Hughes paid Dewhurst a friendly visit the morning before he decided to suspend the two-thirds rule. Whatever tipped the scales, the lieutenant governor found a rationale for throwing out the two-thirds rule so that a bright up-and-comer such as himself could give the party's heavy-hitters in Washington what they wanted.

He was a step behind the Democrats in the Senate, who had already fled the state to Albuquerque, New Mexico, before Dewhurst had made his intentions known. By running out again, the Democrats gave Dewhurst a shove in the wrong direction. Governor Perry set his jaw and resolved to wait the senators out. The Albuquerque Eleven were cut off from their homes, their families, and in most cases, their jobs. And by then the national media had found a story that was sexier than Texas redistricting— Arnold Schwarzenegger's campaign for governor in California. The Texas senators took turns strolling out to the camera pool and answering questions from reporters who were as bored as they were. They were living in motel rooms and going broke.

TRMPAC's Jim Ellis told DeLay in an August memo that it was good the Democrats had marooned themselves in New Mexico; the GOP troops in Austin had worked out a plan that should deflect any challenge based on the Voting Rights Act. Still, Ellis wanted to make sure the plan was entirely clear: "We must stress that a map that returns Frost, Edwards, and Doggett is unacceptable and not worth all the time invested into this project."

Spoken more in bars than in churches, a prayer went around Austin: "God, please bless Tom DeLay and Rick Perry, for they have done what we could not do. They have united the Texas Democratic Party." But it had been spring when redistricting started forcing aside all other business of the Legislature; now it was heat-stricken summer. In September, Senator John Whitmire of Houston—who had hung out with DeLay in the hard-partying days of Macho Manor—flew home without informing his Democratic colleagues. The Republicans had their quorum; the war of attrition was over. Punished in the polls, savaged on talk radio, the weary losers straggled back to their hometowns. A short senator of imperial airs who lately wore his head shaved, Whitmire claimed he was still a loyal Democrat: "We just didn't have an exit strategy."

Having lost the war, Democrats watched in delight as the victors fell snarling, snapping, and yelping over the spoils. Final resolution got so hung up in a fight between west Texas Republicans that Perry was just days away from having to call another special session, which would prolong the agony into the Thanksgiving and Christmas seasons and force rescheduling of spring primaries in a presidential year. Craddick insisted on creating a new district around Midland that would be tailored for K. Michael Conaway, an old friend and oil patch business partner of President Bush. Based on equal division of population as set by the Census, every district must meet the fundamental legal requirement of one-person, one-vote. And every jiggle of district boundary lines sets off a clatter of dominoes in others. "We're fighting over Deaf Smith County," said one Republican negotiator, "a place most people couldn't find with a map."

Recognizing that his master plan might come to nothing, Tom DeLay hurried to Austin, and in the pink granite State House, where he had once been ridiculed, he set about proving who ran this joint now. As he shuttled between meetings with the leadership teams of Craddick, Dewhurst, and Perry, reporters could never get close to him. An aide of one House Democrat looked across an atrium and saw DeLay wearing a dark blue suit, rocking thoughtfully in the office chair of a Republican member. He must have felt her gaze. DeLay looked around at the window and smiled at her briefly, then blinds dropped so hard they bounced and snapped shut.

DeLay's friend Tom Craddick won the dispute. Midland got a new district customized for the pal of the president while Democratic and GOP incumbents in west Texas had to run against each other. The last few days DeLay hovered in the map room, reviewing every tweak. In a subsequent deposition Phil King said that DeLay told the legislators to forget one nudge of the lines of his district—it would take away too much of his base. Was it seemly for DeLay to personally design a district in which he would seek election? Was it *ethical?*

Rick Perry signed the redistricting bill into law in October 2003. A week later DeLay downplayed his role at one of his tightly controlled press briefings on Capitol Hill. "I am a

Texan," he said of his redistricting victory. "It's a process that af-
fects Texas. I am also a leader in the House, and the Republican
Conference's point of view, I felt strongly, should be represented. It's an open process, and I have every right as a citizen
of the United States to participate in the process."

He had subjected government in Texas to seven months of
acrimony and gridlock, and the bill for the special sessions was
passed on to tax rolls in the amount of about $5 million. As
Christmas approached, the battleground in Austin shifted from
the Capitol to a nearby federal courtroom. Before a three-judge
panel, several organizations had joined in a suit to have the congressional districts thrown out on grounds they violated the
Voting Rights Act. During the trial reporters learned one day
that DeLay was in town raising money for his perpetual revolution at a closed affair in the Stephen F. Austin Hotel. Security
officers wouldn't allow the reporters near the stairs to the chan-
deliered room downtown, but they milled in the lobby, craning
their necks and joking. This time they thought they had him
cornered. He would have to run their gauntlet as they hammered him with questions. But once more, DeLay was ahead of
the game. He shook hands and basked in the adulation and gratitude of GOP donors and raked in the dough. Then his heels
rang and his short legs pumped as he and aides jogged down a
fire escape and gave those clowns the slip.

Greg Abbott, the Republican attorney general in his first term,
is a handsome and friendly man in a wheelchair; a tree had broken, fallen, and paralyzed his legs when he lived in Houston. He
attended the trial just one day. To argue the case he hired a high-
priced trial lawyer named Andy Taylor—the attorney of choice
in partisan matters of Texas Republicans. Taylor had a pronounced widow's peak and a way of smiling that involved no
parts of his face but his mouth. The large team of plaintiffs'

lawyers put on a lively show of Texas Democratic congressmen, prominent state representatives, and an expert on redistricting from Harvard. They projected on the wall a copy of the e-mail in which TRMPAC's Jim Ellis wrote bluntly to his boss Tom De-Lay that all of this had not been worth the cost and effort if they did not eliminate three particular congressmen: Lloyd Doggett, Martin Frost, and Chet Edwards. Taylor listened to the witnesses say terrible things about the Republicans' motives and character then dismissed one after another without cross-examination. Taylor knew this case was a slam-dunk. All he had to do, at least for these judges, was cast doubt on the premise that Republicans discriminated against blacks or Hispanics in order to accomplish their partisan aims.

Most of the Democratic congressmen called to testify observed the trial for no more than half a day. One, the east Texan Max Sandlin, had started out in politics as a lower court judge. He wore his hair in a lightly oiled modified crew cut that he brushed straight back from his forehead. His attire was a dark suit, white shirt, tie, and a polished pair of black cowboy boots. Sandlin perched alertly on a pew-style bench in the back of the courtroom and watched and listened with his chin raised slightly, often sitting with his legs crossed, jiggling the toe of one boot. Sandlin was a moderate conservative who had always run well among rural and small-town blacks. In the language of redistricting and the Voting Rights Act, his political domain was known as a "minority interest district." That meant blacks in that locale did not have enough population to overcome historic resistance of Southern whites and elect a black to Congress; a politician like Sandlin campaigned for their support to build his coalition, hired them on his staff, and professed to represent their interests. Sandlin would run again no matter what happened in this trial, but in this plan drawn by DeLay he would have to balance the interests of the rural and small-town communities that were his base against the competing interests of much more populous suburbs of Dallas, which were strongly

Republican, and where he was unknown. He was exactly the kind of white Southern Democrat who, according to DeLay, Karl Rove, and Grover Norquist, had to go.

As the trial neared its close, Andy Taylor's star witness was Ron Wilson, the black entertainment lawyer and Democratic state representative from Houston. Wilson was jaunty and wealthy and at fifty worked hard to project an air of street cool. He had been in the Legislature since 1976 and claimed among his mentors the Democratic hero Barbara Jordan, but he had always delighted in being a pain in the ass of people he considered party hacks. In accepting the courtship of Tom Craddick and turning his back on Pete Laney, Wilson had won key committee assignments and an important chairmanship. Wilson did not go to Ardmore, and he supported this map drawn by Republicans, he said, because it would send an additional Houston black to Congress. Taylor asked Wilson what he thought of representatives of minority-influence districts. Wilson gave a snort of contempt. "I call them step and fetchits. . . . My opinion is there is no influence."

Max Sandlin bristled.

Taylor passed the witness to a plaintiff's lawyer, who pressed Wilson on the worth to the black communities of congressmen such as Sandlin, whose voting records were ranked highly by the measure of the NAACP. "A *deathbed* conversion," Wilson sneered. "'We're all for minorities now!'" All that those Democrats had ever done for African-Americans was keep them saying, "Please! Please! Please!" Wilson snapped his long fingers theatrically, so nobody would miss his allusion to soul singer James Brown.

Gary Bledsoe, an attorney for the NAACP, next asked Wilson what in the world he thought blacks would receive from Tom DeLay. Wilson snorted about the people Tom DeLay represented in Fort Bend County: "Have you *seen* his constituents?" He was saying that realpolitik was the only option blacks had in dealing with someone like DeLay (whose suburban white constituents Wilson had just characterized as freaks). Bledsoe asked again: what did Wilson think African-Americans were going to *get* from DeLay now that he had the power to impose a plan like this?

As much as they'd ever gotten from white Democrats, Wilson shot back—and good riddance to white Democrats. "Next election, Martin Frost will be running around in *blackface* trying to get votes."

He was branding all white Democrats as racists, hypocrites, and whores. In the back of the room the ex-judge Max Sandlin spoke out with more volume than he realized: "Throw him off the stand!"

A hush descended on the courtroom as everyone absorbed the weight of Wilson's cynical outburst. Andy Taylor and his team of assistants had the case won, but they looked as stunned and melancholy in their triumph as the plaintiff's lawyers and Democratic partisans at the other table. In Texas this was what Tom DeLay's politics had come to, and there was an inescapable word for it:

Poison.

Apocalypse Now

Unlike the president, a member of Congress, even one of its leaders, can fly below the national media radar. Which is what Tom DeLay did when he flew into San Antonio in November 2002. DeLay traveled 200 miles from his suburban Houston district to pay a visit to John Hagee's Cornerstone Church. Pastor Hagee is a long way from the mainstream—even by Texas standards. And Cornerstone Church is not your grandfather's Christian church. Rev. Hagee reaches out to the world from a 5,000-seat sanctuary situated in a 50,000-square-foot media complex in the suburbs of San Antonio. Broadcast over 115 television stations and 110 radio stations, his fiery sermons are sometimes complemented by guest homilies of such luminaries of the American right as Ollie North. Politicians flock to Cornerstone to ask Hagee's blessing and sign on to his foreign policy agenda. A select few, like DeLay, are invited to address the congregation.

John Hagee is a Lion of Zion—even if he is more porcine than leonine. He's a Christian Zionist and a premillennial dispensationalist doing all he can to bring on the biblical prophecies that are a prelude to the Second Coming of Christ. There are a few rough detours on the Christian Zionist road to salvation, such as the disappearance of all but 144,000 of the world's Jews and a fierce and final conflagration that will take place on a plain near Armageddon.

Premillennial dispensationalism is not native to America. It is the theological elaboration of John Nelson Darby, an Irish

Anglican minister who left the church in the 1820s and founded his own sect. Darby developed a theology obsessed with eschatology—or "end times." The apostate Anglican divided all of human history into seven dispensations or epochs—based on his literal reading of certain biblical texts. Each dispensation ends when mankind becomes so sinful that God's punishment is required to set things right. According to Darby's eschatological calendar, mankind is nearing the end of the penultimate dispensation. The next and final dispensation will be the 1,000 years of peace that follow Christ's defeat of the Anti-Christ and Satan at Armageddon. So we are living in the *pre*millennial dispensation. Texas fiddle virtuoso Erik Hokkanen wrote "It Ain't Over Till It's Over," echoing Yogi Berra. According to Darby's disciples, it's about to be over. Soon—even if the millennial Y2K clock was off a few years or decades—we will enter the final dispensation: Anti-Christ, Christ, Satan, Armageddon, Tribulation, Second Coming, Epoch of Grace, and all that.

Darby's theology is as elaborate as it is fantastic. (Some might even say unbelievable.) It long ago played itself out in the secular societies of Europe, where primitive Christianity doesn't sell like it does in the U.S. But after a vigorous start in the fertile soil of Texas, it took root in the United States. (The home state of the Branch Davidians and Baylor University always has been fertile ground for peculiar religious hybrids. The best-selling *Scofield Reference Bible,* written by the Dallas Theological Seminary's Cyrus Scofield in 1909, became the guidebook for many American fundamentalists.) Christ defeating the Anti-Christ, whom many Christian Zionists believe will be an apostate Jew leading an army to defeat on the Plain of Armageddon, is not the sole prerequisite prophecy of the Second Coming. Christ will also defeat Satan at Armageddon. The "in-gathering of the Jews" in Israel and the unification of the biblical kingdoms of Judea and Samaria is another. As is the rebuilding of the Third Temple in Jerusalem. The Rapture—that is, saved Christians physically ascending into Heaven at one given moment—is another. There's also the conversion to Christianity of 12,000 Jews from each of the Twelve Tribes of Israel, whom prophecy promises will survive Armageddon. (Presumably because fundamentalist Christians, who oppose the corrupting influence of higher education, will require dentists, doctors, bankers, lawyers, and stockbrokers to make civil society work.) The solution for the unfortunate Jews who don't make the cut, and others who have not accepted Christ as their personal savior, is, well, final.

Dispensationalists saw the creation of the State of Israel in 1948 as a sign that the "end times" Darby promised had finally arrived. The Jews' return to Israel surely would be followed by their occupation of Judea and Samaria, despite the best-laid plans of Lord Balfour and President Truman. Israel's political control of Jerusalem after the 1967 war was another prophetic event. As Billy Graham's fundamentalist father-in-law wrote at the time in his magazine *Christianity Today:* "for the first time in 2,000 years Jerusalem is now completely in the hands of the Jews." That's important because only Jews can rebuild on the spot where Solomon built and Herod rebuilt the Temple that, until it was razed nineteen centuries ago, was the geographic and spiritual center of Judaism. And Christ cannot return until the Temple is rebuilt for a third time.

But a 21st-century foreign policy based on a 19th-century literal interpretation of the beliefs of nomadic Semites living in the Middle East 3,500 years past can be a hard sell. As political entities, Judea and Samaria no longer exist—except in historical memory. If they did they would lie within the boundaries of the land President Bush (and Carter and Clinton before him) mapped out as a Palestinian homeland. There are United Nations resolutions and international law that define territorial boundaries. Three and a half million Palestinians live in modern-day Judea and Samaria. The land on which the Third Temple would be built is occupied by the Al-Aqsa Mosque—one of the three holiest sites in Islam. In brief, a Christian Zionist foreign policy requires an Israel that extends across the Jordan River and perhaps to the Euphrates, the destruction of the Al-Aqsa Mosque, the violation of international law, and the expulsion of the Palestinians from the land on which they now live.

Even if any of this made sense, it would be difficult to achieve. Yet when he shared the Cornerstone Church pulpit with Pastor John Hagee, the then majority whip of the House of Representatives stood cheek to jowly-jowl with a Christian Zionist praying and working to make it happen. When he spoke to Hagee's congregation, the congressman made it clear that he, too, is working to make it happen. And as majority leader of the House of Representatives, Tom DeLay is in possession of something John Hagee, Pat Robertson, and a score of lesser-known revivalists who folded up their tents and moved onto the public airways do not have: constitutional political power.

Hanging on the wall in Tom DeLay's Capitol office, along with a pair of marble tablets with the Ten Commandments chiseled into them, is a plaque that bears five words: "This Could Be The Day."

The Day is that day in biblical prophecy when things fall apart in Megiddo—today a crumbling architectural ruin known in the Book of Revelation as Armageddon. Tom DeLay knew better than to preach to the 5,000 congregants who turned out for Cornerstone's "Twenty-second Annual Night to Honor Israel." DeLay is an adequate speaker. John Hagee is a latter-day Savonarola. DeLay left the preaching to Rev. Hagee.

And preach Rev. John Hagee did.

For an hour he blustered and thundered his way from Old Covenant to New then back to Old. The sermon Hagee delivered on this Night to Honor Israel was rooted in the Old Testament, and it began and ended with Israel. Or, as Hagee mouths it: *Ishrul. Ishrul* and God's covenant with Abraham, Isaac, and Jacob.

John Hagee is a big, physically imposing man. Dressed in a bright blue suit with a brighter blue tie to match the blue gowns of the choir behind him, he's the televangelist from central casting. He reminds the congregation that they've heard him speak "from this platform to this nation and the nations around the world." He tells them they're being watched by 210 million households in the U.S. tonight. (That would be roughly 80 percent of the U.S. population.) He tells them they'll be on the air in *Ishrul* and in all the Holy Land. He runs through the list of religious networks that are broadcasting the event. He mentions the twenty-six satellites transmitting his message around the world. It requires a stout body to bear this preacher's hubris.

Hagee's sanctuary could easily be the new home of the Grand Ole Opry. It's not so much a church as a huge soundstage. No stained glass. No choir loft. No organ. No hardwood pews. Enter the semi-circular sanctuary through any of the twelve doors and you are looking at a huge elevated stage where you would expect to see an altar. There are risers for the two hundred singers in the choir. An orchestra pit for the eighteen members of the band. A large Plexiglas lectern for the pastor. On the walls not a single religious icon.

Within his sanctuary, John Hagee always preaches to the converted. Tonight, fronting a band and full choir, he's smokin'. The sanctuary is filled up to a few scattered empty seats in the balcony. The congregation, except for a delegation of Jews from Houston and San Antonio, accepts Christ as its savior and Israel, Judea, and Samaria as land God gave to "the Jewish people for ever and ever and ever and ever." To make sure everyone's clear on that point, Hagee defines forever: "For ever is for ever! The Jewish people have the Bible mandate to possess and build in the land of Ishrul. Forever. Including Judea and Samaria: the media's West Bank."

The congregation stands and applauds like members of Congress responding to applause lines in a State of the Union Address. They applaud when Pastor Hagee says "God's foreign policy" is laid down in Psalm 89, where David declares that God's covenant with Jacob conveying Israel to the Jews will endure as long the sun and the moon remain a faithful witness in the sky. They applaud when he tells them the Palestinians—or *Palesteenians*—never ruled any part of Israel. And never will. They applaud when he says Jerusalem is not up for negotiation. And never will be. They applaud when he says, "the Bible is an aggressive book." And they rise and applaud on cue when he says, "Christians of America, will you let Israel and the nations of the world hear your response tonight?"

But the congregation reserves its longest and loudest demonstration of support for their pastor's promise of war in Iraq, when John Hagee looks into the eye of television camera and says: "So listen up Saddam, because we're being seen in your country tonight. You can sleep in a different bed every night trying to escape the judgment you so richly deserve. It's not going to help you. There's a Texan in the White House. And he is going to take you down!"

It's not common to see a large number of Jews in the working-class congregation at Cornerstone Church. But the Night to Honor Israel is promoted in some synagogues and the secular pro-Israel community. A rabbi from San Antonio opens the service. The newly appointed consul general of Israel from Houston makes her remarks. Hagee has done a good job selling John Hagee to the Jewish community. He's filled pamphlets, speeches, and sermons with the small details of his own Hageeography—such as an account of the emotional moment in 1948 when he and his father sat weeping for joy at the family kitchen table, listening to a radio news reporter's account of Truman's recognition of Israel. Hagee is a fierce opponent of all forms of anti-Semitism. And he cuts Jews in on Christian salvation. His theology includes a loophole for Jews, or to borrow a phrase from Liberation Theology, "a preferential option" for the Jews. Unlike his dispensationalist brethren, Hagee allows that

Jews can be saved from eternal damnation because they're covered by the First Covenant between God and his people. They get into Heaven by what might be called a grandfather clause. So Jews might feel comfortable, even if not at home, at Cornerstone Church. It also helps that Hagee is tonight contributing $1.5 million to the United Jewish Communities to fund Jews emigrating from the former Soviet Union to Israel. And it also is noteworthy that Hagee is much friendlier to Jews when they are visiting his sanctuary. Two years after sharing the pulpit with DeLay, he told his congregation: "God only hears your prayers when you pray to Jesus Christ." Something of a corollary to the claim of Texas Baptist Preacher A. E. Criswell, who famously proclaimed: "God doesn't hear the prayers of a Jew." It's a canonical position that is endemic among Texas Christians.

Benjamin Netanyahu is also on the marquee for his second consecutive Night to Honor Israel at Cornerstone Church. But events of the Intifada require his presence in Israel. So the congregation watches a video of the speech he gave here the previous year, followed by a live satellite feed of a brief, sober message delivered from his office. Tom DeLay lacks Netanyahu's eloquence, authority, baritone, and tall-and-tan good looks. And DeLay is an unremarkable public speaker. When Hagee introduces the congressman, he begins tentatively, almost conversationally. "Pastor Hagee said everything I was going to say," DeLay says. "If he didn't, Netanyahu did. So I think I'll just sit down." He takes a stab at a joke about how difficult it is to follow "animal acts or Pastor Hagee." He says he's never been to Cornerstone before but "gets the tapes." And he starts into a pedestrian delivery of his Israel stump speech.

DeLay never achieves Hagee's rhetorical force (few people do), but by the time he hits his stride, he is as good as Tom DeLay gets. The speech is a straight-ahead run at Yassir Arafat. It's a celebration of George W. Bush's "moral clarity." It's an attack on Bush critics who remain "mired in the intellectual swamp of moral equivalence." It's a denunciation of the Oslo Peace Accords that Bill Clinton extracted from Arafat and former Israeli Prime Minister Ehud Barak. It is a radical redrawing of the tortured lines that divide Israel from Syria and the West Bank. And it's an argument for the expansion of Israel into the territory defined by God's covenant. "I've stood on the Golan. When I looked to the southwest, I don't see occupied territory. I see Israel. I've walked on the streets of Jerusalem. I've been to Judea and Samaria."

All of this is a carefully coded argument for an Israeli negotiating position that requires no negotiation. At least no negotiation that would involve returning any land or removing any settlements—legal or illegal—from the West Bank. Nor does it allow for a Palestinian state. At least not for a generation of two. DeLay tells the congregation he has dedicated himself to the support of Israel because he is a Christian and an American. He solemnly promises that as long as he is in the House leadership, he will use every tool at his disposal to ensure that the House of Representatives continues to preserve and insure the American alliance with the nation of Israel.

Then he looks up from his prepared text and makes a statement so bold and outrageous that he himself seems surprised to have said it:

"Ladies and gentlemen. What has been spoken here tonight is the truth from God."

From his office in Washington, D.C., Rabbi David Saperstein has watched the Christian Zionist courtship of Israeli and American Jews, and what he sees concerns him. Saperstein is executive director of the Religious Action Center of Reform Judaism, the political and educational arm of some 900 Reform congregations in the U.S. and Canada. In an interview in the DuPont Circle brownstone that houses the RAC offices, Saperstein said he understands why some American Jews are willing to work with Christian Zionists. They believe they risk nothing in return for the unqualified support of Israel. "On one level most Jews just kind of ignore eschatology. They don't believe it. They tend to shrug and literally say, 'if they're right, they're right. If they're wrong, they're wrong. We'll find out.'"

Christian end-times theology is the business of Christians. Beyond his disagreement with Christians using Israel as a pretext to proselytize Jews, Saperstein's concerns are more of this world. "There are some Christian Zionists," he said, "who believe that the government's role is to move us closer to the day when the end of times events will occur. They're pressuring the government to take action aimed at bringing such a cataclysm closer. That's neither good for America, for Israelis, nor for American Jewry."

Hagee is a preacher who might worry Saperstein. Hagee is working to bring on the Apocalypse and while he's at it getting two bangs for each of the three million bucks he's spent resettling Russian Jews in Israel. He's underwriting the prophetic "regathering of the Jews in Israel." And "the Jewish people's return to Judea and Samaria." Not only does he tell his congregation the Palestinians will never rule Palestine, he pays to resettle Jews in the future nation of Palestine. Who knows? With a little luck maybe he'll create enough Israeli-Palestinian tension that things will finally start jumping around the ruins of a historical site once known—in the original Hebrew—as *har Meggidon*.

Tom DeLay's November 2002 appearance at Cornerstone Church was rehearsal for a similar speech he would deliver eight months later at a venue far bigger than John Hagee's church. The ink was still wet on the road map to peace that George Bush and Tony Blair laid out in April 2003, when DeLay traveled to the Middle East in July. The signal he sent to the White House, the Israeli government, and the Palestinian Authority was unequivocal: "The road map to peace is a road map to destruction."

DeLay had already staked out his own far-right position on Israel, quietly outmaneuvering Bush national security adviser Condoleeza Rice, defying the president, and passing a harsh anti-Palestine amendment opposed by the White House. (Bush tried to stop him by backing a more moderate Senate resolution sponsored by Senate minority leader Tom Daschle.) Yet Bush had enough regard for DeLay's position with the evangelical right that he reportedly allowed DeLay to preview his June 24, 2002, speech on the Israeli-Palestinian conflict. ("Does that make him a major player? I'm not sure," said a former State Department official who spent several years negotiating with Israel and the Palestinian Authority.) The president's speech, delivered after two years of neglect of Israel and Palestine, stunned even some of Bush's conservative supporters, said a State Department source. Suddenly there were no longer any shades of gray in the complex and nuanced Middle East conflict. It was your standard GWB black and white: freedom vs. democracy and on with the fight against terrorists. It was definitely pro-Israel, and, along with the opportunity to preview it, it should have pleased DeLay. It was not enough. The timing of DeLay's trip the following summer, after Bush had somehow engaged the Israelis and Palestinians in discussions of his road map to peace, was a calculated public affront to the president. DeLay departed Washington as Bush was concluding meetings with Palestinian Prime Minister Mahmoud Abbas and awaiting the arrival of Israeli Prime Minister Ariel Sharon.

Not only was DeLay openly defying Bush, he was betraying him. While DeLay was in Israel in July 2003, Bush was in Washington. There the president was trying to breathe some life into his moribund peace plan, while his party's House majority leader was in Israel undermining it. To members of the Israeli parliament in the Knesset's Chagall Hall, DeLay delivered a speech so pro-Israel and anti-Palestine that it caught the Israeli far-right by surprise. "If Palestinians continue letting violent men speak for them," DeLay said standing, before the haunting mosaic work of modernist Marc Chagall, "they will remain terrorized under the boot heel of terrorism." The three-month ceasefire the Palestinian factions had announced in response to the road map was meaningless because "murderers who take ninety-day vacations are still murderers." Arafat was one of the Palestinians' "minions of the lie." And: "Israel has no choice but to use its own measures to fight terrorism if the Palestinians are unwilling to do so."

The speech and every public statement DeLay made in Israel placed the entire burden of the peace process on the Palestinians. Then, while Mahmoud Abbas was meeting with the president, DeLay challenged the Palestinian prime minister's commitment to peace: "I want to hear what he plans to do to comply with his part and his agreement of the road map. In all these peace processes in the past it has been more process than peace. And it's because people say a lot of words and they do very few actions and what we are looking for is action. If we are going to go through this process, we want people to actually do things they promised they would do."

The White House kept a cool distance from DeLay. "The House majority leader is an elected leader in Congress," said Bush spokesman Scott McClellan. "We are trying to keep the parties focused on the path forward on the road map and work with them to keep them talking between themselves."

DeLay played better in Israel. "As I shook his hand, I told Tom DeLay that until I heard him speak I thought I was the farthest to the right in the Knesset," said National Union Party deputy Aryeh Eldad. "The Likud is nothing compared to this guy," said Danny Yatom, a former director of Mossad, Israel's security force. The conservative *Jerusalem Post* was enthusiastic. As was DeLay adviser Jack Abramoff, an Orthodox Jew thrilled to hear some Israelis refer to Tom DeLay as the "King of Israel."

It was a remarkable moment. In four days in Israel, DeLay

had engaged in something like the opposite of "shuttle diplomacy." Everything he did or said was loaded with meaning, his stop at the Western Wall of the Temple, his visit to a camp for children who had survived terrorist attacks, his tour of the Golan Heights, occupied by Israel since the 1967 war. He had, as a State Department critic observed, "set the peace process back." On future trips, DeLay won't have Palestinian Prime Minister Abbas to kick around anymore. A month after DeLay's visit to Israel, Abbas resigned. Tom DeLay didn't force the resignation. But his visit undermined the peace process—and the Palestinian prime minister Bush ushered into office to make that process happen.

By the time Tom DeLay arrived at the Grand Ballroom of the Manhattan Hilton to pick up his Defender of Israel Award, his ambition to succeed Denny Hastert as Speaker of the House seemed too modest by a half. "DeLay makes Sam Rayburn look like a lightweight," said a man waiting to hear DeLay's keynote speech to the Zionist Organization of America. "Did Sam Rayburn ever stand up to a president from his own party?"

A voluble middle-management telecom exec was more enthusiastic. With his wife he had driven in from New Jersey to have his picture taken with the Texas congressman he said "already is Speaker of the House and ought to be looking for something bigger." ZOA president Morton Klein was talking bigger: The presidency.

On this mid-November 2003 night in this crowd not even the American presidency was big enough for Tom DeLay. Klein, who had worked for three presidents, couldn't stop with the hyperbole. He compared the former exterminator from Sugar Land, Texas, to one of the Lamed Vav: the "36 Just Men" of Jewish tradition whose very existence sustains mankind. But Tom DeLay is a gentile. That—and his temperament, voting record, and

fundraising shakedowns—make him as likely a candidate for
Lamed Vav as Michael Jackson is for father of the year. So Klein
looked to the Old Testament for a comparison that better suited
his subject. "Moses wanted to know if there was one righteous
man in Canaan," he said. Tom DeLay is as righteous a gentile as
the man Moses went looking for in Canaan. Maybe even more
so. The pugnacious, middle-aged Texas Baptist had earned his
place on the list of righteous gentiles who risked their lives and
careers to defend the Jewish people. Klein ran through his list:
Emile Zola, Lord Balfour, Oskar Schindler. And Tom DeLay.

The praise was over the top. But the 2003 ZOA awards banquet might have been billed "Over the Top on Tom DeLay." Almost 800 people paid $360 or more for a plate of conventional
convention chicken and a speech by the majority leader of the
House of Representatives. There were other honorees, but De-
Lay was the star, picking up the Defender of Israel Award (from
a group that, despite its connections and wealth, also defines
the American extreme on Israel Policy) and delivering a speech
that placed him well to the right of Ariel Sharon.

DeLay—like Dick Nixon, always slightly ill-suited in black-
tie attire—couldn't have found a friendlier room to work. "My
father saw him speak at someone's house in Englewood today
and he promised to get rid of all the Arabists in the State Department if we elect Bush one more time," gushed a young man
seated at the Young Jewish Leaders table.

"We need all the help we can get in Congress," said a bearded,
beatific man with a nimbus of gray hair that floated like a halo
around the rim of his *kippah*. "Tom DeLay believes in Israel.
He's Israel's strongest supporter. And Israel needs all the support it can get. We need people who understand that if we have
to kill 5,000 of them to make them understand that either
they're with us or against us, that's what we have to do."

"We're here to show our support for the congressman," said a
Park Avenue matron waiting for her table assignment. She wondered if the congressman would be bringing any of his Christian

group from Texas with him. But the Christians had stayed home. And maybe that's just as well. A flesh-and-blood encounter with one of the primitive, Texas televangelists who inform Tom DeLay's biblical worldview might have scared the pearls off this urbane woman who disagrees with most of what DeLay does. But it's support of Israel that matters here and she's grateful that this politician with whom she shares nothing else occupies a top spot in Congress. She makes that deal with herself because DeLay uses his position as House majority leader to "pull Bush to the right on Israel."

But Bush's Middle East policy has moved a long way from what the most of the international community considers mainstream, and it requires a rich imagination to envision Bush moving further to the right. Clinton was obsessed with Israel and Palestine and considered himself a legatee of assassinated Israeli Prime Minster Yitzak Rabin. Not only did Clinton maintain what was almost a small private White House shrine to Rabin—earth from his grave site, the *kippah* Clinton wore at his funeral—he doggedly fought to advance the peace process.

Bush came into office and pursued a policy of calculated neglect and within a year the Palestinians and Israelis were engaged in mutual slaughter. Then Bush gave the green light to Sharon, who had come to power after the far more moderate government of Ehud Barak fell. Sharon's aggressive policy toward the Palestinians, his refusal to consider abandoning Israel's West Bank settlements, and his assault on the compound of Yassir Arafat seem sufficiently conservative and militant—without DeLay leaning on Bush to make them more extreme.

But DeLay wanted more. As soon as Bush responded to British Prime Minister Tony Blair's entreaties and patched together an Israel-Palestine policy as ass-covering before going to war in Iraq—the "road map to peace"—DeLay attacked. When Bush argued that Yassir Arafat had to be isolated, DeLay called Arafat a thug and backed a House resolution declaring him a terrorist. When Bush promised Palestinians a state, DeLay said the state would become a nation of terrorists and declared Judea and Samaria (the West Bank) part of Israel. When Bush expressed high hopes for his handpicked Palestinian prime minister, Mahmoud Abbas, DeLay said Abbas didn't have the chops to stand up to Arafat. When Bush tried to pressure the Israeli government to make some small concessions on the occupation of Palestinian territory, DeLay pressed House Republicans to sign a letter urging the president to back off.

For two years before he was recognized by Mort Klein's Zionists, DeLay had been talking his president into a corner, taking his case to the Christian base that always threatens to "take a walk" on a general election if the party doesn't deliver on god, guns, and gays. It's a threat Republicans have had to take seriously. A Frank Rich column in the *New York Times* cited dramatic, if surprising, polling results which found that more than 50 percent of the American public now identify themselves as fundamentalist or born-again Christians. And many of them have found a home in the Republican Party, where they represent 35 to 40 percent of the party's primary voters. If enough evangelicals sit out a general election, Republican candidates lose.

George Bush and Karl Rove know that. They also know that DeLay is the perfect liaison between the Republican Party and its Christian conservatives—whose voting power has even led the devoutly secular Rove to Jesus. According to Rev. William Murray, DeLay "is more preacher than he is politician." That might be overstated, but the born-again son of the late American atheist Madalyn Murray O'Hair has shared the pulpit with the Republican Party's go-to guy for the Jews-and-Jesus crowd. At an October 2002 Christian Coalition demonstration in Washington, D.C., DeLay joined Murray and Pat Robertson and got so caught up in the moment that he made two separate speeches.

"Are you tired of all this?" DeLay shouted kicking off his first speech to the crowd in the Washington convention center. "Noooo!" they responded.

"Not when you're standing up for Jews and Jesus," DeLay said to an audience that considers Christ fundamentally Christian.

At a "Stand for Israel" rally put together for former Christian Coalition director Ralph Reed, DeLay attacked Department of State functionaries working on the Bush road map. "The moral ambiguities of our diplomatic elites notwithstanding, Israel is not the problem; Israel is the solution."

"Negotiating with [the Palestinians] is folly and any agreement arrived at through such empty negotiations would amount to a covenant with death," DeLay said to a Washington gathering of the Conference of Christians and Jews. "Experience and common sense lead to one conclusion about America's proper role in the Middle East: We are absolutely right to stand with Israel, and our opponents are absolutely wrong."

"I'm sure there are some in the administration who are smarter than me," DeLay told the *New York Times* in July 2003. "But I can't imagine in the very near future that a Palestinian state could ever happen. I can't imagine this president supporting a state of terrorists, a sovereign state of terrorists."

The United States, the United Nations, the European Union, and Russia—the "quartet" Bush assembled to work on a diplomatic solution to the Israel-Palestine conflict is "a quartet of appeasement." Like the angry gray-haired Zionist in the *kippah*, Tom DeLay finds no middle ground in the Middle East.

Unlike Mort Klein's angry, bearded follower, the majority leader is in a position to ensure there will be no middle ground. He is the nation's most powerful Christian Zionist. DeLay's Zionist zealots live in a zone of their own. Again, consider their core beliefs: certain biblical prophecies must come to pass before the Second Coming of Christ can occur. Most of the prophecies involve Israel. And none of them square with Bush's Middle East policies. As odd as this is for secular Americans to grasp, Jesus cannot return if the president's modest Middle East policy goals are put in place. Faced with a choice between the foreign policy of G. W. Bush and the Second Coming of Jesus

Christ, DeLay might recall something John F. Kennedy said more than forty years ago: "Sometimes party loyalty asks too much."

The Zionist Organization of America's Defender of Israel Award is not a cash prize. But it's paying off for DeLay and his party. It's not a state secret that the Republicans are exploiting Israel's security to peel voters away from the Democrats. The Jewish vote doesn't win elections, but it swings elections. And there are concentrations of Jewish voters in several of the states where the 2004 presidential election will be won or lost: Michigan, Pennsylvania, and in particular Florida—where discarded ballots of elderly Jewish voters bewildered by confusing butterfly ballots might have cost Al Gore the presidency in 2000.

Then there is money.

With Tom DeLay, it's always about money. Pro-Israel interests have contributed a total of $41.3 million to candidates and party committees over the last ten years, with Democrats taking in $28.6 million. For the majority leader from Texas, Israel is the perfect nexus of ideology, faith, and fundraising. It's where his coming to Jesus in the office of Representative Frank Wolf pays off. *Newsweek* reporters looking at the marriage of Christian Zionist and Jewish Zionists found big donors from New York's Jewish community shifting their contributions away from the Democratic Party. Journalists are so jaded that little surprises them, but the *Newsweek* team seem stunned to find Tom DeLay standing before a public gathering and saying kaddish, the Jewish prayer for the dead. In Hebrew!

DeLay is doing more than speaking Hebrew. Since Bush moved into the White House, the majority leader has become a frequent flyer to Jewish communities where Southern Christian conservatives were considered exotics only ten years ago. In March 2003, five months before he traveled to Israel, DeLay was in Englewood, New Jersey, for a fundraiser for ARMPAC, his top-dollar political action committee. After a brief speech before a group of Orthodox Jews and a pitch for money, he returned to

Washington with $100,000. He was back in Englewood on the day he received Morton Klein's Zionist benediction in Manhattan. (Fundraising totals from that Englewood event were not yet in as we concluded our reporting.) Three weeks later, he was speaking in a Houston synagogue and connecting with Jewish donors closer to home.

Benjamin Netanyahu working the Bible Belt breakfast circuit. Jewish pilgrims traveling to John Hagee's Christian temple. Tom DeLay becoming a Shabbas goy. Maybe we are living in end times after all. Yet if the end is to come, let us pray that it is a result of a Divine plan laid out in Revelation. Or the inexorable laws of physics laid out by Einstein. Not the worldly machinations of preachers and politicians working in collaboration to get us to that moment when they can say: "This *Is* The Day."

Troubles in Texas

Tom DeLay has come a long way from the chaparral of Mirando City, American enclaves in Venezuelan oil towns, and the pest control business in Sugar Land. DeLay relies on people who live in Texas suburbs to certify his stature at the polls, but he is a creature of Washington now, and he is at the height of his power. In fundraising, mastery of governmental process, and domination of the content of the nation's legislation, DeLay has become the most powerful Republican in the House, perhaps the whole Congress. But power corrupts, or at least makes the unscrupulous careless. DeLay's methods and the company he keeps have always caused problems for him. But the higher one rises in politics, the greater the visibility—and perhaps even the greater the demand for accountability.

"A zebra does not change its spots," Al Gore said during his campaign for the presidency, slipping into the peculiar idiom that was actually the signature mark of his opponent in the presidential race. Tom DeLay was one such zebra. To ride an equine metaphor for a few more sentences, he was a zebra utterly unlikely to change his spots while looking a gift horse in the mouth. Enron was one of many gift horses. By 1997, for example, as Enron CEO Ken Lay grew tired of waiting on states to deregulate electricity markets, DeLay was in place to take the lead.

Enron didn't generate electricity (although it would later,

when it acquired Portland General Electric). It wanted the absolute right to buy and sell electricity anywhere—and to use the existing grid to move the electricity it was selling. Enron ultimately became somewhat overzealous in its use of the grid, buying electricity in California then giving it a round trip to an adjacent state, so it could resell it in California at the much higher rate state regulators had set for energy generated in and purchased from another state, which helped prop up a failing company in 2000-2001. Two years after the company collapsed and went into bankruptcy, Enron traders were caught on tape talking about a "Grandma Millie" in California—who wanted "all her fucking money back for all the power you charged right up, jammed right up her fucking ass at $250 a megawatt hour." (Crude and cruel, but that, after all, is what makes Texas a great state.) Enron would have to break up existing monopolies. Electricity, Lay believed, was like any other commodity—like grain, oil, or bottled water. All he wanted was the right to sell his electricity to any consumer who would buy it from him.

It was a position to which Tom DeLay was committed with an almost religious fervor. It was also one that would allow him to express his gratitude to Lay and his colleagues at Enron, for the quarter of a million in seed money they provided his PAC in 1995—and bring him increased contributions from Enron.

States were deregulating their electricity markets, and members of Congress were drafting legislation to encourage deregulation or to set dates by which markets had to be deregulated. On the final date of the 1996 session, DeLay filed the single most drastic deregulation bill, compelling states to deregulate their markets by a fixed date in 1998. Thomas Bliley, a Virginia Republican chairing the Commerce Committee, which would mark up the bill, knew what DeLay was up to. "We sometimes refer to that as the Enron bill," Bliley said.

The bill got nowhere but when the 105th Congress convened in 1997, DeLay was back, embracing deregulation of the elec-

tricity market with the same enthusiasm that once had him
fighting for trucking deregulation on sunny Saturdays in Austin.
He refiled the bill. He delivered a major deregulation speech at
the conservative Heritage Foundation, published op-ed pieces
in newspapers, and flogged the issue relentlessly on the Hill.
Enron didn't get all it wanted out of the Congress, but they
couldn't fault DeLay or his effort. There was even a brief moment where DeLay found himself working alongside the consumer and environmental groups. One of the big questions
involved in deregulation was what to do with "stranded costs"—
the huge debts many utility companies had taken on building
nuclear plants when the energy they promised to generate
promised to be "too cheap to meter." It wasn't, of course, and
the hugely expensive plants placed a giant economic burden on
the companies. As they moved out of state regulation, where
regulators would look at a company's books and determine what
was fair to pass on to ratepayers and to stockholders, utilities
that had built big nukes wanted a legislative mandate to let consumers pay the bill. Consumer advocates, environmentalists,
and Tom DeLay disagreed, insisting that the utilities had built
the plants, and they and their shareholders were responsible for
paying the bills. So Tom DeLay joined with Consumers Union,
Public Citizen, Greenpeace, and the Sierra Club. Enron, it
turned out, owned no nuclear plants. Generating electricity was
old-paradigm business. Enron bought and sold electricity. If the
utilities had to pay for huge stranded costs, Enron, with no
stranded costs, would only be more competitive.

After Bush was elected, Enron CEO Lay got personally involved with the Federal Energy Regulation Commission. He
convinced Bush to get rid of the commission chairman, who opposed the big open regional electricity markets Enron needed,
and to appoint two FERC commissioners who shared his philosophy. If Congress couldn't do the dereg deal DeLay was
working for, FERC could. Perhaps one might say that it was be-

cause of the collaboration of Tom DeLay, George W. Bush, and
Enron's Ken Lay that Grandma Millie got FERCed.

By 2002, Enron was synonymous with corporate corruption
and public disgrace. What had been the political system's premier corporate campaign gift horse was dead. Association with
it was a political liability. So, although Ken Lay had contributed
more than $750,000 to W.'s two campaigns in Texas and earned
the Bush nickname "Kenny Boy," Bush was now describing Lay
as only a casual acquaintance. Public officials, though Tom De-
Lay was not one of them, were scrambling to return their Enron
contributions—or donating them to relief funds set up for Enron employees who had lost their jobs and their retirement accounts.

Enron was a devastating loss for the national economy. And
for Enron workers whose retirement accounts vanished as the
company melted down. And for retired public employees whose
state-managed retirement accounts had invested in the seventh
largest corporation in the world and were considerably dimin-
ished by its collapse. It was also a loss for elected officials who
had come to depend on the regular support of the Houston-
based company. Politicians, however, had it better than workers,
teachers, or retired public employees. For politicians, there are
always other gift horses and cash cows.

Consider Westar. Westar was a Kansas-based utility with a
stranded-cost problem. And a solution that would shift those
costs to the one group that utility companies always conclude
can best manage any big debts companies incur: consumers.
Ratepayers, it's assumed, can always accommodate a monthly
increase in their electricity bills.

In May 2002 a reporter for the *Kansas City Star* was poring
over corporate records made public by members of the board of
directors at the state's largest utility. The material had been released to illustrate to shareholders the poor management decisions made by Westar Energy's executives. Among the records

were internal memos establishing that Westar executives were paying for legislation. Specifically, for one small provision that would result in a huge profit for the company. And a $15 million windfall for the CEO and $12 million for the vice president. Until it was investigated by Public Citizen, a nonprofit, public interest group based in Washington, the pay-to-play-in-Congress story was dying on the pages of a few Kansas newspapers.

The story was not that complex. If Westar could separate its regulated utility from the rest of the businesses it owned, it could move $3 billion in non-utility debt over to the regulated utility, then structure it into customers' electricity bills. It was a brilliant accounting trick that would create a new version of "stranded costs" to be passed on to the consumer. Westar couldn't do it alone. The company management team needed help in Washington. The Public Utility Holding Company Act of 1935 was an archaic law enacted to protect shareholders from precisely the sort of scheme Westar executives had devised. To change the law, Westar executives decided they would have to contribute $56,000 to members of Congress and candidates in congressional races.

If Tom DeLay opposed stranded costs while he was advancing Enron's deregulation agenda, Westar changed his mind. Perhaps Westar's $25,000 contribution to his Texas PAC helped him see things differently. Or maybe Enron had just burned him out on the issue. By 2002 DeLay had changed his position on stranded costs and seemed perfectly willing to have Westar ratepayers pick up the tab for the company's bad investments — even if the investments had nothing to do with the generation and sale of electricity. He had come a long way in a short time.

Massachusetts Democrat Ed Markey smelled a rat when Texas Republican Joe Barton drafted a provision in an energy bill. clearly designed to benefit one company. Markey warned that Westar was trying to spin off losses from its failed burglar alarm business. The company was asking, just as Enron had asked in 1996, for an exemption from a law that protected investors.

Markey even produced a letter from the regulatory agency in Kansas, urging Congress to deny Westar the exemption.

Barton's Westar provision made it into neither the House nor the Senate versions of the bill. Barton took another route. Employing a tactic once considered all but unthinkable, members of Congress now use carefully selected conference committees, in which the majority often shuts off minority participation, to insert new provisions into bills. Barton did Westar's deal in conference. And he let everyone on the committee know that De-Lay wanted this deal done.

There is no doubt that Westar was looking for a custom-tailored provision in the 2002 energy bill. It was all spelled out in a memo. In May 2002 Westar vice president Doug Lawrence sent twelve company executives an outline of a plan to use the House-Senate conference committee to insert a special exemption from the Public Utility Holding Company Act (PUHCA). The memo itemized $56,500 in political contributions and listed a half dozen members of Congress who would get the money.

Westar Vice President Douglas Lake didn't get it. "Who is Shimkus, who is Young. Delay [sic] is from TX what is our connection? . . . I'm confused," he wrote. Lawrence explained that with political contributions to DeLay, Louisiana Republican Billy Tauzin, and Texas Republican Joe Barton, Westar could get what it wanted out of the conference committee. The language Lawrence used in his memo was not intended for a readership beyond the small cabal of executives discussing how to pay members of Congress to do their bidding.

> Right now, we are working on getting our grandfather provisions on PUHCA repeal into the senate version of the energy bill. It requires working with the Conference committee to achieve. We have a plan for participation to get a seat at the table, which has been approved by David [Whittig, the company CEO] the total package will be $31,500 in hard money (individual), and $25 in soft money (corporate). Right now, we

have $11,500 in immediate needs for a group of candidates asso-
ciated with Tom Delay [*sic*], Billy Tauzin, Joe Barton, and Senator Richard Shelby. Delay [*sic*] is the House majority leader. His
agreement is necessary before the House Conferees can push
the language we have in place in the House bill. Shimkus is a
close associate of Billy Tauzin and Joe Barton, who are key
House Conferees on our legislation. They have made this request in lieu of contributions to their own campaigns.

The memo goes on to explain that Tom Young is Senator
Richard Shelby's former aide, then running for a House seat in
Alabama. And that Shelby, Westar's "anchor" in the Senate, had
made a "substantial request of us for supporting Young's campaign."

"These men seem disconnected," the memo concluded, "but
ultimately the plan is directed at getting a strong position at the
table on both the Senate and House Side [*sic*]."

Of the half-dozen "disconnected" men mentioned in the
memo, Tom DeLay got the best deal. Of the $56,000 in contri-
butions, $25,000 was paid to DeLay's Texas PAC. After the
check cleared, a group of Westar executives joined DeLay for a
two-day energy conference—and golf at an exclusive Virginia
resort.

And Westar got its provision inserted in the energy bill. Barton introduced it, then prevailed on a straight party-line vote to
keep it there. The provision was quietly removed after Westar
CEO Wittig was indicted for falsifying bank documents regarding a $1.5 million personal bank loan. Massachusetts Democrat
Ed Markey added to the embarrassment by writing to House
Energy and Commerce chair Billy Tauzin and Senate Energy
and Natural Resources Committee Jeff Bingaman to inform
them that Westar was under investigation by the U.S. Attorney
in Topeka, Kansas, then releasing his letter to the public.

DeLay press flack Stuart Roy is almost nondescript. An elegant, trim, middle-aged white guy with close-cropped hair and

an easy demeanor, he disappears into rooms dominated by his boss. But Roy has those rare qualities that distinguish the good from the great. He's quiet, steady, certain, thorough, and slow to anger. But most importantly, he's the kind of guy who can stand in front of you and piss on your shoes while telling you with a straight face that it's raining.

In June 2003, AP writer Pete Yost might have been looking to buy a new pair of wingtips. Yost was connecting the dots on the Westar story. A $25,000 Westar contribution to DeLay's Texas PAC, followed by two days of golf and face time for Westar executives with the majority leader, followed by a Westar provision inserted in the energy bill at conference committee after neither House of Congress had approved the provision.

And the memos. Memos that stated specific requests had been made, money delivered, and help with a two-line legislative provision worth $3 billion to the company and millions to two executives was on the way.

It was hardly a big deal, Roy insisted. It was just golf. They didn't spend two days "sitting around talking about energy issues." It was golf.

"If you were a contributor to ARMPAC or TRMPAC of $25,000 or more, you could get invited," said Roy. Golf with the majority leader was a "donor fulfillment event." If you made your contribution, you got to spend a couple of days golfing, dining, and drinking with the leader. It was golf and general talk about energy policy. That was all.

And forget the little guys returning their $1,000 checks—minor players in the congressional drama who tried to distance themselves from Westar. "DeLay didn't solicit the contribution," Roy said. He had no intention of giving it back.

Roy isn't always on the defensive. The pen-and-pad briefings he oversees in the Capitol dining room are almost formal events. Thirty to forty reporters take their seats at a long table and at a second tier of chairs placed against the east and west walls of an elegant carpeted room. "The leader" enters, escorted by two aides, Roy and Jonathan Grella. Roy closes the door at the south end of the room and stands beside his boss, who sits at the head of the table. Grella takes his position at the opposite end of the room. DeLay takes his seat, opens with a bit of friendly banter, and begins to work through his agenda. There's so much decorum that DeLay's arrival and departure are almost ceremonial. The fifty-six-year-old congressman is smart, agile, aggressive, and in complete control.

Tom DeLay runs his own show. Grella helps. A huge muscle of a man with a shaved head and a permanent scowl, Jon Grella stands at the east end of the long dining table. Without the coat and tie he'd look like a bouncer in a biker bar. When it's time to get his boss to the House floor, or when reporters bore in with questions that are off the agenda, he signals that the conference is over. Although Grella plays the part of the enforcer, standing, scowling, arms folded across his chest, DeLay can take care of himself. Since he was elected majority leader in January 2003, or claimed the position without opposition, DeLay has been careful, working to soften the hard-ass image he earned over twenty years in Congress. But if a question, or an attitude, rubs him the wrong way, he will cut a reporter off with a monosyllabic answer. Or, as he did to one young woman pressing him about his failed scheme to book a cruise ship to house delegates attending the 2004 Republican convention in New York, simply grin.

"The grin" is not exactly a grin or even a fixed smile, but rather a baring of the teeth. Complemented by a stare that seems to pierce the subject, it conveys to a reporter, or a recalcitrant member of the Republican Conference, or an uncooperative lobbyist, both contempt and incredulity. It is important to deliver a nonverbal message: "Not only are you insufferable, but I can't quite believe you are so fucking stupid as to pose such a question." Almost always effective, it worked on the young reporter at the mid-November 2003 press conference, when she asked DeLay if he still intended to bring a luxury cruise ship to his party's national convention in New York. Grinning and staring as she posed the question, DeLay said he wasn't bringing the ship to New York. It was already berthed there in the harbor. He stared and grinned as the woman continued with a question about why he persisted with a plan to house delegates on a cruise ship when there were vacant hotels in the city. "Because it's a good idea," he said. The rictus on his face never relaxed.

Unwelcome questions are deflected by the grin. Or Grella's menacing scowl. Or the leader's occasional flashes of anger. Or all of them. Reporters had better heed the leader's rules. No TV or still photography is allowed during the weekly briefings. Audiotape is okay, but not for broadcast. There is an agenda, and questions are expected to address the agenda. Sometimes there's a guest, usually another member discussing current policy issues: Budget Chair Jim Nussle on the budget; Intelligence Chair Porter Goss delivering a bizarre and oddly uninformed disquisition on terrorism in Spain. The press exposure, like the caps Christine DeLay recommended for the gap between her husband's front teeth, and the blown-dry look suggested by Washington Representative Jennifer Dunn (who provided the name of the guy who does her hair) are all part of the makeover that has to be complete before DeLay becomes Speaker of the House. This is the new public Tom DeLay, a kinder, gentler version of the whip once known for the fixed smile and the knee to the groin.

Press reports of the $3 million in convention spending the Swedish luxury liner would suck out of New York's hotels, bars, and restaurants sank DeLay's project by December. (Press reports that it was a liner usually booked by gay vacationers made the convention Love Boat scheme even more unlikely for De-Lay.) And by February the leader and his press aides probably wished they had the distraction of the love boat back. The leader was beleaguered by questions related to civil litigation and criminal investigations in Texas. And the *Washington Post* was reporting a lobbying scandal that involved two of DeLay's closest associates.

When the *Post* reported that Jack Abramoff and Michael Scanlon had collected a staggering $45 million in lobbying fees from four Indian tribes, DeLay went on the offensive. "Jack Abramoff has never been on my payroll," DeLay said at a February press briefing. "I have no idea how their operation is run or what it is," he added. "What I can tell you is that if anybody is trading on my name to make money, that is wrong and they should stop it immediately."

He might as well have said, "I didn't have sex with that man." Abramoff has been one of his closest advisers for years. The warning about trading on his name was equally unrealistic. Taken at face value, it would have Susan Hirschmann, Tony Rudy, Rev. Ed Buckham, Karl Gallant, Drew Maloney, Jim Ellis, Mike Scanlon, and Jack Abramoff fighting over *Roll Call*'s "Good Jobs on the Hill" page. Every insider (and most outsiders) in Washington knows that a year on DeLay's staff is the ticket to big-league lobbying. Even the minor players are cut in on the deal. "His influence on K Street has reached a point where former staff members are even moving into the lower level lobbying positions that pay $200,000 a year or less," said American Enterprise Institute congressional scholar Norman Ornstein.

The Indian lobbying story the *Post* picked up and developed, after it first ran in a small Louisiana newspaper, threatens more than the lobbying careers of his associates Abramoff and Scanlon. Its sheer magnitude threatens DeLay's hold on power. It has encouraged Arizona Senator John McCain to open a Senate investigation, forced John Ashcroft's FBI to investigate close associates of the majority leader. DeLay will claim that he is being tarred with guilt by association, but the rip-off of the Indian tribes is going to be a full-blown scandal, and it has the potential to reveal the shady network of money hustlers behind DeLay's massive fundraising operation and his subjugation of K Street.

After all, the value of trading on Tom DeLay's name is illustrated by the meteoric rise of Mike Scanlon. One of the Republican congressional leaders in the Gingrich years said, "Everybody knew who Scanlon was. We thought he was a juvenile delinquent." Scanlon was just twenty-seven when he was cheering on the ruthlessness and orchestrating publicity for the Clinton impeachment proceedings in 1998. He had been one of the aides who went with DeLay on the New Year's junket to the Marianas. While taking a leave to help out in the Marianas, the world of lobbying in league with Tom DeLay opened before him. Scanlon was still paying off his college loans when he moved from DeLay's press office into the offices of Preston Gates Law Firm with Jack Abramoff, his mentor in the Marianas. Scanlon followed Abramoff to the Greenberg Traurig lobbying firm and registered to work as a lobbyist for the Coushatta Indian Tribe. Branching out on his own he set up two public relations firms, Capital Campaign Strategies and Scanlon-Gould Public Affairs. The *Post*'s Susan Schmidt reported that the address on Scanlon's company correspondence is a mail drop on Pennsylvania Avenue.

Because he was doing public relations work rather than lobbying for the four Indian tribes who retained his and Abramoff's services, Scanlon did not have to disclose his fees; $31.5 million of the $45 million the tribes paid out were paid to his businesses, according to contracts the Indian tribes provided the *Post*. It must have been a great mail drop.

The fees paid to Abramoff and Scanlon were ten to twenty times what the tribes paid the previous lobbyists they had used. Once Abramoff and Scanlon showed up, the Indians were paying top dollar. General Motors had a $30.4 million lobbying tab in the same time period. The big four pharmaceutical firms paid $34.8 million while they were heavily involved in lobbying Medicare and prescription drug benefits for seniors. The fees were paid to Abramoff and Scanlon, in fact, at a time when there were no major pending issues regarding Indian gaming—too often the central focus of high-dollar lobbying on Indian affairs.

Abramoff justified his fees, in part, by trumpeting his success in persuading DeLay to block a move to tax Indian gaming profits in 1995. It was an incredible deal while it lasted. But by 2004, leadership changes in tribal councils were working against Scanlon and Abramoff. Tribes were beginning to ask what they were getting for their money—and in some cases canceling their contracts. The tribal council of the Michigan Saginaw Chippewas ended their relationship with Scanlon and Abramoff, after paying $3.9 million to Greenberg Traurig for Abramoff's work and $10 million to Scanlon's firm—*25 percent of the tribe's entire 2002 budget*. "These guys come in and say, 'They are going to take your sovereignty or your land or you livelihood unless you pay us outrageous amounts of money,'" said a Saginaw tribal council member who fought to sever the tribe's relationship with Scanlon and Abramoff. "They need to be exposed because the tribes don't know."

In Alexandria, Louisiana, the *Daily Town Talk* broke the story, reporting that the "lion's share" of the Coushattas' lobbying and public relations fees, $13.7 million in a one-year period that ended in 2001, went to Scanlon's Capital Campaign Strategies firm. "We got involved with them around 2002 when we had to get a gaming contract," said Bert Langley, who had served as the tribe's secretary-treasurer. "Scanlon and Jack were around for a few meetings. They said they had a good network going. They would mention Tom DeLay and all that bunch but I'm not sure what they did or who they talked to."

One can say that businesses can charge whatever the market will bear—it's the American way. But these guys took business ethics back to the grand old days of the Robber Barons. Ten days after the *Washington Post*'s first story, Senator John McCain set out to find who Scanlon and Abramoff had talked to. McCain called the lobbying fees "disgraceful" and ordered Senate Indian Affairs Committee staff to investigate. When Abramoff abruptly resigned from Greenberg Traurig, McCain said it was predictable. "From what I've seen," he said, "I'm not surprised."

The investigation hadn't even begun and McCain had already seen a lot. Some money from the Indian tribes was funneled to the American International Center, which turned out to be domiciled in Rehoboth Beach, Delaware. It was directed by a former lifeguard and a yoga instructor—both beach buddies of Scanlon. While it's not easy to determine exactly what the AIC does, it describes itself as "a premiere international think tank . . . determined to influence global paradigms in an increasingly complex world." Which sounds like important stuff, considering the state of global paradigms. Senator McCain found it odd that the Louisiana Coushattas contributed $566,000 to the AIC. And that it had paid Abramoff's firm $1.5 million for lobbying and public relations—the steep fees probably reflecting the large number of congressional committees and regulatory agencies with global paradigm jurisdiction.

This all could be laughable. But McCain isn't laughing. He is, instead, asking why some tribal members are living below the subsistence level while $45 million was spent on lobbying fees.

The investigation McCain will direct as a senior member of Senate Indian Affairs will, in the tradition of Woodward and Bernstein, "follow the money." For example, did the American International Center serve as a vehicle to move money from Scanlon, who is no longer registered as a lobbyist and therefore not subject to the same disclosure requirements, to Abramoff, who is? It's a question McCain already posed in a letter to Abramoff, in which he demands records of all "Scanlon companies from which you received anything of value from 1998 through the present."

Are tribal council members who approved the lobbying contracts in any way benefiting financially because they signed off on the deal? What did the Indian tribes get for $45 million? The four big pharmaceutical companies who paid $34 million over the same two-year period at least had the satisfaction of knowing their lobbyists wrote the prescription drug bill, banned government involvement in negotiating drug prices for seniors, and blocked the re-importation of prescription drugs from Canada.

When asked what he had done to justify his huge fees, Abramoff told the *Post:* "I think we bring an order of magnitude in terms of our success and our approach on behalf of the tribes. A lot of these tribes who have thrown off the relatively inexpensive lobbyists basically come to us with the comment of 'you get what you pay for.'"

Indeed.

Greenberg Traurig is cooperating with McCain's investigation, after sending Abramoff on his way because of "personal transactions and related conduct which are unacceptable to the firm." Abramoff and Scanlon are lawyered up. Abramoff has hired Abbe Lowell, who worked for Democrats on the House Judiciary Committee during the impeachment of Bill Clinton. Scanlon has retained both Baker and Botts (the Bush family law firm best known for Bush consigliere James Baker III). And Plato Cacheris, a Washington lawyer who represented Monica Lewinsky and Fawn Hall, Ollie North's secretary accused of shredding government files during the Iran-Contra investigation.

The reformers on the tribal councils are talking and sending documents to newspapers. In a word, or two, these guys are in deep shit. And quite literally and no doubt permanently off the reservation.

All of which portends political trouble for Tom DeLay. In an interview not related to the Indian tribe story, Norman Ornstein observed that not only are DeLay staffers and other congressional staff members moving directly from the Hill to K Street, but the lobbying positions come with an understanding that contributions will be made to the GOP. "Everyone is expected to contribute part of that money back into Republican political campaigns. It's Tammany Hall all over again," Ornstein said.

How much of Abramoff and Scanlon's money was finding its way back to Tom DeLay and his extended funding network?

And how much of the $200,000 Abramoff has committed to raise for George W. Bush's 2004 campaign involves Indian Giving? DeLay has, after all, sat lobbyists down in his office and demanded that they stop giving to Democrats and start giving more to Republicans. Abramoff and Scanlon would require no such persuasion. How much are they paying to whom? Not the sort of questions political candidates like to see asked (or answered) in an election year.

It is difficult to imagine two politicians more divergent in interests and distinct in character than Tom DeLay and John McCain. Other than a shared political party and a predisposition toward frankness, the two men might as well have come from different countries. The difference goes as far back as McCain's heroic conduct in Vietnam and DeLay's explanation that he didn't serve because he was reluctant to deprive blacks and Hispanics of the opportunity and good pay that service in the military provided them. Nowhere is the difference more pronounced than in the positions the two men hold on campaign finance reform. DeLay's position is simple, and he has repeated it often: unlimited contributions and full disclosure. There's not enough money in politics, he has said. McCain has dedicated ten years to the enactment of campaign finance reform, which was finally realized in 2002 when Congress enacted what has come to be known as the McCain-Feingold campaign finance law. DeLay was an implacable foe of McCain's work, managing to keep passage of McCain-Feingold at bay for almost as long as John McCain and Wisconsin Democratic Senator Russ Feingold worked on it.

In 2001, when he was whip, DeLay sank the House version, breaking it into fourteen parts and making floor debate impossible, even though Speaker Hastert had promised that the bill would come to the floor in one piece for an up-or-down vote. DeLay fought it again in 2002. "I'm working very hard to see that it doesn't pass the House," DeLay said at the time. "This is big government regulation of our most basic freedom of speech, our freedom to assemble, and our freedom to petition the government. They in this bill even gag groups that come together to petition their government." The passage of McCain-Feingold was considered a rare failure of DeLay's whip organization.

Though McCain has been discreet in public, it is known that he doesn't hold Tom DeLay in high regard—or perhaps not even in low regard. This is not to suggest that DeLay will end up the focus of the investigation, though it will be hard for him to avoid the fallout. Nor is it to suggest that McCain will not conduct an utterly impartial investigation. But the sheer excess of the money extracted from the Indian tribes, and the long and close relationship between DeLay, Abramoff, and Scanlon almost ensure that some of the money raised by the two ended up in one of the many fundraising accounts that have been nicknamed DeLay Inc. There's Abramoff's bundled Bush money. And Scanlon contributed $500,000 to the National Republican Governors Association in 2002—the largest individual donation made that year. Indian Affairs Committee Chair Senator Ben Nighthorse Campbell, who is half Northern Cheyenne and is the only Native American in Congress, is letting McCain lead on the investigation. McCain has hired an investigator to work on the case. And with Campbell's approval, for the first time in history, the committee has issued subpoenas.

DeLay will have to work very hard to distance himself from Abramoff, as he tried to do at a March 2004 press conference. There are too many connections. Abramoff is part of DeLay's kitchen cabinet, the group of advisers (and funders) DeLay regularly consults. He has been DeLay's man in Israel and in the Marianas. And he is a friend, confidant, and former College Republicans associate of Grover Norquist, the brain behind the muscle DeLay provides for the K Street Project.

For Abramoff, such separation will be painful. "Thank God Tom DeLay is the majority leader of the House," said Abramoff, introducing DeLay to a cheering group of College Republicans at their 2003 convention. They were cheering "We Love Tom."

Abramoff went on, "Tom DeLay is who all of us want to be when we grow up."

Of DeLay's troubles, the Indian Giving scandal has gotten the most play in Washington. Celebrity lawyers and a senator with real star power are driving the story. But DeLay also faces real problems in Texas.

Though chances are remote that voters in Sugar Land and the other suburbs will soon turn him out of office, his pipe-wrenching of Texas politics has taken some turns that have Democrats smiling for the first time in years. National Republicans predicted that DeLay's redistricting would gain them at least four House seats in the 2004 election. But some of the white Democrats were hanging tough. Austin had been fractured in thirds. White urban liberal Lloyd Doggett had been separated from his white Austin constituency and forced to run in a bizarre district that stretched from Austin's ethnic east side to McAllen in the Rio Grande valley. Republicans drawing the maps gave that district to Democrats, but to help ward off the Voting Rights accusations created it in such a way that it was certain to elect a Hispanic. To the amazement and woe of right-wing Republicans, Doggett hit the road, spent the money he always penny-pinched, and handily beat the Hispanic woman who was supposed to end his career. The Republicans quickly found a woman who is nominally Hispanic to run against him in the general election, but in all likelihood Doggett is going to be back on Capitol Hill in 2004, yowling in his nasal drawl and shaking his bony fist at Tom DeLay. In Waco, Democrat Chet Edwards has the good fortune to face a candidate who defines the extreme right and as a state rep was largely responsible for draconian cuts in health care to the poor, in particularly children. Dallas Democrat Martin Frost seems to have a shot at winning in a district that is largely Republican and represented by Pete Sessions.

Meanwhile, Ronnie Earle is a name that few in the Capitol press pack—except the D.C. bureau chiefs from Texas dailies—would recognize. But Travis County DA Ronnie takes his responsibility seriously. The veteran prosecutor in his early sixties, with the unsmiling face of an old Texas hanging judge, is as great a threat to Tom DeLay as is John McCain. Perhaps greater. John McCain cannot put the majority leader in jail. Earle can. Because Travis County includes the state capital, the Legislature has provided him with a mandate and a budget to investigate and prosecute political corruption. Armed with a statute passed when the dominant and triumphant politics of the state was a populism shaped by suffragettes, small farmers, and prohibitionists, Earle is in a position to send DeLay and his fundraising cronies to ten years in the big rodeo. The 100-year-old statute, enacted to save some of the state from the Robber Barons, makes it a felony to spend corporate money on election campaigns.

What Earle describes as "an attempt to steal an election" might have been overlooked if the alleged perps had kept quiet. But braggadocio is as deeply ingrained in the Texas psyche as remembering the Alamo. When the head of the Texas Association of Business (TAB) boasted that his organization "blew the doors off" the 2002 election and sent the Republicans' whooping to total power in Texas, it could scarcely not attract the attention of the Travis County DA. Republicans had pilloried Earle since 1994, when he indicted State Treasurer Kay Bailey Hutchison for using state employees for personal and campaign tasks then destroying state agency files that documented the abuse. At the time, Hutchison was running for the U.S. Senate seat she now holds. On the first day he was in court Earle pulled out when the state district judge handed down an evidentiary ruling that would have made prosecuting the case very difficult. "You don't go to the brink of nuclear war and then *fold*," laughed a Democratic trial lawyer who observed Earle's performance in the

Hutchison fiasco. But Earle's public integrity unit has prosecuted many more Democrats than Republicans, and he took able care of the other business of his office. The DA is articulate, handsome, and popular enough in Austin that the Republicans had stopped running against him. He is also the last remaining Texas Democrat in a position of real power. Even Karl Rove had no hooks or screws in him.

Earle observed amid all the boasting and glad-handing that the Texas Association of Business dispersed nothing *but* money donated by corporations. Well-acquainted with the century-old law, he smelled enough smoke to start gathering data on a possible fire and prepared to share his investigation with a grand jury. That scent led quickly to Tom DeLay, his top political aide Jim Ellis, and the organization they had founded, Texans for a Republican Majority. It appears that DeLay's Texas PAC, something of a state franchise of his national leadership PAC, coordinated its campaign spending and consulting with the TAB. And that much of the money DeLay's Texas PAC spent on the elections was raised from corporations (including Westar).

TRMPAC raised approximately $600,000 from corporate benefactors. They could have evaded prosecution if they could reasonably explain the expenditures as administrative. But it was too hard a sell. Utilities and rent are administrative expenses. TRMPAC spent the corporate money on polling, phone banks, and fundraising events. Their own 2000 IRS filings came back to bite them on their asses. TRMPAC's accountant explained expenses of $1,027,086 on the 2002 IRS form as "campaign expenses." On another line, $1,168,513 for grants and donations, the accountant was more explicit and helpful: "Activities related to support of Republicans for state legislature and statewide offices in the state of Texas." Another glaring problem was $190,000 in corporate "soft money" that TRMPAC wired the Republican National Committee. Two weeks later, the RNC sent out as legal "hard money" checks to seven GOP legislative candidates in the exact amount of $190,000. "Money laundering" is a charged term, but its use appeared much more plausible than what the national party called it: "coincidence."

Then there was TRMPAC's executive director John Colyandro's order to the accountant to send $152,000 to Midland for delivery to fourteen House candidates by Tom Craddick. Texas also has a law prohibiting outside interests from trying to buy the selection of a House Speaker. In his days as a reformer, Craddick had helped craft that law himself. Three decades later, he retained one of the state's top criminal lawyers to help him respond to subpoenas and the possibility of indictment by a Travis County grand jury. (The attorney would explain that Craddick's office mailed or expressed those checks; he didn't hand-deliver them. Perhaps that helped.) Ellis, Colyandro, and officials with the Texas Association of Business were braced for indictments. Texas is still the Wild West of campaign finance. Any individual can donate any amount to any candidate, as long as it is reported to the Texas Ethics Commission. But Texas law specifies that knowingly spending corporate money on a political campaign is a felony. And if Travis County D.A. Ronnie Earle finds that DeLay or anyone working for the Texas PAC did so, they could face criminal indictment. Suddenly, the big rodeo began to look like a real possibility.

In February 2004 Maria Recio of the *Fort Worth Star-Telegram* disrupted one of DeLay's Capitol Hill briefings by asking about the investigation and grand jury in Texas. The leader didn't grin but he did glare. "This is nothing more than a vindictive, typical Ronnie Earle process," DeLay lashed out. "The district attorney has a long history of being vindictive and partisan. He did it to Kay Bailey Hutchison and lost that case. He's done it to other people so that he can get press but he doesn't follow through and file charges. This is so typical. This is an attempt to criminalize politics, and we have a runaway district attorney in Texas."

"Being called vindictive and partisan by Tom DeLay is like being called ugly by a frog," Earle responded. "My job is to prosecute felonies. Texas law makes it a felony for corporations and labor unions to contribute to campaigns."

Republicans clamored for Governor Perry and the Legislature to disband Earle's public integrity unit or reassign it to attorney general Greg Abbott. (Apart from political appearances and certain conflicts, there was a constitutional problem with that: the attorney general is a civil office in the state's judiciary system.) DeLay had all but dared Earle to come after him; and it appeared quite likely he would. Taking his time, the prosecutor released one grand jury and convened another. DeLay's daughter, Danielle Ferro, was summoned to the courthouse to explain what she had done for TRMPAC as a $27,600 consultant. All she did was buy some flowers! a DeLay spokesman cried in outrage. ("How do you get *that* gig?" wrote the *Texas Observer*'s Jake Bernstein.) Ferro was believed to have little criminal exposure because she had done what she specialized in doing—organize political fundraisers. When Ferro brought in Florida GOP hero Katherine Harris for an event advancing the cause of Texas redistricting, she may have had no idea where the money that she spent came from. But the grand jury was going to be looking at how directly DeLay had involved himself in fundraising. And phone records, memos, and e-mails obtained in a separate civil suit filed by one of the Democrats DeLay's PAC defeated all point toward the Republican majority leader. Also, members of TRMPAC's board arguably had a legal obligation to know how the organization's money was being raised and spent. Tom De-Lay had been a principal officer of that board and allowed his name to stay on it for a long time.

Like all of DeLay's fundraising operations, TRMPAC traded on the brand: the DeLay name. Corporate donors were offered packages; $100,000 brought a private dinner with DeLay or other board members, $50,000 a group dinner. Jack Dillard, a veteran tobacco lobbyist in Austin, even got an invitation to a brief meeting with DeLay for a mere $10,000. The TRMPACers seemed contemptuous of Texas law that barred corporate money in political campaigns. "Corporate checks are acceptable" read an invitation to a Houston Petroleum Club event where DeLay was speaking.

When Democracy 21's Fred Wertheimer* observed that "these guys all overreach," and that overreaching ultimately brings them down, he might have been writing Tom DeLay's political epitaph. DeLay certainly overreached in May 2001, when he went back to the dependable Ken Lay to ask for $100,000 "in combination of corporate and personal money from Enron

---

*The majority leader disparages Werthimer as a "leftist" who picks on Republicans. Yet it was DeLay's good fortune that the campaign-finance advocate focused so much attention on one fundraising scheme that DeLay himself decided to shut it down. Celebrations for Children was a convention shakedown that seemed to defile the cause to which Tom and Christine DeLay have given their time, their money, and their name. Sold as a children's charity, CfC offered golf on Long Island, cruises, tickets to Broadway shows, dinners with the DeLays, and a "Members reception" after President Bush's speech at the 2004 convention in New York, at which lobbyists and corporate executives could spend an evening with House Republicans. High-dollar "Upper East Side" packages with golf, yachts, and discrete diners with the leader, were offered for $500,000. The cheap seats, "Greenwich Village" packages, sold for $10,000. (In 2003, DeLay overturned a Gingrich-era House rules reform measure that banned members from accepting golf, dinners, and other entertainment paid for by lobbyists' contribution to charity events.) While a small amount of money would be directed to the children's charity, most of what was collected would cover the cost of events open to a select group of insiders willing pay for quality time with House Republicans. It was the perfect DeLay deal; he provided convention meals, golf, and entertainment for his House delegation, underwritten by corporate lobbyists who in turn got facetime with House members. Wertheimer filed a complaint with the IRS, challenging CfC's non-profit charity status, because so little of the money raised would be used for charitable purposes. Had the IRS revoked Celebrations' nonprofit charter, lobbyists who had paid $500,000 for convention events could not have claimed the expense as a charitable tax write off. The complaint, and the bad press it created, was more than DeLay could handle while he faced civil and criminal litigation back home in Texas. Like the cruise ship he had booked to house convention delegates who would avoid the mean streets of Manhattan, Celebrations for Children was quietly retired.

executives. . . ." The request made it clear that some of the money would be spent on "the redistricting effort in Texas." One of the Enron lobbyists DeLay was asking to get the money out of Lay was Linda Robertson—a former Clinton administration aide whose hiring by Enron had been fought by DeLay and the K Street Project.

By the time the *Washington Post* broke the Enron memo story in July 2004, DeLay already knew he was in a real bind. In March the *Houston Chronicle*'s R. G. Ratcliffe had reported that DeLay had told a group of Houston supporters that he might need their help in raising money for a legal defense fund. One man quoted him as saying, "I fully expect to be indicted." Observers of the drama in Austin were startled by the report. Most believed that the indictments would fall as close as DeLay's top political aide but only scorch the leader with headlines. DeLay's press aides hotly denied that he said he would be indicted. At his D.C. press conference DeLay denied that he had discussed a legal defense fund and suggested that someone "who has given me money but isn't working in my interest" got into the Houston meeting then talked to reporters. But Ratcliffe is one of the state's most thorough political reporters and he cited several sources at the meeting. And the retainers required by the D.C. criminal defense lawyers are certain to cost DeLay far more than his annual congressional salary.

The redistricting DeLay directed won't be undone. But he might. His Texas PAC put $1.5 million into the successful races of seventeen new Republican members of the Texas House, wresting it from the Democrats and putting in place a hand-picked Speaker to do DeLay's deal on redistricting. For a year of redistricting, DeLay had been flaunting his authority and power as he presided over the sort of political cartography Texans haven't seen since Mexico gave up half of its nation by signing the Treaty of Guadalupe Hidalgo. DeLay's in big trouble in Washington. But the machinations in his home state might ultimately be his undoing.

That March, DeLay's House colleagues and the Capitol Hill paper *Roll Call* suddenly realized that the majority leader had a genuine problem on his hands in Texas. If DeLay were indicted, under a rule imposed by congressional Republicans, he would have to stand down from his leadership position. Loyalists said that in that worst-case scenario it would only be a "step aside," a temporary surrender of power. DeLay denied that report, too, calmly telling reporters seated around his elegant antique dining table that it was never discussed. But could he count on time standing still for him? Are his collaborators in Texas willing to go to jail for him, or will they talk? What would become of Tom DeLay if he lost the leverage of his power? Who would even want to play golf with him? All at once the Hammer was looking like Humpty Dumpty.

Division of the House

The modern House of Representatives was divided by design, largely the design of Newt Gingrich and Tom DeLay. It is a design that will create—and one hears this phrase from Democrats, impartial observers of the political process, and in private, Republicans—a "permanent minority." DeLay prefers a polarized House in which the adversarial relationship between Republicans and Democrats is institutionalized. "A number of times the Republican majority could pass a bill by 300 votes," said a veteran House staffer who has worked for the Democratic leadership. "A bill that has that type of potential. Then they yank it to the conservative side so it passes 220–210. . . . There's a mentality in the Republican leadership that if a significant number of Democrats support a bill somehow it's tainted.

"Part of it goes back to the K Street thing, where they want to be able to say to their funders that the only people who can deliver anything for you are Republicans." If House Republicans can make their Democratic counterparts irrelevant to the process of passing the nation's laws, they can make them irrelevant to big political contributors. Despite the best intentions of the McCain-Feingold campaign-finance law, big money is still required to win elections. Without access to it, Democrats become the permanent minority party. (DeLay spokesperson Stuart Roy openly refers to House Democrats as "irrelevant.")

"Tom DeLay needs ten or twelve more conservatives in the Republican conference to ensure he will be Speaker," said a congressional staffer. "That's why he was so aggressive in redistricting in Texas. If he can pick up four or five or six seats there, he's that much closer." DeLay made Denny Hastert Speaker and Roy Blunt majority whip. Both men were his assistants when he served as whip. He is the first majority leader in the history of the Congress to decide who holds every position in the leadership, including his own. Hill handicappers now say when the time is right, DeLay will announce and Hastert will renounce. The only question is when. Countless articles have been written about Hastert's "growing into the job" DeLay forced him into. DeLay has said Hastert turned "white as a sheet" when DeLay told him he had to run for Speaker in 1998. In truth, Hastert has grown into a role, not a job. "He likes being Speaker but isn't at all engaged or interested in policy," said a House committee staff director who has worked on the Hill since before Hastert was elected. The real power, some would say the de facto Speaker, is Hastert's chief of staff (and D.C. roommate) Scott Palmer—who matches Hastert in physical stature and surpasses him in understanding of policy and enthusiasm for political infighting. "Scott's DeLay's real adversary in the Speaker's office."

Palmer's considerable political skills and loyalty to his boss won't be enough to stop Tom DeLay when he decides it's time for him to replace Hastert. If he pulls it off, he will have ridden a river of political money into the position that is one step below the vice president in order of presidential succession. Everything Tom DeLay has achieved in leadership derives from the tens of millions of dollars he raised and then contributed to Republican House races. From the loyalty engendered by campaign contributions came his upset victory in the 1995 whip's race. The whip organization he built became another mechanism by which DeLay expanded the party's power while building and consolidating his own. During the eight years he served as majority whip, DeLay made it his business to know everything about every one of his members. He knew who had money problems, who had marital problems, who had drinking problems, and who had deviated from the official mores of the

Republican House: abstinence, heterosexual relationships among consenting unmarried adults, marital fidelity, and discreet infidelity. (DeLay can accommodate homosexuality when pragmatic politics requires it. On one occasion he told a closeted gay Republican member he would advance no further and that it was time for him to leave. On another occasion, he warned a colleague that he could either be a gay Republican congressman or an effective and productive member of the caucus.)

But it's not all about threats. "He is better than anyone I've ever seen when it comes to care and feeding of House members," said Ken Bentsen, a former Democratic House member who served with DeLay. "Feeding" is literal. Once a week, DeLay's whip organization would serve lunch to the entire Republican Conference, providing members with meals and marching orders. On late nights when the House was conducting business, DeLay would open his office to the Conference and provide barbecue, pizza, and sandwiches for all. The whip operation also included a House travel agency and service desk. If a member needed reservations at a restaurant or hotel, DeLay's staff would see that it was taken care of. "What he is," said one former GOP leader, "is a concierge, not a hammer." If a member of the Republican Conference needed to organize a fundraiser in his district, DeLay made it his business to know about it and to make it happen. He was a leader of the majority conference, director of a cadre of more than sixty deputy whips, and the concierge who provided for all their needs. "The most effective whip in the modern Congress," said American Enterprise Institute scholar Norman Ornstein.

Since he was elected to the leadership in 1995, DeLay has spent millions to elect Republicans to the House. But he has also worked (and spent his PAC money) to eliminate Republicans who refuse to get in harness when he needs them. Marge Roukema is one example of a casualty of DeLay's strategic plan to create a House dominated not only by Republicans, but by right-wing Republicans. Roukema is a social moderate and fiscal conservative. DeLay had no use for her pro-abortion-rights position and generally moderate voting record on social issues. Yet as the senior majority member of the committee in 2001, she was in line for the chair of the House Financial Affairs. Iowa Republican Jim Leach had served his six years as chairman, and was termed out by one of the reforms put in place when Gingrich became Speaker in 1995. Roukema was next in line. She had served for twenty years on House Financial Services. If the term limits Gingrich imposed on Republican committee chairs worked for Roukema, there was an unwritten rule that worked against her: for the first time in the history of the House, committee chairs are required to raise money and distribute it to Republican candidates. "It's one of the things DeLay pays careful attention to," said a Republican House staffer who requested his name not be used.

Roukema was beloved in her district, but she wasn't exactly a money magnet. "Since the seniority system is gone, candidates have to interview for chairmanships," the staff member said. "They provide a statement about their philosophy and their position on bills. But that's not what matters. When they are interviewed by the leadership, around this horseshoe table, everyone has the [philosophy] statement. But they also have a book sitting on the table. It lists the money they raised and how much they contributed to other campaigns." Smart candidates for chair competition even attach a fundraising activity report to make it easier for the steering committee that picks chairmen.

It's the money audition that matters. "They actually flip through the book as they question you," said the Republican staff member. Not only was Marge Roukema a weak fundraiser, she had spent all she raised to defend herself against a primary opponent lavishly funded by the Club for Growth—a conservative and ostensibly nonpartisan PAC to which DeLay would contribute $50,000. "It shouldn't be necessary to buy a chairmanship," Roukema said in an interview. Even if she had agreed with the money audition, Roukema said, she had no money to give to other candidates: "I had run two very expensive primaries."

Michael Oxley, a fundraising machine from Ohio, became chair of Financial Services and Roukema was sent packing. "Oxley's not that bright," said a member of a Republican House staff. "But he's always been close with the credit card companies." His ability to raise money from credit card (and insurance) companies, whose fortunes are tied to bills written by House Financial Services, won the day. "They see that committee as a good place to raise money. That's the way it's done these days," Roukema said.

The leadership tried to provide Roukema a graceful exit, shopping her around to the Bush administration as a candidate for U.S. treasurer. She refused, telling the *Washington Post* she was "gravely disappointed." With good reason. Not only had she lost the committee chair she had worked and waited for, she faced a third primary challenge from a candidate who was a far better fit for the new Republican majority DeLay is building. Because replacing Roukema with Scott Garrett would guarantee DeLay a genuine conservative in her place, neither DeLay nor his PAC provided her any help. Garrett had run two primaries against her and was gearing up for his third. The Club for Growth that had contributed $350,000 to his second primary campaign was standing ready. Her chair was denied her. So in 2002 Marge Roukema announced her retirement, after twenty-two years in the House. "I suppose it had to do with money," she said. "And Tom DeLay is very motivated in the party regarding money."

Jim Leach is a moderate, maverick Republican. Yet he got a better deal from DeLay—even if he didn't get the committee chair he was in line for. The message from DeLay was, you can stay in office, but not in power. Leach, an Iowa Republican, went through the motions in the committee chair audition. Termed-out at Financial Services, he submitted to a pro forma grilling and review of fundraising by the twenty-seven members of the Republican Steering Committee. But he was a man out of

time. He accepted no PAC money, no contributions from outside his home state, even while he was chair of Financial Services. By DeLay's standards, Jim Leach is a loser. After deluding
himself with his audition for House Foreign Relations, where he
was the senior member and next in line for the chair, Leach accepted the chairmanship of the tiny East Asia and the Pacific
Subcommittee.

Yet DeLay wasn't prepared to abandon Leach completely, as
he had Roukema. In 2002, after his district was redrawn to his
disadvantage, Leach was losing to a well-funded, popular Democrat. Leach was an independent moderate who at times voted
against the leadership, but he wasn't expendable. Tom DeLay
poured campaign staff and ARMPAC money into Leach's race,
even though Leach is far more moderate than some Democrats
(for example, he voted against the Iraq war). "DeLay's pragmatic," said a congressional source close to Leach. "He knows
he'll get one vote from Jim Leach, the vote to organize the
House." That is, the vote for House leadership that occurs at
the beginning of each Congress.

In the long run, DeLay will get more. He saved Leach's
twenty-six-year career. In doing so, he laid claim to the support
of one of the remaining Republican House moderates, sometimes referred to as the Main Street Caucus. The two dozen
centrists might have some influence—if they had backbone and
would hang together on important votes. It was, after all, the
Main Streeters (under a different collective name, they change
every year as they lose ground) who joined Democrats to kill the
appropriations riders DeLay wrote to destroy the EPA in 1995.
That was another time. The moderates have since been house-
broken. Ornstein uses a technical term to describe them:
"wusses."

The 2004 and 2006 elections will diminish the "Wuss Caucus" even further. (If the Club for Growth can field and fund a
candidate who can win Iowa's Second District, DeLay's loyalty
to Jim Leach will disappear.) The consensus on the Hill is that

they have missed their moment to organize and negotiate with the conservatives who dominate the Republican Conference. They are no longer an obstacle for DeLay. Their lack of independence is ridiculed by what he calls his "catch and release" program, by which he has the House floor whips hold the moderates in line for critical votes—until the bill he is promoting passes. Then he turns them loose to vote their convictions—if that's a term that can be applied to them.

Tom DeLay and George W. Bush are almost the same age. The two began their political careers in Austin, share the same anti-regulatory, anti-tax political philosophy, and are both born-again Christians. When DeLay became majority leader, he was immediately included in the weekly leadership meetings at the White House. That invitation was never extended to Dick Armey, whose last two years as majority leader coincided with the first two years of the Bush presidency. The president extended the invitation in deference to DeLay's power, although the decision was probably informed by Lyndon Johnson's observation that it's "better to have him inside the tent pissin' out than outside the tent pissin' in."

Despite the presidential courtesy and deference to the real and not titular power in the House, DeLay is the one member of the Republican leadership in Congress who cannot be counted on to do the president's bidding. Bush first antagonized DeLay during the 2000 presidential campaign, when he criticized House budget cuts and said DeLay shouldn't try to "balance the budget on the backs of the poor." DeLay responded that Bush didn't understand how Congress works. After the election, DeLay embarrassed the president by refusing to extend Bush's tax cuts to 6.5 million low-income families earning between $10,500 and $26,625 a year. Denying tax breaks to the poor families who were cut out of the bill was unseemly if nothing else, making it difficult to sell as compassionate conservatism a tax cut package that primarily benefited the wealthy. Yet DeLay refused to accommodate the White House—unless he got additional tax cuts that would never be passed by the Senate. And the Senate, which responded with the quick fix Bush demanded, would never concede to the tax cuts DeLay wanted in the bill. The majority leader was openly contemptuous of the president. "Ain't going to happen," he said when asked about Bush's request that the House fix the tax-credit provision. When Bush spokesperson Ari Fleischer reiterated the president's request, DeLay was resolute: "The last time I checked they [the White House] don't have a vote." Bush even pulled DeLay aside at a White House function and told him he "didn't appreciate" DeLay using his position to block the low-income tax-credit. According to a congressional source, "DeLay never blinked."

DeLay has crossed Bush on other issues, such as his Middle East policy and the No Child Left Behind bill, which DeLay voted for but described as "that awful education bill." But nowhere has the majority leader's obstructionism been so disappointing to the president than on the energy bill. "Tom DeLay killed the bill," an energy lobbyist said in an interview in late December 2003. "It would have been signed into law now if he would have agreed to compromise on one issue."

George Bush wanted his national energy policy as a campaign issue for the 2004 election. Before he was sworn into office, he enlisted a coal and gas lobbyist he would later appoint as second in command at the Interior Department to convene a meeting of energy lobbyists at the American Petroleum Institute and find out what they wanted in an energy bill. After the election Bush assigned Dick Cheney the task of drafting a comprehensive energy policy, developed in a series of closed-door meetings of an energy working group. The result was an energy bill informed by Cheney's industry working group and loaded down with tax breaks and deregulatory incentives befitting an administration directed by two former oilmen. Yet it was unacceptable to DeLay because it stiffed one of his constituency groups while rewarding a group he has resolved to destroy.

So DeLay said no.

The bill died because DeLay insisted on a provision that would protect producers of MTBE from civil lawsuits. MTBE is a gasoline additive that is also an environmental and public health hazard. "It was a tort reform measure forced into an energy bill," said the energy lobbyist. DeLay wanted to protect the producers of MTBE, who do business in Texas and Louisiana and contribute generously to his and to other Republican PACs. He also wanted to ensure that no trial lawyer made any money suing on behalf of states or individuals harmed by MTBE. "Trial lawyers are bloodsuckers," DeLay said at a press conference. "They don't create any wealth. They don't create any jobs. They suck blood."

DeLay guaranteed the failure of the bill by inserting a "reach back" provision on MTBE lawsuits, according to a source on the House Energy Committee. "There was no way," she said, "that the Senate was going to accept a provision that basically voided lawsuits filed since the previous October." Not all the suits were opportunistic, frivolous, and driven by blood-sucking plaintiffs' lawyers. Several states had gone to court, or were in the process of going to court, to force industries to pay for expensive cleanups of MTBE. Despite personal entreaties from a president and vice president in his own party, DeLay didn't move.

"It was a lousy bill. It was an industry bill. And DeLay did the country a great favor, regardless of his intentions," said a public interest lobbyist who spent the fall of 2003 working against the bill.

All in all, it was an impressive demonstration of the power base that Tom DeLay has built in the House—and something few believe that Speaker Hastert could have pulled off even if he had had the resolve to stand up to the president.

The failure to pass an energy bill was a huge loss for the White House. Yet Bush knows that more often than not, DeLay has used the power he has cultivated over the past ten years to advance the administration's legislative agenda—often in the face of what seems like opposition that cannot be overcome. After getting his two tax-cut bills through the Congress and signed into law, Bush badly needed a big domestic policy set piece, if for no other reason than to ensure working-class Americans that their president knew they were out there. To that end, the Bush administration wanted to pass Medicare reform with a prescription drug benefit before the 2004 campaign began in earnest. Yet the $400 billion bill was in trouble. (It wasn't even a $400 billion bill; the White House had an executive agency actuary withhold the report that determined the cost of the bill will be greater than $500 billion.) Only DeLay, working with Speaker Hastert, could save it.

They did. In one of the most bizarre and contentious floor votes ever seen—or perhaps not seen—in the House, Hastert, DeLay, and Majority Whip Roy Blunt passed the president's Medicare reform bill. And they did it while almost no one was watching. And even those watching couldn't see; sometime between three and six in the morning, two days after the November 2003 meeting at which Blunt and DeLay whipped Republican members toward the big Medicare vote, the C-SPAN television camera in the House chamber stopped its slow panning across the floor and focused its cold eye on the Democrats. To their own surprise, Democrats and (a handful of Republican budget hawks concerned about adding a $400 billion to the ballooning Bush deficit) had stopped the Medicare reform bill that DeLay was trying to push through the House. The vote tally board indicated the Medicare reform proposal was failing, and the numbers on the board held fast for almost two hours.

At five o'clock on the morning of November 22 it was over. "Our whipping of that bill was perfect," said a Democratic member who watched the entire process. "We won that vote. The Republican leadership couldn't believe that we held our members together." The House Democrats had won—despite the record length of time the vote was kept open. In the House, a vote is called and the clock begins to run. By a tradition that is almost a hard rule members are allowed fifteen minutes to cast their votes. Democrats had abused the process on occasion when they were in the majority. But never to this extreme. In 1987 Democratic Majority Jim Wright added ten minutes to a vote and a Republican whip named Dick Cheney called it "the greatest abuse of democracy" he had seen in his lifetime. It was the only time the Democrats substantially exceeded the fifteen minutes during the thirty-two years since the electronic voting system was put in place.

C-SPAN televises all House proceedings. But the leadership controls the movement of the camera. The C-SPAN camera looked the other way in the pre-dawn hours of November 22 to allow DeLay and Hastert to go to work on uncooperative Republicans. "They were working the floor looking for members they could bully," one Republican representative said. At almost six in the morning, with the camera focused on the Democratic side of the aisle and no videotape record of what the Republican leaders and whips were doing, the House leadership prevailed. After prowling the floor for three hours, DeLay and Hastert forced two Republicans to change their votes. A few others followed. The presiding officer banged the gavel. And the largest single entitlement ever enacted by any Congress passed in the longest open vote in the history of the House—by a 220-215 margin.

The process was not only flawed by the extended vote. In the course of the three hours Hastert and DeLay kept the vote open, someone working with the Republican leadership team got a little overzealous and offered a colleague a $100,000 bribe. On the day after the vote, Michigan Republican Nick Smith told a reporter he was offered $100,000 for the campaign of his son who was running to succeed him. And warned that if he didn't change his vote, House Republicans would work against his son's election. Smith repeated his charge on radio.

Then something odd happened. Nick Smith changed his mind and said it never happened.

At a DeLay pen and pad conference in the dining room beside his office, the leader was asked about Democratic whip Steny Hoyer's suggestion that the House Ethics Committee investigate Smith's initial claim. "I think the Democrats in the House ought to leave their campaign plan out of the chamber," DeLay said. "They are trying to politicize the ethics committee, and I think that's wrong. They are starting to throw mud and try to burn down the House. They are going to find out that the mud is going to get all over them." When a Fox News reporter asked a follow-up question, DeLay cut him off and the session abruptly ended. DeLay knew it was unlikely that the Ethics Committee would take up the issue, because it was unlikely any Democrat would file a complaint. A complaint would end the ethics truce, and inevitably lead to complaints filed by Republicans. And by a House rule passed seven years earlier, no outsider party can file an ethics complaint in the House. "Mud all over them" can be interpreted as "end the truce and begin filing complaints before the moribund ethics committee, and we will come back at you." Such a threat was a powerful restraint, considering Republican lack of restraint in using their majority position to punish the Democrats. (The truce would later blow up over Texas redistricting: A defeated Houston congressman, Chris Bell, filed an ethics complaint against DeLay; the GOP immediately filed a complaint over the tactics of Dallas Democrat Martin Frost.)

The Medicare bill passed the Senate, and not one Democrat was appointed to the conference committee that resolved minor House and Senate differences, while the Senate leadership refused to allow minority leader Tom Daschle to sit on the committee. And George Bush got his Medicare reform, with a prescription benefit for seniors—drafted by the pharmacy lobby.

As Barney Frank saw it, a month after he stood sputtering in anger on the House floor at six in the morning, the Medicare vote was the most egregious example he has yet seen of the new Republican order. "They kept it open for three hours," he said in his office. "Their fall back was to move for reconsideration and adjourn. That means keep it open indefinitely. Indefinitely. If you are the Republican and you are told at six in the morning that this is never going to end until you give up, you give up. You can't outwait them."

"This is transformative," Frank said of the Republican House. "Unlike anything we have seen in the past 100 years. De-Lay has the power and inclination to sweep aside any constraint . . . any institutional or procedural constraint."

With all the institutional and procedural constraints removed; with former DeLay chief of staff Susan Hirschmann working for the big health providers and leading the lobbying effort; with the president on the phone with members in the middle of the night and the Secretary of Health and Human Services making an unprecedented visit to the House floor; with the true costs of a "$400 billion" entitlement kept out of legislators' hands by order of Medicare director Thomas Scully; and with a promise of $100,000 contribution made on the floor of the House, the Medicare bill passed at sunrise—as the public eye was literally turned the other direction by the Republican leadership. (Even the AARP was domesticated, having hired former Nixon supporter and Gingrich enthusiast William Novelli as CEO to accommodate the K Street project requirement that Republicans get the big jobs in the lobby.)

In a system of results-oriented democracy, the results are preordained by the leadership. "They have the same kind of discipline as the British Conservative or Labour Party," Frank said. "That's why anybody who votes for a Republican in November is voting for Tom DeLay."

It was a partisan observation but nonetheless valid and insightful. Tom DeLay will someday be elected Speaker. When he does, he will in effect be the first prime minister of the United States.

Sources

Prologue: Kicking Ass and Taking Names
The Republican majority of winning by narrow margins was reported by Juliet Eilperin, "House GOP Practices Art of One-Vote Victories," *Washington Post* (October 14, 2003), Republican relationships with Democrats are described by Norman Ornstein, "To Boost Power, Unity Is Key for Both Parties," *Roll Call* (September 8, 2003).

Interviewed for the prologue were Norman Ornstein (Telephone, April 2004), Representative Barney Frank (Washington, D.C., December 2004), Representative Henry Waxman (Washington, D.C., April 2004), Representative Deborah Pryce (Washington, D.C., November 2003).

Chapter 1: Born in the USA
Tom DeLay's early years have been described in several profiles. The most penetrating and compelling was by Peter Perl, "Absolute Truth," *Washington Post* (May 2001). Also useful are Jeff Godell's "The Exterminator of Capitol Hill (*Rolling Stone,* May 5, 2001) and Timothy Noah, "The Exterminator," *George* (February 1999).

The wide range in reaction to the man and his politics has been demonstrated by the sympathetic and respectful Richard E. Cohen, "The Silent Hammer," *National Journal* (February 2002) and Hanna Rosin, "Whiplash," *New Republic* (February 1996)—personally offended and aghast.

Interviewed on the general subject of Webb County history and politics were *LareDOS* editor and publisher María Eugenia Guerra, State Representative Richard Raymond, and State Senator Judith Zaffirini, all of Laredo. Frank Stagg, a longtime friend of the DeLay family, contributed a valuable interview and morning-long tour of Mirando City and the area's once-booming oilfield.

Among many other sources, authoritative capsule histories of Texas politics, the oil boom along the Texas-Mexico border, and the birth and decline of Mirando City can be found in the multi-volume *The Handbook of Texas* (Austin: Texas State Historical Association, last updated 2002).

DeLay described his years in Venezuela in a lecture at the Churchill Memorial of Westminster College, in Fulton, Missouri, in October 2003. He told the story about his family's harassment on a Cuban airstrip early in Fidel Castro's regime in an appearance on *Meet the Press,* April 2003.

Chapter 2: Sugar Land

The rich history of Sugar Land is explored in several articles in *The Handbook of Texas* and on the city's website. The experience of the town's football star, Ken Hall, was related by Jim Dent in *The Junction Boys* (New York: St. Martin's, 1999). As a prism into the politics and power of DeLay, Sugar Land was well-described by Carolyn Lockhead, "GOP Leader's Texas Sweet Spot," *San Francisco Chronicle* (January 2003) and Helen Thorpe, "The Exterminator," *Texas Monthly* (April 1999).

From a range of perspectives and emphases, Texas's change from a Democratic to a Republican state is explored by David Richards, *Once Upon a Time in Texas: A Liberal in the Lone Star State* (Austin: University of Texas Press, 2002); Lou Dubose, Jan Reid, and Carl M. Cannon, *Boy Genius: Karl Rove, the Brains Behind the Remarkable Political Triumph of George W. Bush* (New York: PublicAffairs, 2003); Molly Ivins and Lou Dubose, *Shrub: The Short but Happy Political Life of George W. Bush* (New York: Random House, 2000); Bill Minutaglio, *First Son: George W. Bush and the Bush Family Dynasty* (New York: Times Books, 1999); and Patrick Cox, *Ralph W. Yarborough: The People's Senator* (Austin: University of Texas Press, 2002).

Tom DeLay's initial run for the Texas Legislature was covered sketchily by the *Houston Chronicle* and the *Houston Post* in 1978. His voting record in the Legislature is provided by Kate Fain.

Interviewed for this chapter were musicologist Bob Simmons, who confirmed the Sugar Land past of convict and blues singer Huddie Ledbetter; Hilmar Moore, Hilmar Moore, Jr., and Chip Briscoe, on the political past and terrain of Sugar Land and Fort Bend County; and Texas author Vallie Fletcher Taylor, one of the Republican women drawn to and supportive of DeLay's candidacy in 1978. Former state senators A. R. "Babe" Schwartz and Carl Parker, former state representative Debra Danburg, former Texas land commissioner Garry Mauro, Austin attorney Shelia Cheney, and longtime Texas political correspondent Sam Kinch shared their perspectives on DeLay's record and social swath while a member of the State Legislature.

Chapter 3: Freshman Year: The Exterminator Meets Jesus

DeLay's first campaign for Congress in 1984 was covered by the *Houston Chronicle* and the *Houston Post*. During his freshman term, Kathy Kiely of the *Post*'s Washington bureau provided rich coverage of DeLay's adjustment to his new life on Capitol Hill and his assault on the budget and taste in poetry of the National Endowment for the Arts. Prescient in its analysis of DeLay, Dick Armey, and the importance of that freshman class to the Texas GOP was Peter Applebome, "The Texas Six-Pack," *Texas Monthly* (June 1985).

The books of Minutaglio and Ivins and Dubose, op. cit., convey the unusual circumstances of the religious conversion of George W. Bush. The material on Rev. James Dobson is adapted from his website and his address at Trinity University in San Antonio, "Where's Dad?" The *Washington Post* magazine profile of DeLay by Peter Perl, op. cit., contains revealing information on DeLay's spiritual life and beliefs.

Interviewed during the research of this chapter was Peter Applebome, a reporter for the *New York Times*. In 1985, then on the staff of *Texas Monthly*, Applebome interviewed DeLay at length while reporting an article on the significance of the "Texas Six-Pack" of GOP House members who were freshmen that year. Author's visits to worship and Bible Study at First Baptist Church of Pearland provided insight into Rev. Scott Rambo's congregation. An interview with several members of the congregation who requested their names be withheld provided some insight into how the DeLays fit into First Baptist's congregation.

Chapter 4: Solidifying the Base

Tim Fleck of the *Houston Press* witnessed the congressman's ill-advised press conference at the Republican national convention in 1988 and has made sure that DeLay's perspectives on military service in Vietnam, offered in defense of Dan Quayle, continues to be part of his public record.

Fleck's colleague at the *Press,* Michael Berryhill, rigorously covered DeLay's performance in the twenty-second district through the 1990s. Berryhill wrote about DeLay's attitudes toward highway construction and environmental protection, his personal and professional relationship with his younger brother Randy DeLay, and the lawsuit against Albo Pest Control, which triggered Tom DeLay's rancorous behavior in Fort Bend County during 1994. Berryhill's instructive articles included "The Exterminator" (November 1995), "Buggy Business" (November 1995), and "Road Hogs" (November 1997). Berryhill shared his extensive files of documents, including IRS forms and court depositions, with the authors of this book. In a well-researched article for a Houston magazine, Joe Conason shed light on longtime associates of the Bush family, the Cinco Ranch development on the outskirts of Sugar Land, and its connection to the Grand Parkway real estate and highway building scam—"Texas-Fried Ethics," *The Voice* (March 1989).

Peter Perl, op. cit., skillfully portrayed the deep estrangements of the DeLay family in his article in the *Washington Post.* Ray DeLay described his ministry on a Net Ministries Web page. His continuing legal troubles were reported by Perl and by the *Houston Chronicle.*

Chapter 5: Now the Revolution

Elizabeth Drew's *Showdown: The Struggle Between the Gingrich Congress and the Clinton White House* (New York: Simon and Schuster, 1996) is a remarkable account of Newt Gingrich's House.

Also cited are: Dick Armey, "Down with the Palace Guard," *New York Times* (November 26, 1991), Dan Balz, "GOP Contract Pledges 10 Tough Acts to Follow," *Washington Post* (November 20, 1994), Gareth Cook, "Laws for Sale," *Washington Monthly* (July 1995), Robert Dreyfuss, "Political Snipers," *American Prospect* (Fall 1995), Mike Feinsilber, "How the Republicans Would Get the Deficit to Zero," Associated Press (May 19, 1995), Ira Flatow, "Carol Browner's Tenure as EPA Administrator," NPR Radio: *Talk of the Nation* (December 22, 2000), Dick Goldstein, "Pit Bull Vies for House Whip," *Philadelphia Inquirer* (December 4, 1994), Julie Hollar, "The DeLay Chronicles: A Nice Guy in Austin," *The Texas Observer* (February 2, 2000), Karen Masterson, "Money Boosts DeLay's Prestige," *Houston Chronicle* (January 5, 2003), Dan Morgan, "Environmental Laws Under Ax," *Washington Post*, (March 16, 1995), Grover G. Norquist, "Whipped into Shape," *American Spectator* (February 1995), Benjamin Sheffner, "McCollum's Last-Minute Blitz," *Roll Call* (December 19, 1994), Peter Stone, "Taking Care of Business," *National Journal* (March 2, 1996), Michael Weisskopf and David Maraniss, "Inside the Revolution," *Washington Post* (March 12, 1995), Robert Worth, "Asleep on the Beat; Environmental Laws," *Washington Monthly* (November 1, 1999), John E. Yang, "Reps. Walker, a Gingrich Ally, and Geren Decide to Retire," *Washington Post* (December 16, 1995), "House Passes Controversial Bill Cutting EPA's Budget," *Chemical Marketing Reporter* (August 7, 1995).

Interviewed for this chapter: Ken Bentsen (Washington, D.C., March 2004), Carol Browner (Washington, D.C., October 2003), Scott Lilly (Washington, D.C., March 2004), Representative David Obey (Washington, D.C., March 2004). A Former EPA official interviewed for this chapter requested his name not be published.

Chapter 6: Everything Is Deregulated

To his probable regret, DeLay agreed to let two reporters for the *Washington Post,* David Maraniss and Michael Weisskopf, observe the sessions to massively revise or eliminate federal regulations during the 1995 Congress. The four-part series, which ran between November 1995 and January 1996, won them the Pulitzer and first established DeLay as a national figure and front-line player in GOP politics.

Lending further meaning to the Contract with America Congress was DeLay's appearance on a Walter Cronkite documentary report, "Environment Beware," on the Discovery Channel in October 1996.

Jan Reid, in "Poison and Pork," *Mother Jones* (October 1996), described the close cooperation of Congressman DeLay and his attorney-lobbyist brother Randy, pushing legislative priorities that included a Mexican cement monopoly, the merger of the Union Pacific and Southern Pacific railroads, and routing of the I-69 interstate highway through Sugar Land. The subsequent ethics investigation in the House cleared Delay but resulted in a total break in relations with his brother, as described by Perl, op. cit.

Bushwhacked: Life in George W. Bush's America, by Molly Ivins and Lou Dubose (New York: Random House, 2003), is our source for the 2001 reversal of the OSHA Ergonomic Rules; also Stephen Greenhouse, "Senate Votes to Repeal Rules Clinton Set on Workplace Injuries," *New York Times* (March 7, 2001).

Other sources are: Federal News Service Transcript, "Hearing of the Veterans Affairs, HUD and Independent Agencies Subcommittee of the House Appropriations Committee" (April 15–18, 1996), *Congressional Record,* Senator Chris Dodd (March 6, 2001), *Congressional Record,* Senator Paul Wellstone (March 6, 2001), Property Records, Alexandria, Virginia (January 1, 2003), Property Records, Fort Bend County (Texas) Tax Assessor-Collector (2004).

In interviews conducted in 1996, Houston environmental attorney Jim Blackburn, Lake Jackson and Galveston Bay area activist Sharon Stewart, and Tom Smith of Public Citizen provided insight into DeLay's record on issues of ecology and conservation in his district. Kate Fain assembled and shed light on DeLay's voting record on environmental issues in Congress. Ross Milloy, a *New York Times* correspondent who also worked as a consultant on transportation issues in Texas, discussed the railroad merger and the maneuvering to dictate the route of the new interstate highway. Gary Ruskin, then of the Congressional Accountability Project in Washington, provided the driving force of the ethics investigation of Tom DeLay and his lobbyist brother Randy.

Chapter 7: DeLay Inc.: The Man and His Political Money

The account of Peter Cloeren's relationship with Tom DeLay, Brian Babin, and Triad Inc., is told in great detail in the Federal Election Commission's General Counsel's Reports (MUR # 4783 June 16, 1999), and in Peter Cloeren's August 6, 1998, affidavit delivered to minority members of the House Committee on Government Reform and Oversight.

Juliet Eilperin of the *Washington Post* has thoroughly reported on Tom DeLay. Her "Fundraising Focus Earns DeLay Wealth of Influence," *Washington Post* (July 22, 2003) is an extraordinary account of DeLay's fundraising in Texas as a prelude to the 2002 state elections. Her other articles herein used are: "House Whip Wields Fundraising

Clout," *Washington Post* (October 19, 1999), "Republicans Crying War in Suit Against DeLay," *Washington Post* (May 6, 2000), "Targeting Lobbyists Pays Off for GOP" (with Jim VandeHei), *Washington Post* (June 26, 2003), "Westar Lobbyist's Role Detailed," *Washington Post* (June 10, 2003).

The numbers crunching that provided the documental content for Eilperin's July 22, 2003, article is found in Democracy 21's "DeLay, Inc.: House Majority Leader Tom DeLay and His Money Machine," investigated and published by Fred Wertheimer and Rebecca Webber on July 22, 2003. Additional accounts on money were found in "Congressional Leaders' Soft Money Accounts Show Need for Campaign Finance Reform Bills," Public Citizen Congress Watch (February 2002).

Other reporting that informed this chapter is Greg Hitt, "Republican Had Questions About Groups Tied to DeLay," *Wall Street Journal* (June 1, 2000), Kevin Galvin, "DeLay Urged Illegal Campaign Gifts," Associated Press (October 9, 1998), Janet Hook, "Democrats Target DeLay in Suit That Calls His Fund-Raising Extortion," *Los Angeles Times* (September 24, 2000), David Montgomery, "Democrats Portray DeLay As Enron Poster Boy," Knight Ridder Tribune News Service (March 10, 2002), W. John Moore, "Kindred Spirits," *National Journal* (December 19–26, 2003), "This Story Has It All, Triad, Funneling, Even Tom DeLay," *National Journal* (August 7, 1998).

Interviewed for this chapter were Craig Holman (Washington, D.C., February 2004), Fred Wertheimer (Washington, D.C., October 2003), Rebecca Webber (Washington, D.C., October 2003), Representative Jerrold Nadler (Washington, D.C., December 2003), Gino Karpenksi (Washington, D.C., September 2003), Norman Ornstein (Telephone, April 2004), Craig McDonald (Austin, Texas, August 2003).

Chapter 8: Revolt Within the Revolution

Helen Thorpe's profile of DeLay in *Texas Monthly,* op. cit., conveyed a vivid portrait of the whip's office and team as the center of real power in the House between 1996 and 1997. The congressional career of his close ally Bill Paxon was summarized in the "All Politics" website of CNN/Time.

One former member of the House Republican conference generously provided insight into DeLay's role in the 1997 coup.

Chapter 9: Whipping the President

Peter Baker's *The Breach: Inside the Impeachment and Trial of William Jefferson Clinton* (New York: Scribner's, 2000) is the definitive investigation of that tempest in recent American politics. The impeachment is also thoroughly covered in Sidney Blumenthal's *The Clinton Wars* (New York: Farrar, Straus, and Giroux, 2003). The timing of Helen Thorpe's *Texas Monthly* assignment, op. cit., provided her with unmatched access to DeLay and a perspective of his role during the meltdown of House Speaker-designate Bob Livingston.

Additional accounts of the impeachment were found in Carl Cannon, "How Impeachment Became Inevitable," *National Journal* (December 19,2003), James Carney and John F. Dickerson, "The Big Push to Impeach: It's Coming from Tom DeLay," *Time* (December 14, 1998), Mike Dorning, "DeLay Scolds Clinton Over Allegations," *Chicago Tribune* (March 28, 1998), Juliet Eilperin, "DeLay Mobilizes Hill Effort with Aim of Clinton Resignation," *Washington Post* (August 28, 1998), James Gertenzang, "Tensions Over Impeachment Continue to Flare," *Los Angeles Times* (December 25, 1998), Linda Hennenberger, "DeLay Has Little Need for Hammer," *New York Times* (December 17, 1998), Judy Holland, "GOP Leader Blasts Clinton: House Majority Whip Says Clinton Has No Shame," *Fort Lauderdale Sun Sentinel* (March 28, 1998).

Tom DeLay's speeches on the floor of the House are found in *The Federal Document Clearing House Transcripts* (December 19, 1998) and *The Congressional Record* (September 15, 1998 and September 24, 1998).

Interviewed for this chapter were Sidney Blumenthal, who directed us to other sources and source material (Washington, D.C., February 2004), Ken Bentsen (Washington, D.C., March 2004), Lanny Davis (Washington, D.C., December 2003). Two former House staffers interviewed for this chapter requested their names be withheld. Also interviewed for this chapter were Denver journalist Helen Thorpe, formerly of *Texas Monthly*, and Susan DeQuesnay, a longtime political columnist for the *Fort Bend Star*. DeQuesnay shed new light on the mystery surrounding DeLay's much-rumored "other daughter." Scott McCown, a Democrat, former Travis County district judge, and activist on family issues, described being asked by DeLay to come to Washington and brief the congressman and his staff on new approaches to foster care.

Chapter 10: K Street Kingpin

An account of lobbyists being required to whip bills is found in Robert Dreyfuss's "DeLay Incorporated," *The Texas Observer* (February 2, 2000). Nicholas Confessore's "Welcome to the Machine: How the GOP Disciplined K Street and Made Bush Supreme," *Washington Monthly* (July/August 2003) is a thorough examination of the new Republican lobby.

Other sources cited are Gloria Borger, "Just a Little Respect," *U.S. News & World Report* (October 26, 1998), Kathleen Day and Jim Vande-Hei, "Congressman Urges Republican Lobbyist," *Washington Post* (February 15, 2003), Juliet Eilperin, "No Democrat Need Apply," *Washington Post* (October 14, 1998), Juliet Eilperin, "Business Group Backs Democrat Whose Hiring Irked GOP Leaders," *Washington Post* (October 15, 1998), "Intimidation" (Editorial) *Roll Call* (May 17, 1999), David Jackson, "Connections Make the Lobbyist: Ed Gillespie. . . ," *Dallas Morning News* (February 17, 2002), Louis Jacobson, "The DeLay Factor on K Street," *National Journal* (January 4, 2002), Jim VandeHei and John Bresnahan, "Lobbyists Battle Boiling Over McCurdy. . . ," *Roll Call* (October 15, 1998), Brody Mullins, "K Street Doors Finally Open for GOP," *Roll Call* (January 26, 2003), Timothy Noah, "Who Cares If DeLay Bullies Lobbyists," *Slate* (July 11, 2003), Alison Mitchell, "Enron Efforts to Please DeLay Exceeded Campaign Donations," *Houston Chronicle* (January 16, 2002), "Star Rainmakers: The Hill's List of Top lobbyists," *The Hill* (March 26, 2003), Susan Page, "Field of Dreamers, Finally Some Democrats Who Would Be President," *Newsday* (September 14, 1991), Peter Stone, "One Hammer, Plenty of Nails," *National Journal* (June 12, 1999), Shawn Zeller, "McCurdy's Survival Instinct," *National Journal* (July 17, 1999), Editorial, "The Hammer and His Lists," *Washington Post* (December 3, 1995).

Also: Congressman Lamar Smith, Committee on Standards of Official Conduct, "Memorandum for All Members: Prohibition Against Linking Official Actions to Partisan or Political Considerations, or Personal Gain Officers and Employees, Congressman," Committee on Standards of Official Conduct (May 11, 1999), Hilary Rosen, "Prepared Statement," House Judiciary Committee, Federal News Service (September 17, 1997), "Dave McCurdy: President," EIA website, 2003.

Interviewed for this chapter were: Hilary Rosen (Washington D.C., March 2003), Peter McCloskey (Telephone, Washington, D.C., April 2003), Representative Jerrold Nadler (Washington, D.C., November 2003). Three sources, one House staff member and two lobbyists interviewed in October and November 2003, requested that their names be withheld.

Chapter 11: Saipan

Dennis Greenia's masterful reporting and documentation and his generous sharing of his files deepened the authors' understanding of the K Street network of lobbyist allies, most of them former aides, that DeLay assembled in the nineties. The episode in the Marianas Islands was both an outgrowth of that expanding base of power and a forerunner of the bilking of Native American tribes by certain of those lobbyists and DeLay associates.

Two reports by California Congressman George Miller and the Democratic staff of the House Committee on Resources in 1997 and 1998 revealed the broad outlines of labor abuse and exploitation by textile sweatshops in the Marianas. The Global Survival Network, an international organization devoted to women's issues, published a revealing report on forced-labor trafficking in the Marianas in 1999. The U.S. Department of Labor provided reports of its prosecutions and penalties between 1998 and 2000.

Juliet Eilperin of the *Washington Post* wrote about DeLay's "Petri dish of capitalism" and the GOP junkets in July 2000. Other news organizations that uncovered this exotic state of affairs included the *Houston Chronicle, The Hill, National Journal,* and *Saipan Tribune.*

In several days of interviews in Washington, D.C., and on the Chesapeake Bay in Maryland, Dennis Greenia shared his voluminous knowledge of DeLay's network of allies on K Street, the Republicans' choice of the Marianas Islands as their favorite exotic beach resort, DeLay's high-profile junket to Saipan for the New Year's holiday in 1998, the textile sweatshops, and attempts by DeLay to force the Marianas commonwealth to grant a large power plant construction contract to Enron. Also interviewed at length for this chapter were Congressman George Miller of California and his chief of staff, John Lawrence.

Chapter 12: Remaking Texas . . . and American Democracy

Newspaper and periodical sources include Matthew Berger, "AIPAC, Congressional Trips Are Effective Way to Boost Israel," *JTA Global News Service* (August 20, 2003), Jonathan Broder, "DeLay Flexes Muscles on Middle East Issue," *CQ Weekly* (May 4, 2002), Tom DeLay, "Israel's Fight Is Our Fight," *Jerusalem Post* (August 1, 2003), William Cook, "Armageddon Anxiety," *Counterpunch* (February 22, 2003), Matthew Engel, "Meet the New Zionists," *Guardian* (October 28, 2002), David Firestone, "Tom DeLay Is to Carry Dissenting Message . . . ," *Middle East Information Center* (July 25, 2003), John Hagee, "All the Gospel to All the World," *JMH Magazine* (Vol. 15, No 2. 2003), Johann Hari, "A Writer at Large: Apocalypse Soon," *Independent* (June 29, 2003), Clifford Kiracofe, "President Bush and the Christian Zionist Lobby," *Lebanon Wire* (May 2, 2002), Daniel Levitas, "A Marriage Made for Heaven," *Reform Judaism Magazine* (Summer 2003), Mara Liason, "Profile: Pro Israel Stance Helping to Link American Jews, the Republican Party . . . ," National Public Radio (May 16, 2002), Barbara Richmond, "Texas Evangelical Christians Give $1.5 Million to Israel," *Jewish Journal of San Antonio* (November 5, 2003), Douglas Turner "Christian Zionists Resist Middle East Peace," *Buffalo News* (August 17, 2003).

Also: "The Hammer in the Holy Land," *Chicago Tribune* (August 1, 2003), "Israel's Christian Soldiers," *New York Magazine* (September 29, 2003), "Texas Taliban," *Texas Observer* (December 6, 2002), "Majority Leader Tom DeLay and CoDel Meets Chabat's Terror Victims Project for Children," *U.S. Newswire* (July 29, 2003), "DeLay: Administration Right to Veto Anti-Israel Resolution," *U.S. Newswire* (September 17, 2003).

Speeches cited are Tom DeLay, "Do Not Be Afraid" (Israel, July 30, 2003), Tom DeLay, "ZOA Award Acceptance" (New York, November 16, 2003), John Hagee, "Night to Honor Israel" (San Antonio, Texas, November 2003), Morton Klein, "Remarks and Introduction, Justice Louis D. Brandeis Awards Dinner" (New York, November 16, 2003), Benjamin Netanyahu, "Night to Honor Israel" (San Antonio, November 4, 2001).

Interviews for this chapter were with Representative Barney Frank (Washington, D.C., December 2003), who addressed Jewish political contributions in an interview on another topic (Washington, D.C., December 2004), Morton Klein (New York, November 2003), Rabbi David Saperstein (Washington, D.C., December 2003), James Zogby (Washington, December 2003). Also interviewed were one State Department official and two former State Department officials who requested their names not be used for publication and five attendees at the November 2003 Zionist Organization of America awards banquet, who requested their names not be used for publication.

Press releases cited are Jacob Goodman: "ZOA Strongly Supports Majority Leader Tom DeLay's Statement" (July 31, 2003), William J. Murray, Religious Freedom Coalition, "Washington School Prayer Rally a Success" (September 21, 2001).

Chapter 13: Apocalypse Now

The authors are deeply indebted to Fred Lewis of Campaigns for People for his patient explanations and sharing of documents regarding the congressional redistricting controversy that consumed Texas politics in 2003.

Jake Bernstein and Dave Mann provided the most comprehensive interpretation of the complex events in *Texas Observer* articles that included "Scandal in the Speaker's Office" (February 2004) and "Rate of Exchange" (March 2004). Their colleague Felix Gillette measured the political aftershocks in "Cleaning House" (March 2004).

Juliet Eilperin of the *Washington Post* did a masterful job of connecting the dots and describing the span of the story in a "Fundraising Focus Earns DeLay Wealth of Influence . . ." that ran July 23, 2003. Coverage of the affair in the daily Texas press was too voluminous to list all the important pieces. Often written in short dispatches, the work of several reporters stands out: R. G. Ratcliffe and Clay Robinson of the *Houston Chronicle,* María Recio and Jay Smoot of the *Fort Worth Star-Telegram,* Michael King of the *Austin Chronicle,* and Harvey Kronenburg of the *Quorum Report.*

In multiple interviews, Fred Lewis of Campaigns for Change was a sure and knowing guide to an understanding of the chronology of events in the redistricting saga and the legal significance of the small mountain of documents that the research of that saga produced. John Hall, a government consultant in Austin, offered observations and leads on DeLay's relations with ethnic minorities in his district. State Representatives Richard Raymond, Elliott Naishtat, Garnet Coleman, and State Senator Judith Zaffirini provided much insight and detail into the chain of special sessions required by redistricting, on the orders of DeLay. The staffs of Raymond and Naishtat bolstered the information conveyed in those interviews. Congressmen Chet Edwards and Max Sandlin and Texas Attorney General Greg Abbott provided thoughtful perspectives and comments during recesses of the federal redistricting trial in Austin in late 2003.

Chapter 14: Troubles in Texas

As it often happens, the small-town press broke important facets of the story about the outrageous fees that two lobbyists closely aligned with DeLay, Jack Abramoff and Mike Scanlon, charged Native American tribes. Following up on reports in Alexandria, Louisiana's *Daily Town Talk,* Susan Schmidt of the *Washington Post* projected the likely investigation led by Arizona Senator John McCain.

Concerning the Texas grand jury's investigation into allegations of illegal corporate donations channeled into legislative race, see the stories in the *Texas Observer,* op. cit. Patricia Kilday Hart provided a careful analysis of the growing scandal in "Speakergate," *Texas Monthly* (May 2004).

DeLay's rewriting of the House rules are explained by Damon Chappie, "DeLay Foundation Exploits New Rules," *Roll Call* (January 20, 2003), Jim VandeHei and Juliet Eilperin, "House GOP Erodes Its Gift Ban: New Rules Let Lobbyists Offer More Meals, Tickets and Trips," *Washington Post* (January 21, 2003), Jim VandeHei and Juliet Eilperin, "Power Play: Goal of Reforms in House Gives Way to Tough Tactics Party Once Criticized," *Washington Post* (July 26, 2003), Representative Tom DeLay, *The Congressional Record* (November 16, 1995).

Evolving coverage of Abramoff's fall from grace in 2003 was found in the following stories: Susan Schmidt, "A Jackpot from Indian Gaming Tribes," *Washington Post* (February 22, 2004), Susan Schmidt, "Probe Is Sought on Indian Corruption," *Washington Post* (February 22, 2004), Susan Schmidt, "Think Tank's Director Tied to Lobbying Firm," *Washington Post* (February 27, 2004), Susan Schmidt, "Lobbyist Quits As Firm Probes Work with Tribes," *Washington Post* (March 4,

2004), Susan Schmidt, "A Jackpot on Indian Gaming Probe Finds $10 Million in Payments to Lobbyists," *Washington Post* (March 30, 2004), Stephen Pizzo, "DeLay's Godfather," *AlterNet* (May 14, 2002).

Our account of the Westar contribution scandal is informed by Public Citizen Complaint filed with the House Committee on Standards of Official Conduct (June 17, 2003), Public Citizen Letter to Charles Q. Chandler, Chairman of the Board, Westar Energy (February 9, 2004), Public Citizen Letter to Noel Hillman, Department of Justice, Criminal Division, New York (June 17, 2003), Kansas Corporation Commission Letter to Representative Edward Markey (September 27, 2002), Congressman Edward Markey's Letter to Congressman Billy Tauzin and Senator Jeff Bingaman (September 7, 2002),

Other reporting cited: Paul Kane, "McCain to Probe Lobbying Contracts," *Roll Call* (February 26, 2004), Paul Kane and Brody Mullins, "McCain Seeks Files in Abramoff Probe," *Roll Call* (March 4, 2004), Paul Kane, "McCain Makes Progress in Indian Probe," *Roll Call* (March 24, 2004), Judy Sarasohn, "Mine Project Is No Jewel for Tiffany . . . ," *Washington Post* (March 25, 2004), Andrea Seabrook, "House Majority Leader Tom DeLay's Rise to Power," National Public Radio (February 27, 2004), Nicholas Thompson, "The Exterminator," *Salon* (September 3, 2003).

Letters of complaint filed with the IRS by Common Cause (December 5, 2003) and Democracy 21 (December 4, 2003) explain allegations regarding Tom DeLay's use of charitable institutions for partisan purposes. Celebrations for Children, Inc.'s New York convention packages are listed in Celebrations for Childrens [*sic*], Inc., brochure: contacts Craig Richardson, Dani DeLay Ferro, Rob Jennings.

Interviewed for this chapter were Fred Wertheimer (Washington, D.C., January 2004), Melanie Sloan (Washington, D.C., March 2004).

Conclusion: Division of the House

Matt Bai, "Fight Club," *New York Times Magazine* (August 10, 2003), Richard E. Cohen and David Bauman, "The State of Congress," *National Journal* (January 10, 2004), Senator Tom Daschle, "Removing Protections for Polluters in Energy Bill Will Boost Ethanol Production," *Black Hills Pioneer* (March 23, 2004), Juliet Eilperin, "Taking a Right Turn on K Street," *Washington Post* (March 14, 2001), Norman

Ornstein, ". . . And Mischief," *Washington Post* (November 26, 2003),
Jim VandeHei, "DeLay Nears Top of House He Reshaped," *Washington Post* (November 13, 2002).

Author Interviews: Representative Barney Frank (Washington, D.C., December 2003), Representative Henry Waxman (Washington, D.C., April 2003), Former Representative Marge Roukema (Telephone, February 2004).

Index

PUBLICAFFAIRS is a publishing house founded in 1997. It is a tribute to the standards, values, and flair of three persons who have served as mentors to countless reporters, writers, editors, and book people of all kinds, including me.

I. F. STONE, proprietor of *I. F. Stone's Weekly,* combined a commitment to the First Amendment with entrepreneurial zeal and reporting skill and became one of the great independent journalists in American history. At the age of eighty, Izzy published *The Trial of Socrates,* which was a national bestseller. He wrote the book after he taught himself ancient Greek.

BENJAMIN C. BRADLEE was for nearly thirty years the charismatic editorial leader of *The Washington Post.* It was Ben who gave the *Post* the range and courage to pursue such historic issues as Watergate. He supported his reporters with a tenacity that made them fearless, and it is no accident that so many became authors of influential, best-selling books.

ROBERT L. BERNSTEIN, the chief executive of Random House for more than a quarter century, guided one of the nation's premier publishing houses. Bob was personally responsible for many books of political dissent and argument that challenged tyranny around the globe. He is also the founder and was the longtime chair of Human Rights Watch, one of the most respected human rights organizations in the world.

. . .

For fifty years, the banner of Public Affairs Press was carried by its owner Morris B. Schnapper, who published Gandhi, Nasser, Toynbee, Truman, and about 1,500 other authors. In 1983 Schnapper was described by *The Washington Post* as "a redoubtable gadfly." His legacy will endure in the books to come.

Peter Osnos, *Publisher*